ESTORICK, ERIC. Stafford Cripps: prophetic rebel. 285p pl $2.50 Day

B or 92 Cripps, Sir Staffo[rd]
—Politics and governmen[t]
(Great Britain)

Largely a sociologist's pictu[re of a]
labor leader who became ministe[r to Moscow in]
1940 and from that vantage point predicted the
coming of Germany's attack on Russia in 1941.
Index.

——————

Booklist 38:157 Ja 1 '42

"Mr. Estorick has written his sketch of
Cripps's personal life against a background of
British political history over the last ten years.
Neither is full, nor clearly stated. His attitude
toward his subject is one of frank adula-
tion." Joseph Barnes

Books p18 N 23 '41 900w

Reviewed by S. K. Ratcliffe

Nation 153:542 N 29 '41 950w

"This volume by a young American sociologist is an attempt to introduce Cripps to the
American public. The reader will find much of
interest and value in Mr. Estorick's pages. The
essential biographical data are briefly set forth;
so too is the story of Cripps's early activities
in the peace movement and his political debut
as Solicitor-General in the second Labor government. Most of the book, however, is given
over to Cripps the rebel, to an account of his
differences with the Labor Party in the past
half-dozen years. . . Mr. Estorick has done a
good job in presenting the facts of those differences. But he has been somewhat less successful as a biographer." D. W. Petegorsky

+ — **New Repub** 105:739 D 1 '41 800w

STAFFORD CRIPPS:
PROPHETIC REBEL

Lady Cripps and Sir Stafford on a holiday.

STAFFORD CRIPPS:
PROPHETIC REBEL

ERIC ESTORICK

ILLUSTRATED

NEW YORK

THE JOHN DAY COMPANY

For

MOTHER, DAD, AND ALMA

ABOUT THE AUTHOR

ERIC ESTORICK was educated in America and Europe, and from 1938 to 1941 was a member of the sociology department of New York University, first as a Hayden Fellow and then as an instructor. He was also in Europe during the Munich crisis and at the outbreak of war. In the late spring of 1941, before entering government service, he was associated with a research project sponsored by the Rockefeller Foundation, studying totalitarian communications. His articles and reviews have appeared in *The New Statesman and Nation, The American Journal of Sociology,* the *Annals* of the American Academy of Political and Social Science, *The New Republic, The Nation, Asia,* and other magazines in the United States and abroad.

CONTENTS

ILLUSTRATIONS

STAFFORD CRIPPS:
PROPHETIC REBEL

Why did England hold back?

In what direction is she heading?

How is it that the Labour party in particular stood helplessly by while Mussolini brought "civilization" to Ethiopia; while German technicians, Italian bombers, and Moorish conscripts brought "Christianity" to Spain; while Hitler "freed" the Sudetens from the Czechoslovakian "yoke"; while the National Government at home adopted such measures as the Sedition Bill, the Means Test, and other equally insidious legislation?

The career of one man in England affords answers which I have tried to reveal in this presentation of Stafford Cripps. He is a man about whom we Americans want to know and about whom we shall want to know much more. Two to three years ago his activities in England interested me as a sociologist and at that time most of the material for this book was assembled. Here was a man in the heart of politics who was no politician. One of London's leading newspapers published an article setting forth Sir Stafford's abilities as challenged by none and regretting only the fact that he was not a trained politician. A chemist, and then a lawyer, he had entered the so-called political field less than a decade previous to this publication, and, according to the judgment of the writer of this article, he was wont to "bash his head against the wall" whereas an experienced politician would "slip his head through a hole in the wall." Recent events indicate that the head has not been "bashed." When war was declared, Cripps gave up what was undoubtedly the most brilliant as well as lucrative law practice in England and offered his services to the Chamberlain Government as a technician. When Churchill came to power, he was the man selected to handle Britain's most difficult diplomatic assignment—in Russia. During the previous year he had been invited by Chiang Kai-shek to visit China. He went also to India, Russia, and the United States before his return to England. Needless to say, my interest today is more than that of the sociologist. I watch, along with other Americans, the international situation in which our immediate national destiny is yet undetermined. As we watch and wait, we not only discuss the above questions, but we also think about "politics." I am glad of the opportunity to introduce Stafford Cripps to my fellow Americans as a man in international affairs who is a leader rather than a politician. I can assure them that the wall will continue to give way to this man who has not slipped his head through the holes it offered but who, upon one occasion when it seemed as if his head might therefore very well be "bashed," had said: "Failure is no test of right or wrong; of that there is but one test—your conscience and reasoning powers."

Sir Stafford Cripps has been British Ambassador at Moscow since the debacle in France. A whole year passed during which time he had ample opportunity to impress upon the realistic-minded Soviet officials the stamp of his provocative personality and the earnest vigor of his social philosophy.

Hitler's invasion of the Soviet Union on June 23, 1941, produced in Moscow immediate proof of the latter's very cordial relationship with Sir Stafford, who had been able to smooth the path toward wartime co-operation between his own country and the Soviet Union. Whether these warm relationships will continue in the future, only time will tell; but a story which gained currency in Europe prior to the Russian-German hostilities hits the nail right on the head.

Upon one of his visits to the Kremlin, Cripps was reassured that Anglo-Russian relations were smoother than they ever had been, but one problem still puzzled the Russians.

"Tell us, Sir Stafford," they asked, "who really stands for British foreign policy? You here in Moscow, or Lord Halifax in Washington?"

I

THE LIBERAL CONSCIENCE

I⊤ MAY SEEM SURPRISING, at first sight, that a wealthy and titled
gentleman of the ruling class, with a fine old eighteenth-century
name, should be a leading figure in the English working class
movement. Indeed, the connection of such an aristocrat with the
working class movement at all—leaving aside for a moment his
evidently significant position—requires no little exploration. Such
a phenomenon, however, is much less remarkable than might
be expected.

In England it is not at all unusual for scions of the aristocracy
to place themselves at the head of resurgent movements of the
working class. The leaders of the Levellers and the Diggers,
revolutionary sects which flourished for a time as the left wing
of Cromwell's army, were for the most part sons of the minor
nobility. The Labour party at present is represented in the House
of Lords by peers who inherited their seats, as well as by those
created under the Labour governments of 1923 and 1929. The
first of these political aberrations (or so they must have seemed)
can be accounted for in terms of religious equalitarianism. The
second represents an instance of the operations of the liberal
conscience, whose convolutions can be clearly traced by an examination of the family background of Sir Stafford Cripps.

Sir Stafford himself tells us, somewhat inaccurately, that he
sprang from "a traditional, conservative middle-class family." It
is true that the Cripps-Potter family were not aristocrats; they
had no hereditary titles and were not, like the Woods (Halifax)

and Guinnesses (Earl of Iveagh), both nineteenth-century titles, assimilated into the aristocracy. But neither were they middle class, as the term is generally understood today. They were what Beatrice (Potter) Webb, an aunt of Cripps, calls "such country gentlemen and public service families as the Hobhouses, Farrers, Aclands, and Stracheys," with their tradition of "cultivated refinement and sense of social obligation." They are the same class of people who, in the latter half of the nineteenth century, comprised such groups as the Charity Organization Society, Toynbee Hall, the Christian Socialists, the Socialist League, the Fabian Society, and even the Social-Democratic Federation. They were found before the outbreak of World War II, active as ever, organizing in the League of Nations Union, the Peace-Pledge Union, and various refugees' relief organizations, and, to a lesser extent, in the leadership of left wing parties.

This tradition of the "enlightened lower upper middle class" is peculiarly English. It must be explained as a hangover of the liberal idealism of the English *bourgeoisie,* retained from the days when they were in reality an oppressed class who—to emancipate themselves from the constraints of feudalism—broke the power of the Stuart kings. Naturally, their claims against the monarchy were formulated in general terms, and seemed to promise freedom for *all* men—a fact which gained them some measure of support from the lower classes. But, after the triumph of Cromwell and the economic consolidation of the *haute bourgeoisie,* it became apparent that the freedom for which Englishmen had fought was the freedom of Newcastle, and later on industrial capitalism to exploit the population and build an Empire. A residue of liberal ideology did remain, however, as the skeleton in the family closet of the English upper classes. And, when this was placed in juxtaposition with the naked exploitation of the Industrial Revolution, it produced those strange contradictions which go to make up the liberal conscience.

Unlike the French Revolution, which was largely anticlerical, however, the liberal conscience of England was also evolved as part of a peculiar religious history. The great English revolutionaries of the seventeenth century, from Cromwell to Winstanley, to say nothing of the "turbulent priests" of earlier ages, St. Thomas à Becket, Wycliffe, John Ball, Jack Straw, More, and Latimer, clothed their campaigns from beginning to end in scriptural texts and formulae. And this practice has not died out in England as so largely it has elsewhere. Many of the Chartist leaders were clergymen, like J. R. Stephen, Richard Oastler, G. S. Bull, Vicar of Brierley near Bradford, and Ernest Jones, who claimed "to preach the democracy of Christ." Labour today is still largely Nonconformist. As Mr. Attlee, Lord Privy Seal in Mr. Churchill's Government and leader of the Parliamentary Labour party, has said, "Leaving aside Owen and the early pioneers, I think that the first place in the influence that built up the Socialist movement must be given to religion. England in the nineteenth century was still a nation of Bible readers. To put the Bible into the hands of an Englishman is to do a very dangerous thing. He will find there material which may send him out as a preacher of some religious, social, or economic doctrine. The large number of religious sects in this country, and the various tenets that many of them hold, illustrate this. The Bible is full of revolutionary teaching, and it is not surprising that, in a country where thought is free, many men and women have drawn from it the support which they needed for their instinctive revolt against the inhuman conditions which Capitalism brings. I think that probably the majority of those who have built up the Socialist movement in this country have been adherents of the Christian religion—and not merely adherents, but enthusiastic members of some religious body. There are probably more texts from the Bible enunciated from Socialist platforms than from those of all other parties."

The Nazis, those most consistent modern defenders of class rule, are perhaps right in their perception of the dangers of Christianity, especially in its Anglo-Saxon varieties infused with liberalism and humanitarianism. If Marxists have regarded Christianity as the "opium of the people," so can it become, the Nazis point out, the narcotic of the ruling class. Nothing can be more dangerous to the preservation of a class society than a "degenerate" ruling class, a ruling class that no longer believes in itself; that no longer believes in its "divine" right to rule. "Christianity," cried Baron Wolsogen, "has offered promises of happiness to the materially and spiritually poor, the cripples of body and soul, the slaves and weaklings; it has heaped menaces on the rich. . . ." "It is in Christianity," said Klages, "that the proximate causes of 'Progress' in universal history are rooted," and Progress to the Nazis means decadence. If "interpretations" of Christianity are as many and as varied as the fishes of the sea, that species which led Ernest Jones to speak of Christ as the "first Chartist" has at least had quite a widespread effect on sections of the British upper and middle classes. Among others, it brought Sir Stafford Cripps to the Labour movement.

As far back as the eighteenth century, when no working class movement existed, John Potter, Sir Stafford's maternal great-great-grandfather, a well-to-do farmer and retail draper of Tadcaster, was getting his windows smashed by a "deluded multitude" for not lighting a lamp for a victory of the English over "our American brethren." He continually protested against the war of intervention against France, "when Pitt was in all his glory." He was disgusted that "England's blood and treasure were to be wasted in a contest so unnatural—that of dictating to another country what form of Government it should have."

His son, Richard Potter, who became a prosperous Manchester manufacturer, was even more unmistakably "a consistent Friend of Freedom, abhorring tyranny in all its acts." He tiraded against the French war, advocated justice for Ireland, went to considerable exertions to reduce some of the disgracefully heavy sentences for trifling offenses, which the courts at that time meted out to working class delinquents, and became an enthusiastic adherent of the Anti-Slave Trade Campaign. During the Luddite Riots of 1812 he sympathized openly with the workers and went to London to oppose the Manchester Police Bill. He interviewed Lord Wharncliffe, "who was supposed to be rude and bullying, but we plucked up and let him know we did not care for him." Later he became Liberal M. P. for Wigan in the first reformed Parliament, and a close friend of Cobden, Bright, and Daniel O'Connell. With his brothers he played a part in founding the liberal *Manchester Guardian* in 1834. Richard Potter was certainly no conscious hypocrite. At a time when hypocrisy was in the air, especially among the liberal *bourgeoisie,* who had somehow to reconcile their Christian faith with their commercial practices, Richard Potter was surprisingly free from pretense—noting in his diary the agreeable sensations that accompany charity and observing, "How true the remark of Pope is: 'What a luxury it is to do good!' " We find nevertheless in his diaries not one single mention of the conditions of the workers in his own factories, and we have little evidence to indicate that they were outstandingly better than the standards prevailing at the time—about the worst in English history.

His brother, William "Citizen" Potter, was rather less remarkable for his integrity—but no less so for his freedom from cant. The maxims with which, in his letters, he was fond of regaling his family, show evident traces of "the salient characteristic of the English." "Always *appear* to be busy even if you are not." "Practice economy with an appearance of generosity." "It is the opinion of some people that the shopkeeping trade cannot be carried on without some little deviation from truth, but I am of a contrary sentiment . . . for my part I have the sacred idea of the obligation between man and man. I should shudder as much at being detected in a lie as being detected in a depredation of property"—and then he adds somewhat hastily, "I do not mean for a moment to inculcate a disregard for getting money." Alas, the high principles and worthy sentiments of this highly respected Quaker and Radical proved insufficient to preserve him from the clutches of the "fatal demon," drink, who "drags down through Hell's gaping portals the countless souls of rum-wrecked mortals."

The younger Richard Potter was the father of nine remarkable daughters, one of whom is now Beatrice Webb, and another, Theresa, the mother of Stafford Cripps. In some ways a less advanced man than his father, his salient characteristics seem to have been amiability and a certain lack of cant. Herbert Spencer, his "admirer and close friend," said of him, "I think he is the most lovable being I have yet seen. His amiability is that of reality." But this in no way hindered—on the contrary, it must have aided—Richard Potter of Standish, after he had deserted the Bar for industry, making himself a fortune out of his various directorships—of the Great Western Railway, the Hudson's Bay Company, and, in particular, a Gloucester timber business for which, during the Crimean War, he obtained the very profitable contract for army huts for both the French and the British armies. Richard Potter of Standish was a product of his age, and, like the majority of his bourgeois contemporaries, he was possessed of the English Nonconformist conscience. He was, that is to say, a Unitarian, with its firm insistence on personal merit, industry, integrity, improvement, and a strange patch of insensibility regarding the field of commerce and its economic consequences; a field ably taken care of by the predominant utilitarian theory of which his wife was a great exponent.

Mrs. Potter, her daughter Beatrice has recorded, was "an ardent student of Adam Smith, Malthus, and Nassau Senior. She had been brought up in the strictest sect of Utilitarian Economists. . . . She never visited the servants' quarters, and seldom spoke to any servant other than her own maid. She acted by deputy, training each daughter to carry out a carefully thought-out plan of the most economical supply of the best regulated demand. Her intellect told her that to pay more than the market rate, to exact fewer than the customary hours, or insist on less than the usual strain . . . was an act of self-indulgence, a defiance of nature's laws which would bring disaster on the individual and the community. Similarly, it was the bounden duty of every citizen to better his social status. . . . Only by this persistent pursuit by each individual of his own and his family's interest would the highest general level of civilization be attained. It was on this issue that she and Herbert Spencer found themselves in happy accord. No one of the present generation realizes with what sincerity and fervor these doctrines were held by the representative men and women of the mid-Victorian middle class."

With the end of laissez-faire and the beginning of State economic intervention which set in at the time of the great crisis of 1881, still another crisis occurred for the Nonconformist conscience. Should the old standbys of liberal doctrine be maintained, or should the previous genuine concern for worth, political and intellectual liberty, and the spiritual as opposed to the economic welfare of the remainder of society, spread to include precisely that material welfare on which, it was beginning to be realized, spiritual welfare so largely depended? Gone were the days when Hannah Moore, calling attention to the appalling poverty and misery which existed in the villages during the forties, could console herself with the thought that these trials and privations were specially sent by a wise and beneficent Providence for the spiritual advantages of the poor, affording them peculiar opportunities for the exercise of all the virtues.

Like Sir Stafford's maternal forebears, the Potters and Heyworths, the Cripps family had a long tradition of duty and public service. For many generations they had acted as luminaries of the church and the law in Buckinghamshire and Gloucestershire. Their zealous pursuit of education and self-cultivation rivaled even that of Mrs. Potter of Standish, whose capacity for Greek so impressed the French economist, Michel Chevalier. Here is an extract from the diary of Julia (Lawrence) Cripps, daughter of the great surgeon, Sir William Lawrence, and Sir Stafford's paternal grandmother. "Up at five, read the Psalms and Lessons. Worked. Took geranium cuttings and put fresh glasses on the bees. After breakfast wrote letters, and studied as usual. Writing German, reading French history a.s.o. [and so on] then reading Tasso again that I may not forget my Italian. Reading Wheatley on Common Prayer until bedtime."

Like Richard Potter of Tadcaster, Henry William Cripps, Chairman of the Bucks County Council and Quarter Sessions, and Recorder of Lichfield, "was an advocate of lighter sentences in criminal cases, and thought as a rule that the punishments inflicted, especially for minor offenses ... were too harsh, tending rather to promote criminality than to encourage reform." Unlike the Potters and Heyworths, however, the Crippses were no

Cobdenites—advocates of unadulterated laissez-faire. Neither Henry William Cripps nor his son, Charles Alfred, later Lord Parmoor, ever accepted extreme laissez-faire as advocated by Herbert Spencer. Unlike many upper-class families of the day, they lived in very close contact with the farmers and agricultural laborers in their neighborhood. "I spent much of my time," wrote Lord Parmoor, who died in his eighty-ninth year in July, 1941, "with the farm hands, forming life friendships with some of them. As children we were encouraged to visit their homes and to enter into personal relationships. . . . It was impossible for the farm labourers in Buckinghamshire to live decently on the wage they received when there was a family. In the result, undernourishment was a constant evil. It was part of our duty as children to take round food, in our afternoon walks, to certain cottages each day, where the need was greatest." Such a procedure, needless to say, was in flagrant violation of the Spencerian principle then prevalent, that "generous relief grants were an inducement to idleness." "No doubt," he added, "early associations and the constant care of my father, who showed a continuous interest in the social welfare of his farm labourers by providing better cottage accommodation and by bringing within their reach new opportunities for education, turned my thoughts in the direction of an economic change, now generally designated as a Socialist System."

"It fell to my lot to pilot through the House of Lords in 1924 the Minimum Wage Bill for Agricultural Labour. This Act has done much to improve the general conditions in country parishes. These conditions are, however, not likely to be really satisfactory until there has been a substantial change in the character of our land tenure, and the monopoly of private ownership has been adequately restricted under a fair system of compensation."

Here then, in a characteristically English form, are features of what Marx called "conservative or bourgeois Socialism," to which Lord Parmoor, though with an increasing consciousness of its limitations, was faithful all his life. It can be regarded as the last stage but one in the evolution of the English Nonconformist liberal conscience from the smug self-satisfaction of English capitalists, exploiting their fellow Englishmen in conformity with the Benthamite "laws" of nature, to the benevolence of English Radicalism, with its high-minded idealism and its myopic grasp of economic realities, castigated in different periods and for widely differing reasons by the Tories of the eighteenth century, the ultra-lefts of the nineteenth, and the Fascists of the twentieth.

The political development of Charles Alfred Cripps (Lord Parmoor) followed these lines fairly faithfully. Though at first his Protestantism led him to side with the Liberal Unionists in the Irish controversy, he changed his opinion "as a result of further research and inquiries." Nevertheless, it was as a Conservative that he stood and was elected for Stroud in 1895.

The first question on which he spoke in the House of Commons was the need for reform in parliamentary procedure. This is perhaps significant in view of the attitude which his son was later to adopt in regard to this question, Stafford pointing out that, before it was possible to put any program of social reform into operation, the obstruction of the House of Lords would have to be removed. The question came up again in 1910, as a result of Mr. Asquith's Parliament Bill which limited the power of the House of Lords, and Lord Lansdowne's bill which would have radically altered the character of the Second Chamber. Lord Parmoor, supporting the bill, said, "I think that a Second Cham-

ber which has not representative principle behind it is not sufficiently strong to preserve really popular Government and representative Government in this country." But the "proposals were
not adopted, and the Constitution of a reformed Second
Chamber is still a matter in dispute."

In the years preceding the First World War, a number of
events served to radicalize Lord Parmoor's attitude, notably his
work on the committee on the Jameson Raid of 1895 and the
Taff Vale Case of 1901, which aroused his condemnation as a
constitutional lawyer, and the question of free religious education in the schools, involving the general question of compulsory
education. "The time has now come," he wrote, "when a universal system of compulsory education should be open without
distinction to all children. . . . The costs of such a scheme must
be placed on the Capitalist class, distributed on the principle of
the ability to pay. . . . It is not in elementary education that
the need of a universal compulsory system is urgent. There is
the same need both in secondary schools and universities. In
both secondary schools and universities endowments clearly intended for the benefit of the children of poor parents have been
gradually diverted from their original purpose." He cited particularly the case of the scholarship foundation at Winchester
College, where he himself had been a scholar. Throughout, and
particularly in his attitude toward the House of Lords, to which
he was elevated in 1914 by Mr. Asquith, we find traces of the
resentment felt by the worthy middle-class country gentleman,
scholar of Winchester and New College, Oxford, against the
extravagant and exclusive aristocrats who required scholarships
to ease the burden of their school fees—an attitude as old as the
first Protestant and Dissentist stirrings among the English
squires and burgesses of the fifteenth century.

Fifty-two years ago, on April 21, 1889, Stafford Cripps was born into this family of cultured Christian country gentlemen— the youngest of five children, four sons and a daughter.

At first there was very little indication that here might be a future leader, except perhaps the precocious fondness which he early acquired for "giving advice to the elder members of the family—earning him the name of 'Dad' in family circles," His interests, like those of most of his age and milieu, seem to have been athletics and architecture rather than politics. Though here it must be noted that the species of class oppression which afflicts younger brothers must have had some influence on his character: on the hunting and shooting expeditions which formed the staple recreation of the family at Parmoor, Stafford "as the youngest brother was usually walking with the beaters and hunting on the pony which was used for mowing the lawn. He consequently formed a rather less favorable view than his brothers of sport. . . ."

His architectural activities seem to have been conceived in an ambitious mold. What is more, they seem generally to have been completed. He built underground houses and bridges across the Parmoor pond. In 1906, three years before Blériot's Channel flight, he crowned his achievements by constructing a glider in the face of the ridicule of the rest of the family, who expressed their regard for his project by calling the shed in which the glider was housed "Stafford's Folly." The glider unfortunately— or fortunately—crashed on its first flight "and was irreparably smashed."

Stafford appears early to have shown an organizational capacity of a high order. In very early days, his brother Fred, now Colonel Cripps, tells us, "he was a capitalist." Stafford and Leonard, another brother, organized a teashop on sound capi-

talist lines, cornering the family's supply of tea and cakes and
selling them "to the waylaid guests at the price of sixpence a
head." In 1905, at the age of sixteen, he became intimately connected with a local Conservative paper, the *South Bucks Standard,* and for five years he was director in sole charge of the
business side.

In 1901, he went to Winchester, where generations of Crippses
had preceded him, in the same term as another future socialist
barrister, Mr. D. N. Pritt, who was, however, two years his
senior. At Winchester he came under the influence of Dr. Burge,
then headmaster, who was to be connected with his father and
himself in all the wartime and postwar International Christian
movements.

He studied natural science, particularly chemistry, and in 1907
gained a Science Scholarship to New College, Oxford. He did
not, however, avail himself of it. His papers were considered
by the examiners to show such promise that they were sent to
Sir William Ramsay, the famous chemist, who was sufficiently
impressed to invite Stafford to go to work under him in his
laboratory at University College, London. His chemical studies
bore fruit in 1912, when he became the youngest student ever
to read a paper before the Royal Society. The paper was entitled
"The Critical Constants and Arthobaric Densities of Xenon"—
in connection with which he also invented a pyknometer, or
device for measuring the densities of gases and liquids. In 1911
he dropped chemistry and began to work for the Bar, passing
his final examinations in the summer of 1912, and being called to
the Bar at the beginning of the following year. The first case in
which he appeared was the important case of Bowden Wire
Company, Ltd., v. Bowden Brake Company, Ltd. Cripps and his
father represented the plaintiffs, who demanded injunctions

against the use of a term "Bowden Control" by a firm other
than the original patentees. They lost the case. Stafford, however,
did not address the court.

Stafford did a modest amount of political work in his father's
constituency, South Bucks, in connection with the 1910 election.
It was here that he first met Isobel Swithinbank, a grand-
daughter of Mr. J. O. Eno, of fruit salt fame. "Their meeting,"
wrote Lord Parmoor, "was the beginning of a love affair; they
became engaged and were married two years before the war,"
on July 12, 1912. Their first son, John, was born a year later.

Cripps did not seem to have held his political activities of those
days in much account. "In the days before the last war," he
writes, "I was almost entirely politically unconscious. Brought
up in a traditionally Conservative middle-class family, seldom
meeting anyone other than Conservatives, I accepted that environment quite naturally and from time to time participated in
some election or other political activity in the same way that
I engaged in any other sport or social event. I was neither aware
of democracy nor of politics in any real sense of the word. The
course of events, so far as I was concerned, seemed to run
smoothly and there appeared to me no reason why I or any
other young man of my acquaintance should trouble himself
with political controversies or electoral disputes. Educated as a
chemist and with the prospect of a professional career at the
Bar before me, I concentrated upon my studies, varying them
with visits abroad whenever the opportunity and the money was
available."

It was the war that finally woke Stafford Cripps to political
consciousness and shocked Lord Parmoor out of his Conservatism. As conscientious Christians, regarding themselves as followers of the humanist tradition of Sir Thomas More, Erasmus,
and Colet, the war revolted them. "War," Erasmus had said, "is

so pestilent that it blights at once all morality, so impious that it has nothing in common with Christ."

At first, however, this condemnation of the war scarcely showed itself in any overt conduct. Lord Parmoor accepted a position as judge on the Admiralty Prize Courts, and all the Cripps sons joined the army. Stafford spent the first eleven months of the war driving a medical supplies lorry from the base at Boulogne to various units at the front. While he was engaged in this work he was instrumental in providing a new and special type of slipper for men suffering from frost bite.

The War Office decided that his chemical abilities might be turned to advantage, and in 1915 recalled him to work as assistant superintendent of the government explosives factory at Queensferry. Gradually, as the war progressed, its incompatibility with Christian morality, and especially the conduct of the churches which, "instead of preaching Christ's Gospel of world peace and good will, too often encouraged a war spirit," impressed itself on both father and son. This question was raised still more acutely in regard to the conscientious objectors, who were being victimized, it seemed to Lord Parmoor, for expressing Christian sentiments which were also his. He devoted himself to acting on their behalf, endeavoring to obtain for them less harsh treatment from the local tribunals. It was in this work that he met his second wife, Marian Ellis, daughter of the famous Quaker, the Rt. Hon. John Ellis. (His first wife had died in 1895.)

The Government issued in 1917 a new Defence of the Realm Act, according to which no book or pamphlet dealing with the war or the making of peace should be published without having been submitted to the censor. The Society of Friends felt that this regulation was opposed to the principles of Christian liberty, and proceeded to issue a number of leaflets giving the facts about the treatment of conscientious objectors. The chairman and secretaries of the Friends' committee, who were responsible for the distribution of these leaflets, including Miss Edith M. Ellis, the twin sister of Marian Ellis, were charged and imprisoned for terms varying from three to six months. "Miss Ellis," said Lord Parmoor, "suffered severely in health, but the experience gained enabled her more fully to appreciate the harshness of the punishment inflicted on persons who refused to betray conscientious convictions, which their religious training had made part of their moral nature."

Previous to this, Lord Parmoor had associated himself with Lord Lansdowne's letter to the press, expressing the demand for "moderate" peace terms, and with the first suggestions for a League of Nations. In March, 1918, he placed the first resolution in favor of a League of Nations on the order papers of the House of Lords. The resolution was adopted without dissent, thanks to the support of Lord Curzon.

It was through Marian Ellis that Parmoor came into contact with the efforts of Archbishop Soederblum of Upsala, Sweden, to bring about an International Christian Conference, the task of which, stated the invitation, was "without any prejudice to national loyalty . . . of manifesting the spiritual unity in Christ of all the believers, and to weigh in prayer the duty of the Church to resist the passions of war, and to promote that temper which makes for justice and good will in all the intercourse of Nations." Dr. Burge, then Bishop of Southwark, Dr. Temple, now Archbishop of York, and Dean Inge also took part in the council which was formed to promote the Conference.

The Conference, however, was never called. Peace came, and, in a very different spirit, the Christian governments went on to impose their Versailles terms on their defeated enemies.

Meanwhile, in 1916, Stafford Cripps had had a complete break-down. Left in sole charge of the Queensferry factory through the illness of the director, he had set out to master every job process in the plant. He had succeeded, but the physical strain was greater than his constitution could withstand. "From that time till the end of the war I was largely an invalid with much time for reading and for thinking. In the result, by the time the war was over I had become aware—indeed, very aware—of the appalling and useless tragedy that the world had brought upon itself. At this point my political consciousness was born."

It was still, however, a political consciousness of very definite limitations, bounded by the principles of Christian pacifism. Neither he nor his father was yet a Socialist, though his father gradually moved in the direction of the Labour party, attracted by the same sort of vaguely international, interclass "good will" that constituted, under MacDonald, the stock-in-trade of the party at that time.

"I was still, however, living in a tradition of Conservatism, though the result of the War experiences upon my father had very greatly changed his political outlook. His sense of the interference with all liberty of conscience, and of the injustices wrought upon the common people, had convinced him that some new outlook was necessary if civilization were to be saved from destruction. For some time I concentrated upon inter-national work, especially through the medium of a world or-ganization of Christian Churches."

Until 1929, when he joined the Labour party, Stafford Cripps confined himself, as regards political activity, to work for the World Alliance for Promoting International Friendship through the Churches, an organization of which he became the treasurer, persuading Dr. Burge, late Bishop of Oxford, to become the British president. For the rest, he devoted himself to building up his legal career, to which he returned when his health permitted him in 1920. In the intervals he lived as a farmer and a family man in a Cotswold house, "Goodfellows," in a Cotswold village, Filkins, with his wife and four children.

"The man who is a good citizen is not necessarily a bad husband and father," said Cripps in one of his World Alliance speeches; "in fact he is probably a good one." Of this there can be few better examples than Stafford himself. The Cripps family at Filkins could be held up as a model of the typical English country family. But it was more than that. The typical English country paterfamilias, to be sure, might well be found engaged in improving the breed of his flock of pedigree Ryeland sheep, but we scarcely expect to find him carving himself a hand-loom to weave scarves for his children, or working stone quarries on his estate to preserve the tradition of Cotswold stone building.

A period which could be called the International Conference Epoch was dawning, an epoch which followed the last war and lingered on until the preliminary skirmishes of the next swept its pretenses away. It was an epoch to which, it should be noted, Lord Parmoor's particular outlook was peculiarly suited. "Moderate" statesmen of all shades—Democrats, Social-Democrats, Liberals, Radicals, Centrists, Republicans, and Conservatives, and not a few who professed themselves "Socialists"—vied with each other in professing their loyalty to International Co-operation, the League, Arbitration, Disarmament, Peace. They illuminated their discourses with frequent references to Christian principles, but without endeavoring to eliminate those forces which everywhere were stirring up the demons of international discord, anarchy, armament races, and war. They were for the most part unaware of what these forces really were. It was the era of Briand and Herriot, of Rathenau and Stresemann, of

Robert Cecil and Henderson and MacDonald—essentially of MacDonald, in spirit if not in fact; but always there were a sufficient number of realistic reactionaries, the Churchills, Austen Chamberlains, and Poincarés, turning up at the right moment to sabotage the schemes when they became too grandiose. Cripps's political activities were widening.

The typical Parmoor-Cripps outlook of this time can hardly be better portrayed than by presenting a précis of the pattern which was adopted by Cripps's World Alliance speeches, delivered for the most part in 1923. They run true to form, generally commencing with an account of endeavors through the centuries to eliminate force from international life as it has been eliminated from national life. The various deterrents which have been tried are listed: the strong man armed, the balance of power, international police; but all these are unsatisfactory because all are based on force. The only sanction which is stronger than force, and has not yet been tried, is love—love and Christianity. Thus it is the churches that should be the true protagonists of peace; the churches must organize for peace. There follows a brief history of the origin and development of the World Alliance, a sketch of its contemporary work on such questions as religious minorities and disarmament, and an account of the special tasks of the British Council. The aims of the Alliance are then stated: the creation of an International Christian Conscience, the application of Christ's teaching to our relations with other nations, as we already seek to apply it in our everyday life. The difficulties in the way are listed as "parochialism," unfamiliarity with thinking internationally, ignorance of how the foreigner lives and thinks, and the poisonous prejudices spread by the press against foreign countries. There is no conflict, it is maintained, between patriotism and Christian internationalism. True patriotism does not mean aggressiveness and bullying. Loving our country does not mean hating and despising all the other countries—just as loving one's own family does not mean hating all one's neighbors. Family, parish, country, world loyalties are complementary, not contradictory. To carry all this out needs faith and energy, not lip service. The churches must give a lead, as Bolshevism gives a different kind of lead. Otherwise, youth will drift away from Christianity. But no difficulties can overcome the truly Christian spirit.

Lord Parmoor gained some further insight into the working of aggressive imperialism as he came into closer contact with the effects of the Versailles terms in his work on the "Fight the Famine" Council—a typical and admirable example of the benevolent spirit. His collaborators at first included, among others, the ubiquitous Dr. Burge, the Webbs, Mr. H. N. Brailsford, one of England's best-known progressive journalists, and Mr. J. H. Thomas, a leading trade union official, who, as a member of Baldwin's Cabinet in 1936, had to quit political life because of a budgetary scandal. At their First International Economic Conference, held in November, 1919, resolutions were passed calling for the abandonment of intervention against Russia and affirming "that the economic clauses of the Peace Treaty are in large measure responsible for the disorganization of production and of credit and for the danger with which civilization is threatened by violent revolutions and by famine, and that the vital interests of all countries demand that these clauses should be amended with the least possible delay."

The significance of the first of these demands should not be misconstrued. The abandonment of intervention in Russia was advocated not from motives of class consciousness, but on the grounds that the absence of Russian markets and Russian raw materials would impede the recovery of the "capitalist West."

Lord Parmoor stands out as perhaps the only noteworthy

success that the MacDonald "personal contact" method of introducing Socialism has to record. MacDonald's speech at the Third International Conference, in October, 1921, appears to have impressed him. At this time MacDonald said, "Good service to the cause of disarmament might be done by a campaign to awaken and inflame people's minds with the idealism behind disarmament, and the great moral issues involved in a real attempt to put war and preparations for war out of men's minds and calculations." Lord Parmoor had already moved about as far in the direction of Socialism as he was ever going, as is shown by his conversation with Prince Max of Baden a year previously. It cannot be denied, however, that MacDonald succeeded in persuading him, and through him his son, formally to join the Labour party.

The words of that conversation which Lord Parmoor held with Prince Max of Baden, show us with significant clarity the considerations which finally turned Lord Parmoor toward the Labour party. "He [Prince Max] spoke of Socialism, and said that he was Socialist in the true sense of desiring not to destroy but to distribute more equitably the results of work and industry. He said that he had been told that there was a chance of civil war in England, but that he did not believe it. I told him that, in my opinion, there was no chance of this, unless the reactionary forces which war had created were too aggressive, and this was not probable. He asked about the Labour party in England, and I told him that I thought there was no risk of class war, so long as there was understanding and a desire of capital and labour to get on together. He expressed the view that the Labour party was the only party likely to obtain, or insist on, a revision of the Peace Terms, but did not think that they were likely to come into power."

Mr. John Scanlon has suggested that in allotting the posts

for the first Labour Cabinet, Mr. MacDonald drew the names of the candidates out of a hat. Lord Parmoor's name was never drawn out of a hat; but even if it had been, such a circumstance would not have redounded unfavorably to Lord Parmoor. He was admirably suited for the job Mr. MacDonald had in mind— the job of playing at Geneva a dignified, distinguished, competent, and patently well-intended second fiddle to Mr. MacDonald himself.

On the eve of the formation of the first Labour Government, Mr. MacDonald wrote to Parmoor inviting him to assist by taking a ministerial office. Since "Labour's vision of an ordered world," as expressed in their 1923 Election Manifesto, appealed to him, Parmoor on the advice of Dr. Burge finally consented. He believed that, owing to his close contacts with the international peace movements and with many foreign statesmen and clergymen, "his inclusion in a Ministry would appeal to, and bring out, the latent Peace spirit . . ." On Russia he wrote, "If Russia could be acknowledged in the short time suggested, this is of great importance. Recognition is essential in any progress toward a diminution of unemployment." And on France, "In France opinion is moving against Poincaré. It is to this opinion that an appeal should be made. I believe such an appeal would awaken a real response. There is need of a generous policy toward France; but on the necessity of the evacuation of the Ruhr, England must be adamant." Perhaps it would have been as well if MacDonald had followed this sage advice, instead of launching himself into a whirlwind courtship of the unemotional Poincaré, who was in fact superseded in a few months by M. Herriot and the *Cartel des gauches*.

So Lord Parmoor became Lord President of the Council in Britain's first Labour Government. Though from the point of view of immediate successes the Labour foreign policy was a considerable improvement on that of the Tories both before and after, it cannot be maintained that it underwent any drastic change under his sway or that of Mr. MacDonald.

Imperial policy is a far more serious touchstone of sincerity than international policy in general, and Labour's imperial policy continued to be imperialistic. "The British Empire is a fact," Lord Snowden had written the previous year. "We have our own views about the way it has been built up. But it is a fact, and having incurred the responsibility we cannot lightly cast it off; indeed, we cannot cast it off at all." Nothing seemed further from Labour thoughts; "self-determination" was decisively shelved.

Mr. William Leach, the pacifist Under-Secretary of State for Air, had to announce that in regard to the bombing of disaffected natives, "we have not made any change in the policy of the late Government of Iraq." Lord Parmoor himself had to affirm "in absolutely definite language, that H. M. Government is not going to abandon the Sudan in any sense whatever" despite the representations of Zaghlul Pasha, the leading Egyptian statesman, who was roundly snubbed by the Prime Minister. India received the same high-handed treatment. "No party in Great Britain," telegraphed MacDonald, "will be cowed by threats of force or by politics designed to bring government to a standstill." His telegram was followed by the notorious Bengal Ordinances and the shootings at Jaito. International affairs should have been the sphere of the Prime Minister's most decisive triumphs, judging by the proportion of his time and energies it consumed. But here most of the planks in Labour's Election Manifesto had to wait. Disarmament, "the only security for the Nations," was postponed for a more auspicious time, namely, until the collective security system of the Geneva Protocol should be already in force. As regards the revision of the

Versailles Treaty, the sole achievement of the Government was the hustling through of the Dawes Plan. This was a new and more efficient method for squeezing reparations out of Germany by stimulating prosperity in German industry at the expense of German labour. It contributed in no small measure to the severity of the crisis which broke out five years later. The German counterdemand for the evacuation of the Ruhr—despite Parmoor's protest that the occupation was illegal, even according to Versailles—was overruled, and was not actually enforced until July, 1925, when Baldwin was again in power in Britain. In one respect, however, Lord Parmoor and his colleagues achieved a success, or what might under other circumstances have been a success: the great Geneva Protocol which, by inducing the nations to agree to submit to international arbitration all disputes that might lead to war, was to lay the foundation stone of the edifice of "the new World Peace Policy founded on a sympathetic Christian understanding." The signing of the Protocol was to be followed by the admission of Germany to the League and a general disarmament conference from which, in the atmosphere of collective security induced by the Protocol, substantial successes were hoped for. Seven prime ministers, including those of Britain and France, were present at the discussions—a thing hitherto unknown in international conferences. The Protocol had already been signed by France, Japan, and eight other countries. It required only the ratification of the British Government, which had been delayed at the instance of MacDonald himself. Before it could be signed by the Labour Government, however, the Tories swept away the flimsy Labour coalition at home and with it the Labour delegation at Geneva. The following spring, Austen Chamberlain, the new Foreign Secretary, decisively rejected the Protocol, contending, somewhat lamely, "that the objections to universal and compulsory arbitrations might easily outweigh the theoretical advantages." Thus was undone the work of the Assembly, which Mr. Motta, the Swiss premier, compared to Dante's ascent of the Mountain of Purification. "The light on the horizon," as Mr. Henderson has expressed it, was extinguished.

The refusal to sign the Geneva Protocol was the real end of the epoch of international conferences. Lord Parmoor continued to play the leading role in the organization of the International Christian movement. In particular we may mention the Life and Work Conference that took place in Sweden in 1925, again under the aegis of the venerable Archbishop of Soederblum. His son continued to look after the finances of the World Alliance and to make well-marshaled speeches presenting its aims. The Alliance included at that time representatives of all the leading churches of Europe, with the exception of the Catholic, and had official representative councils from twenty-seven nations. But it was quite obvious that the hand of the old power politicians was tightening once more on the reins of international policy. Lord Curzon and Dr. Burge died in 1925, and Lord Haldane in 1928. Although it lingered on for nearly another decade, culminating in the Disarmament Conference which finally killed Mr. Henderson, the international conference epoch was never quite the same again. One by one the imperialist chickens were coming home to roost.

The "Socialist bourgeois" who held the stage throughout the conference epoch quite rightly perceived that the gravest of the "struggles and dangers" confronting the capitalist world at this time are precisely those interimperialist wars during the first of which the first breach in the capitalist world-system— the Russian Revolution—took place. But they were incapable even of understanding, much less of facing, the real problems involved in the elimination of these struggles and dangers. It had not yet become apparent—to use Cripps's words—"that no amount of good feeling and good will would ever alter the hard economic facts of the world [nor] that direct, political intervention was essential, if an environment was to be created in which peace could be permanently established."

There is every excuse for Lord Parmoor. He was an old man who had traveled a long way from the benevolent Conservatism of the very different times in which he had been brought up. The whole motive force of his development had been simply his sentiment of consistent Christianity, which was sufficiently strong to be horrified by the excesses committed in the name of jealous national gods. The case is different with those leaders and prominent functionaries of working class parties, excepting Henderson, who diverted the public gaze to their antics at Geneva. These people claimed to know something about imperialist wars; they had seen the Treaties of Versailles, of Trianon, of St. Germain. They had seen Brest-Litovsk and the treatment accorded to the newly born Socialist States of Russia and Hungary. They themselves, compelled by the imperialist machine of which they were temporarily in control, had been forced to order the bombing of the Iraqi, the shooting of Indians. But the League of Nations, the international conference, were new toys. A reconstruction of the world by such means, the conquest of imperialism by good will, might have seemed an experiment worth trying in the postwar doldrums, when every second Government was social-democratic.

Today such methods have become not only obsolete, but positively dangerous; and those who use the terminology of pacifism and international arbitration, as Mr. Chamberlain did, usually do so to disguise their real motives. It is pitiful for the average man that this should be so, but recent events leave no other conclusion for those who are not either intellectually blind or dishonest. It is symptomatic of the growing political maturity of the liberal conscience that, more and more, bourgeois Socialists are beginning to realize the economic roots of class antagonisms; and the connection of Sir Stafford Cripps with the British Labour party, no less than his incisive political analyses in recent years of both domestic and foreign affairs, testify to this growth of political maturity. Against the background of a vast struggle which has been steadily increasing, and which now reaches a climactic point on the battlefield of Europe, Sir Stafford Cripps plays a challenging role.

II

CRIPPS AND THE
SECOND LABOUR GOVERNMENT

NINETEEN HUNDRED AND TWENTY-NINE.

The long-awaited opportunity had come for the British nation
to give its verdict on the present Government.

After four and a half years of Stanley Baldwin, who had
broken the General Strike in 1926, the British people were looking for a change. Mr. Baldwin's regime deserved most of the
strictures made upon it by the Labour electioneers:

"Unemployment is more acute."

"Vast areas of the country are derelict."

"The Tory Government has added £38,000,000 to indirect
taxation."

Yet Mr. Baldwin appealed to the impatient electorate with the
uninspiring slogan "Safety First."

This apparent failure of Mr. Baldwin's to strike the right
note of appeal needs explanation. In view of his reputation for
political astuteness, it might be suggested that he had some
inkling of the real state of economic affairs and refused to im-
pugn his party's future position by being optimistic when he
sensed nothing but catastrophe ahead. The period of stabilization
which followed the first World War was, in a sense, a gift from
America to the world. But the economic foundations of stabilization were laid in quicksand. If American capitalism should once
stop expanding, retrenchment of some kind would be inevitable;
and there is no doubt that Mr. Baldwin, if he could have fore-

seen the future, would have been delighted to find a Labour rather than a Tory Government placed in such a predicament. In any event, his miscalculation of public sentiment was a strong factor in the choice of Ramsay MacDonald to head a minority Government.

The line which the new Labour Government intended to take was clear from the outset. The Labour party's credo had contained a running buffet providing everything from pure Socialism to impure reformism, from utopian idealism to sound financial orthodoxy. But the King's speech promptly revealed that Socialism and "impractical" working class demands were out of the question.

The Government maintained that its hands were tied because of its failure to obtain a majority in the House; but it has been seriously doubted, by competent observers, whether this fact was regretted by the Prime Minister and the rest of the Cabinet, who had been responsible for the lines which party policy had followed since the General Strike. In his first speech as Prime Minister of the new Government, MacDonald appealed to the Liberals and the Conservatives to "co-operate," to "put ideas into a common pool" so that "we can bring from that common pool legislation and administration that will be of substantial benefit to the nation as a whole." It was clear that no intransigent measures were contemplated, since they might endanger the continuance of the Labour Government by uniting the opposition.

But while the Labour Government strove, along with the two Opposition parties, "to improve the competitive position of British industries in the markets of the world," there hung round its neck like a millstone a number of traditional working class demands. These had been duly promised in the credo, *Labour and the Nation*, and could not be relegated to the background as easily as the abstract slogan of Socialism.

Perhaps the greatest success scored by the Labour Government in 1929, as five years earlier, was in housing. The majority of all houses built up to 1932, when the Act was repealed, were built under the Wheatley Act of 1924. Mr. Greenwood had taken the place of Mr. Wheatley, who was too far to the left for the taste of the Prime Minister and had been excluded from the new Cabinet. In 1930 Mr. Greenwood introduced a new Housing Act. By this Act provisions were made to build a total of 340,000 houses over a period of five years, though allowances were made for an increase to a million houses. The program also indicated that 95,000 houses would be demolished during the same period by the local authorities. As far as it goes, this stands in glowing contrast to the achievement of the Tories, who, during their four and one-half years in office had demolished only 8,265 houses and built no more than that. The Government passed an Act in 1931, providing £2,000,000 for rural housing, or approximately 60,000 houses. It was on this question of rural housing that Stafford Cripps gave an example to the Government.

In the spring of 1930 the Witney Rural District Council decided to build four new houses in Cripps's own village of Filkins. They were to be modern houses, built of bricks and mortar—and utterly out of keeping with the native stone architecture of the Cotswolds. "Everyone," wrote the local paper, "was against it, but what could be done? The Honorable R. Stafford Cripps, K. C., who lives in the village, came to the rescue. He approached the Rural District Council, and it was ultimately decided that he should be allowed to erect the houses if he agreed to pay the difference in cost between building them in brick and building them in Cotswold stone. Cripps immediately set to work. The stone was quarried on his own estate; all the labourers, including the foreman mason, were his workers. The architect was Mr. R. Morley Horder. The houses were finally built at a cost of £444 apiece, only a fraction above the price of the vermilion eye-sores. They were opened by Mr. Greenwood, Minister of Health, and created a considerable stir in the housing world."

Even if Cripps had not already been a member of the Labour party, and had not invited Mr. Greenwood to perform the opening ceremony, such an example as this would have had a profound effect on the party. For here, in action, was Mr. Mac-Donald's own conception of the coming Socialism—the enlightened landowner, out of the goodness of his heart, caring for the welfare and "raising the cultural level" of the workers. If all landowners followed Cripps's example, MacDonald's dreams would have come true. It is not surprising, therefore, that almost simultaneously with the building of the cottages Cripps was adopted as Labour candidate for Woolwich, and a few months later, in October 1930, was elevated to the position of Solicitor-General, without as yet having a seat in the House.

It might be of advantage to place his appointment to the Solicitor-Generalship in its proper perspective. To do this, we must first trace the meteoric course of Stafford Cripps's legal career from 1921, when he recovered sufficiently from his wartime illness to return to the Bar, to 1930, when as a patent lawyer he was already commanding by far the highest fees in the country.

Almost from the beginning, he took a leading part in every case in which he appeared, and was frequently briefed in important cases without a leader or even another Junior to assist. Consequently, when he "took sick" in 1927 it made very little real difference to the nature of his work. As a King's Counsel he achieved prominence at once and his practice continued to grow in scope and importance.

His first important case, in 1921, he undertook in conjunction with Sir A. Colefax, with whom his father had worked before the war. It was an action of the Aktiengesellschaft für Anilinfabrikation v. Levinstein regarding the patent for a remarkable invention of a black dye. Cripps addressed the court and was largely responsible for the upholding of the patent. His thorough preparation of the case and the profound chemical knowledge he displayed in his cross-examination of expert witnesses immediately established his reputation as a patent lawyer. Technical experts, after undergoing his examination, have often remarked that he appeared to know more of the subject than they did themselves. In such cases it is essential to have an up-to-date knowledge of highly abstruse subjects, which Cripps possesses in a remarkable degree along with a keenly analytical and constructive mind. His subsequent patent cases included such noted actions as I. G. Farbenindustrie v. Imperial Chemical Industries (a case of great importance for the British dye industry); Mullard Radio Company, Ltd. v. Philco Radio Company, Ltd. (the famous "Pentode Valve" case in which his exposition of the history of thermionic valves before the House of Lords took over seven days); and the still more renowned artificial silk case, Courtaulds v. British Celanese. Questions on ecclesiastical law and the law of compensation were other of his specialties, for he had edited his grandfather's work, *Cripps on Church and Clergy* and his father's *magnum opus,* on compensation. His longest case, Duff Development Company v. Government of Kelantan, in which the plaintiff company, thanks to his efforts, was awarded £387,000, lasted from 1923 to 1927, and brought him into contact—not to say conflict—with the Colonial Office. Subsequently the Colonial Office retained him in a number of appeals before the Privy Council.

Other important litigation included his work in connection with the Safeguarding of Industries Act, the Railway and Canal

Commission, the Dock Charges Committee and the Railway Rates Tribunal. Here, in conjunction with Herbert Morrison of the London County Council, he did some particularly good work in connection with Workmen's Fares, as well as for the Royal Commission on Awards to Inventors, and once again on behalf of the London County Council in an action for damages owing to delay in building the new County Hall. He has also appeared in numerous income tax cases in the Court of Appeal and the House of Lords.

It is important to mention his work in connection with the Wrexham Inquiry and the Markham Inquiry as instances of his devotion to the cause of the people. He will long be remembered with gratitude by the ....ers for his efforts on their behalf after the tra....y of the Gresford disaster.

"For many years," writes Geoffrey Wilson, a young Barrister and Cripps's confidential secretary, "Sir Stafford has given expression to his social and political beliefs through his work at the Bar. Litigation in England cannot normally be embarked on by a person who has not got considerable resources at his disposal, but Sir Stafford's services have constantly been available to the Trade-Unions and the working class movement generally. Thus, in 1935, he appeared for certain officials of the National Unemployed Workers' Movement in an action which they fought against the Commissioner of Police for London. The Police had searched the offices of the Movement and removed all their papers, the result of which was an action for trespass in which the Movement was successful, and the damages they recovered were added to their funds as a gift from the Commissioner of Police!

"A more regular feature of Sir Stafford's work in this direction is his appearance on behalf of workmen in the House of Lords in connection with workmen's compensation cases. In recent years, the scope of the Workmen's Compensation Acts has been considerably extended beyond what was previously believed to be their limits, as a result of the cases which he has conducted.

"Perhaps his most spectacular case in this field was the Gresford Inquiry in the autumn of 1934. On September 21st, 1934, 265 miners lost their lives in an explosion at Gresford Colliery. The Inquiry opened at Wrexham in October, and Sir Stafford appeared, free of charge, on behalf of the North Wales Miners' Association. The Miners' Federation of Great Britain, not yet believing that a mere lawyer would know the right questions to ask about a pit, was represented by its own officials.

"Sir Stafford arrived in Wrexham the night before the Inquiry opened without, as far as anybody knew, any detailed knowledge of the technical side of mining. But he was fortunate in having as his technical adviser Mr. D. R. Grenfell [now Minister of Mines in Churchill's Cabinet], one of the South Wales Miners' Members of Parliament, and a fully qualified mine manager. Within 36 hours of his arrival in Wrexham, Sir Stafford began a cross-examination of the manager of the mine, which continued mercilessly for two and a half days. The cross-examination took a form at which Sir Stafford has no superior. So skillfully were the questions selected and put that the manager had no option but to agree with the course of argument put forward by the questioner, and there was universal admiration for the grasp of technical detail which Sir Stafford had acquired. This was, no doubt, partly explained by his long apprenticeship in patent cases where he had to be prepared to meet technical experts on their own ground.

"The Inquiry continued for 35 days, and resulted in a Report which showed little mercy to the way in which the pit had been managed. It also shook the public faith in the system of mines inspection by Government officials, and, at the next big public Inquiry into a mining disaster, that at Markham in Derbyshire in 1938, not only was an independent chairman appointed, but the Mines Department was also represented by counsel as a measure of protection against any attack which Sir Stafford might launch."

Another important service he has rendered to the people is his achievement in clarifying the legal doctrine of "common employment." This doctrine laid down that injuries sustained at work through the negligence of a fellow workman could not be the subject of a claim for damages against the "common employer." In the case of Radcliffe v. Ribble Motor Services, Ltd., Cripps appeared for the orphan daughter of a bus-driver who was killed in a collision with another vehicle belonging to the same company. Cripps succeeded in establishing the view that "common employment" must imply not only the same employer but the same job of work, and in so doing he severely limited the application of this law. Heavy damages were awarded in the Radcliffe case, and the result was of great importance to all transport workers.

In October, 1930, Cripps was appointed Solicitor-General to succeed Sir James Melville, K. C., M. P. At that time Sir William Jowitt, later to hold the same post in Churchill's Government, was Attorney-General, and the two made a powerful combination. Though the office of Solicitor-General naturally gave added prestige to Cripps, it probably did not make a great difference in his practice, for he would certainly have been just as successful without it. There is no doubt that, since Sir Wilfred Greene became Master of the Rolls, Cripps has had a unique position at the Bar apart from jury cases in which Sir Patrick Hastings and Mr. Norman Birkett have an outstanding popular reputation. Cripps has not specialized in jury cases;

had he done so, however, he would doubtless have been equally successful in this branch of the law.

His success is based on solid qualities of judgment, learning, and keen perception. He has an excellent memory, and has often been known to prompt his opponent with details of dates and documents. He is noted for the thorough preparation of his cases, and although his notes are carefully written out beforehand he rarely needs to refer to them in court. It has been said of him that he appears to have a natural instinct for legal principles, and his prima facie view of law is almost invariably supported by authority. He has great ability in extracting principles from a number of authorities and presenting his argument as a logical sequence. Throughout the longest and most complex case he never fails to retain the interest of the tribunal. This is perhaps due in large measure to his happy gift of being able to suggest fertile analogies and to give a simple view of complicated facts.

In these outstanding characteristics of the legal Cripps the germ of his political development is to be found. "Burke," said Lord Parmoor, "has expressed the well-known opinion in favor of a legal education to develop concentration and accuracy. I find no fault with this judgment, but after this education is finished the business of life begins, and it is difficult for a barrister in large practice to give sufficient attention to take a leading part in matters of political interest." It is this "concentration and accuracy," the constant urge (so often expressed in his World Alliance speeches) to "think things out to the bottom" that distinguishes Sir Stafford from the numerous cohorts of Christian semi-Socialists who, after traveling a certain distance, become stuck in the mire of MacDonald's good will. Cripps's primarily moral and emotional attitude toward political questions could not long subsist side by side with the strictly scientific and logical character of his legal work. That it could do so at all can only be explained by the "insufficient attention to matters of political interest" permitted him for almost a decade by his immense practice.

Nevertheless, it was largely through his professional activities that he finally determined to join the Labour party. "My professional work in connection with the acquisition of land for housing schemes and for, new municipal enterprises of all kinds, especially in and around London, took me into slum areas, of the meaning of which I had before been completely unconscious, though I had lived and worked in London all my life! I discovered that in this country of ours the conditions of the workers were appallingly bad. I had long been familiar with the disease-ridden hovels which in many rural areas passed for houses, and the tragically low wage levels of the agricultural workers. But for the first time I began to appreciate what the urban slums really signified in terms of suffering, starvation and ill health."

In spite of these other influences and activities, Christianity was still his most compelling motive for undertaking social activity, and many of his basic conceptions had not altered. In his speeches during his Woolwich candidature in 1930, there are many remarkable similarities of sentiment with those of the earlier World Alliance speeches; but, fortunately, new notes are sounded. The emphasis is less on the international and more on the national defects of contemporary capitalism. In these speeches his views of foreign politics are still substantially the same. The decline of the influence of "idealistic" England, the rise of that of "fear-ridden" France, and the consequent general worsening of international relations are attributed to the rejection of the Geneva Protocol. "England had contributed much, but at the critical time she seemed to lose interest."

("Losing interest" is something of a euphemism for Sir Austen Chamberlain's well-considered action.)

But in his 1930 speeches war no longer appears as the only, nor even the primary, social evil of the present day. Unemployment figures prominently. Mr. Jimmy Thomas's constructive alleviations are praised in contrast to the "quack" schemes of Sir Oswald Mosley (who had just issued his memorandum prior to resigning from the Labour party in March, 1931), as are the "panic" remedies of Baldwin, and the Coal Bill. "Safeguarding" comes in for an orthodox drubbing along the three main lines, "Tariffs mean food taxes," "Tariffs put a premium on inefficiency," and "Tariffs have not helped in America and in Germany." Housing and slum clearance occupy much of his attention. The anticlericalism of Russia is extenuated, but not excused, on the grounds of the corruption of the Russian church. Throughout the speeches runs the leitmotiv of "humanization"— humanization of unemployment relief, humanization of pensions, humanization of housing conditions, of relations in industry, of international relations. Socialism, when it enters at all, enters quietly and unobtrusively. "Eventually," run the notes of one speech, " 'social control,' we hope, as *true solution*."

Upon Cripps's appointment to the Solicitor-Generalship, he was knighted, as is the custom for this position. At the death of Walter Baker, the Labour M. P. representing East Bristol, the National Executive Committee obtained the adoption of Sir Stafford Cripps for the by-election. Mr. G. R. Shepherd, the National Agent of the Labour party, attended a specially convened meeting of the executive committee and general council of the local party on December 13, 1930. He stressed "the important fact which should govern the deliberations referring to the position of the Labour Government, and that Sir Stafford was a Solicitor-General without a seat, and the important necessity of his services being now required inside the House of Commons. I urge the Local Party, nay, I implore you to accept."

There was considerable opposition, led by Alderman Hennessy, who has since become one of Cripps's staunchest supporters. His criticism was the method adopted later by the National Executive Committee. He felt that here was a rich man, very little known to the Labour movement in general, who in addition was a knight and an aristocrat.

"The workers of East Bristol had always been regarded as very radically minded," writes Councillor Herbert Rogers, of East Bristol, "and there was considerable doubt in the minds of Alderman Hennessy and others as to the reactions of the workers generally, together with his own prejudices, which were very proletarian."

As soon as the campaign was under way, Sir Stafford was able to convince the workers of East Bristol that their decision was a wise one. Alderman Hennessy and others who had opposed his selection worked whole-heartedly for his return. The three-cornered contest resulted in a victory for Sir Stafford.

He quickly proved himself one of the ablest parliamentarians and committeemen that Labour possessed. His general capacity and his loyalty to the Labour party earned him the title, and the job, of "maid-of-all work." His first speech was a demure and uncontroversial affair, dealing with an unimportant bill. It was not long, however, before he was given something bigger to handle: the long-awaited Trade-Unions and Trades Disputes Bill, to repeal the Tory monstrosity of 1927. But, in early 1931, Cripps's views on trades disputes were very different from what they were subsequently to become. His handling of the bill, in fact, was designed far more to appease the Liberals than the Trade-Unions and the Labour back-benchers, who, at the 1930 Party Conference, under the leadership of Ernest Bevin, had passed a resolution demanding "without any equivocation at all the complete restoration of the pre-1927 position." The bill was a masterpiece of equivocation. It was presented by Sir Stafford as being designed to remove the widespread "feelings of unfairness and injustice" in Labour circles at the provisions of the 1927 Act. "The Mond-Turner Conference demonstrated conclusively, if any such demonstration were necessary, that the organization of Labour into Trade-Unions was essential to the efficient organization of business. The partners in industry must feel that they were treated justly by the House and by the country and that they were not unfairly hampered in their negotiations." He then proceeded to differentiate between the industrial strike, "the sole weapon of the workers in an industrial dispute," which everyone admitted to be legal, and the "strike or lockout which was in its substance political or revolutionary," and which, they were all agreed, "was, and had been, and always should be illegal." "Under the present Bill, if in substance the object of a strike was non-industrial, it was illegal; and if, in substance, it was industrial, it was legal." Even admitting the strictures on "revolutionary" strikes, there remained the essential difficulty of drawing the line between one type and the other. The key question was whether or not the General Strike of 1926 would have been legal under this new bill.

Cripps gave the answer which was on his own definition correct—that the General Strike, although "primarily" industrial, "in substance" was political and revolutionary, and therefore would have been illegal under the new bill. This caused an immediate outcry in the Labour ranks, to which the Prime Minister contributed by drawing a very pretty red herring across the trail; instead of pointing out that the bill was unsatisfactory, which was evident, he affirmed that the General Strike had been "purely industrial," which is palpably false,

These tergiversations in Parliament apparently satisfied most of the Liberals, and the bill passed in an early reading by twenty-seven votes. But the Tories, with the able assistance of Leslie Burgin, an able lawyer who became one of Chamberlain's standbys during the appeasement period, succeeded in killing it in the committee stage by passing an amendment illegalizing any strike which endangered the food, water, fuel, light, medical, sanitary, or other necessary service—in other words, any major strike whatever. The Government thereupon withdrew the bill, and nothing more was heard of it. Doubtless it is the memory of this Parliamentary debut that has kept alive in many trade-union minds their suspicion of the author of these equivocal speeches.

The other major bill which Stafford Cripps was given to handle (Snowden fell ill about this time) was the highly technical Finance Bill, dealing with the taxation of land values. The bill was not perhaps of great intrinsic importance, but Cripps's forensic handling of its complexities called forth a veritable shower of congratulatory notes from the Opposition and the Liberal benches. The *Yorkshire Post* compared his treatment of his opponents' arguments to the action of a tank. "He has the swift motion of a tank and its crushing power; he produces the rolling up effects of the tank. The metaphor, however, breaks down as regards aspect. The tank is ugly and cumbrous. Sir Stafford is, in personal appearance and externals of speech, graceful."

With that pretty tribute we shall leave Sir Stafford briefly, and pass to events which, by forming the background against which he has moved, have largely conditioned his career.

III

THE CRISIS YEARS 1931-1935

THE WORLD CRISIS steadily deepened all through 1930 and 1931. Unemployment figures kept mounting while Mr. Thomas reiterated at meeting after meeting that the clouds had a silver lining, that a brighter time was just around the corner, that the old country was not yet down and out. But as Mr. Thomas's optimism grew more and more beatific, certain other members of the Cabinet began to perceive more and more clearly the limits that capitalism set to the piecemeal, ameliorative demands which constitutional Socialism asked of it.

In those days even the most modest requests for concessions seemed revolutionary, since the very fabric of capitalism appeared to be threatened. As G. D. H. Cole said, "It was no longer enough to ask how much further the policy of social reform could be pressed without endangering Capitalism. The gradualists found themselves forced rather to consider how much of the reforms already gained it was possible to retain in face of the international pressure to bring down the costs of production."

On every hand demands for economy were heard, and the epidemic reached the Treasury Bench on February 11, 1931, when Mr. Snowden made his famous speech demanding "sacrifices from all."

It was over the question of the maintenance of the pound at the artificial par level that this controversy over the balancing of the budget arose. For the drain of gold from Britain could be counteracted only by borrowing from France and from America; and, according to Mr. Montagu Norman, the Governor of the Bank of England, the French and American bankers imposed the balancing of the budget as a condition of lending. After the Government did abandon the gold standard, with no very alarming consequences, it was frequently questioned whether it had been so desperately necessary to "stand by the pound." But the fact of the matter was, as Sidney Webb admitted, that the Labour Government had never seriously considered abandoning the gold standard. They held that if the pound decreased in value, it would buy less Canadian wheat, less Argentine beef, less American tobacco. The result would be a rise in the cost of living, or even more serious consequences: possibly an inflation such as Germany had experienced.

Two main suggestions were made for balancing the budget—tariffs and economies. Tariffs, of course, were the Tory catchword. But Keynes and Sir Oswald Mosley also were advocating a "scientific tariff" by means of "import boards." A revenue tariff would at least have helped to balance the budget and would, it was argued, have lessened somewhat the adverse balance of payments which in 1931 had turned against Britain for the first time, to the tune of £110,000,000. But Labour's financial theorists, particularly Philip Snowden and Pethick Lawrence, true to the liberal lineage from which so many of them had sprung, refused to countenance any such question.

There remained economies. As the result of an amendment moved by Sir Donald McLean, a Liberal who later joined the "National" Government, Mr. Snowden set up such a committee to recommend economies. The chairman was Sir George May, late President of the Prudential, and the members were in the main businessmen, with Arthur Pugh and Charles Latham as Labour representatives. The committee recommended cuts amounting to £96,000,000. Of this total, £66,000,000 were to be cuts in unemployment benefits, and the remainder mostly summary reductions of pay of schoolteachers, police, the armed forces, health insurance doctors and pharmacists, civil servants, judges, and ministers. In addition, other expenditures on public health, secondary and university education, colonial development, and all forms of scientific research were to be reduced to a minimum.

While this report was being studied, Mr. Snowden made the startling announcement (without explanation) that the deficit would amount, not to £120,000,000 as predicted by the May Report, but to £180,000,000. Mr. MacDonald, who was in continual contact with Mr. Montagu Norman, painted the gloomiest possible picture. For the first time, rumors were heard of the drain of gold. The £56,000,000 which had already been lent by America and France were rapidly becoming exhausted, and at any moment, reported the Prime Minister, the Bank of England might have to refuse the Treasury the £12,000,000 that was required weekly for the Unemployment Insurance Fund.

The story was spread about that actually the French and American bankers determined the issue. As a condition for their lending the £80,000,000 considered essential to maintain the gold standard, it was said that they had insisted not only that the budget be balanced, but that this balance be achieved by cuts in unemployment expenditure.

While the question is still far from clear, the most recent evidence indicates that British bankers took matters into their own hands and used the French and Americans as a blind for their own manipulations. It is certainly clear that they did everything in their power to place the Government at their

mercy by undermining confidence abroad in the financial stability of Great Britain and thus furthering the drain of gold
reserves. Newspapers, including *The Times*, and national leaders
repeatedly drew attention to the serious plight of the country.
A series of articles by the Frenchman, André Siegfried, did the
same.

The Liberal-Labour Cabinet was appalled at the Opposition's
rejection of their proposal. They realized that they were in the
hands of the Opposition leaders, since, by combining in the
House of Commons, the Opposition could outvote the Labour
party Government. Their consent was, therefore, necessary for
a decision. The Cabinet sent the Prime Minister again to the
Opposition leaders, and again the answer was the same. The
Cabinet was in a dilemma. To refuse the Opposition demands
meant defeat as soon as the House met again; it might, Mac-
Donald intimated, mean much worse than that if the loan was
not achieved and confidence not restored. But nothing would
induce the Cabinet as a whole to agree to raise their bid beyond £56,000,000.

They would fight, it was decided; they would rally round
their alternative budget. All would stand together to save the
unemployed. But Mr. MacDonald had a new shock in store
for them. He put before them another ultimatum, this time his
own—either accept the cut in unemployment benefits or resign from the Cabinet. He already knew definitely from Mr.
Baldwin and Sir Herbert Samuel what the attitude of their
respective parties would be toward him and the National
Government he had in mind.

The members of the Labour Cabinet naturally assumed on
that Sunday night, August 23rd, that Mr. Baldwin would be
asked to form a government. But without consulting them at

all, without even informing them of his intention, Mr. Mac-Donald proceeded to set up a National Government with himself as Prime Minister.

When the Cabinet assembled next morning, MacDonald came in and announced to them that a new Government had been formed—in short, that he was in and they were out.

"Some day, no doubt," Sir Stafford Cripps later wrote, "the true story will be told of the trans-Atlantic telephone conversations which preceded the fall of the Labour Government, but these were of small importance compared to the real issue that was fought out within the Cabinet whether consciously or unconsciously. The moment had arrived when reformism had to be abandoned. It had necessarily decreased the difficulties of the capitalists with their rapidly contracting markets, and would no longer be tolerated without the danger of a complete collapse of the whole system. Two paths were open: to allow reaction to take charge and to give up the concessions which had been extracted from capitalism; or to proceed to risk the breakdown while making a rapid change-over to Socialism."

The defection on the part of hitherto "beloved leaders" now pushed the surviving Labour leadership into a wave of "uncompromising Socialism" such as the Labour party has seldom enjoyed before or since. In the demure words of Mr. Attlee, "the revulsion from MacDonaldism caused the Party to lean rather too far toward a catastrophic view of progress, and to emphasize unduly the conditions of crisis which were being experienced. . . ."

The effects of this drive from the left are clearly seen in the next Labour election manifesto, studded as it is with such phrases as "Capitalism has broken down"; "The only issue is Capitalism versus Socialism"; "No more patching-up of Capitalism but only a drastic Socialist policy." Mr. Herbert Morrison, Miss Susan Lawrence, Mr. Cramp, and even Mr. Clynes uttered Socialist sentiments which would have done justice to Jimmy Maxton, Independent Labour party leader.

From the very start of this campaign, Stafford Cripps moved into the leadership. It was clear that none of the old Cabinet Ministers, profoundly compromised by Labour's "Economy" epoch during the summer, and particularly by the last few fatal Cabinet meetings, could lay down the new "ultra-left" line. At the time of the fateful mid-August discussions, Cripps had been on a holiday in Germany where he had fallen ill. Although certain newspapers hinted rumors that he proposed remaining as Solicitor-General in the Government, his unhesitating condemnation of MacDonald from the time of his return, established him at once as the *Chevalier sans peur et sans reproche* of the Labour party. His speech opposing the Government's Economy Bill was a decisive rejection of it, and was received by the Labour back-benchers with more enthusiasm than any speech since the Labour Government had come in. He followed this up by appearing at the Labour Party Conference in October as the champion of the unemployed. He created a yet profounder stir with his speech in connection with the by-election at Hull, when he bluntly stated that Labour had a "complete scheme to take over the Bank of England," to be followed by the control of the joint stock banks, the discount houses, and the complete financial apparatus of the City. He announced that all foreign securities would have to be mobilized with a view to ensuring the stability of the currency—a phrase which explains many of Labour's waverings on the question of imperial policy, since the liberation of the Colonies would involve automatically the liquidation of a high percentage of these securities. Finally, he advocated the immediate establishment of a National Investment Board to control the distribution of capital.

During this period, Cripps was frequently canvassed for the leadership of the Labour party as well as of the Parliamentary Labour party, the organization of Labour Members of Parliament. Newspaper after newspaper, gossip column after gossip column, raised the question, "Will Cripps supersede Henderson?"

Although he did not, the Labour election manifesto made it plain that temporarily the Cripps election policy had won all along the line. Foremost in the program, among the fervid appeals for Socialism, stand the demands for national ownership and control of the banking system, for an international conference to arrive at a concerted monetary policy, and for a National Investment Board. It proposed to "reorganize the most important basic industries—power, transport, iron, and steel —as public services, owned and controlled in the national interests." Import boards were to be set up to control foreign purchases. The land was to be nationalized.

Rapid conversion to Socialism did not save Labour from overwhelming defeat at the 1931 elections. The conversion had, perhaps, been too rapid for many of those who remembered the attitude of prominent Labour functionaries toward the unemployed, the coal miners, and the cotton workers, during the period of Labour rule. The poll for Labour, the "panic" atmosphere, was only a fraction higher than that of 1929, and considerably less than that of 1924. On the other hand, it did not serve to reassure the "investing public" in the face of the "National" spokesmen's warnings that the Labour program represented "Bolshevism Run Mad," and that among other "wild-cat" schemes Mr. Henderson's "hooligans" planned "seizure of the deposits in the Post Office Savings Bank." The *Daily Mirror* even published a picture of Petrograd during the "June Days" of 1917 with Kerensky's machine guns posted at the street corners against the anticipated Bolshevik rising.

Nearly all the most venerable Labour leaders—Henderson, Graham, Morrison, Dalton—were defeated. The only former Ministers who remained to lead the Labour platoon of forty-six in the House were George Lansbury, Clement Attlee, and Stafford Cripps.

"Cripps had been associated with East Bristol for only seven months when the crisis of 1931 broke out," writes Herbert Rogers, Sir Stafford's agent in Bristol. "During the General Election, which followed in October, a vile campaign was conducted against him, and his opponents adopted the most unscrupulous methods. The following is an instance: There is one area (which usually polls 75% to 80% Labour) in which a large factory is situated, employing in normal times upward of 1,000 hands, and in recent years this had been converted to the manufacture of artificial silk. With the slump in the artificial silk industry, the whole district had been reduced to poverty, aggravated by the fact that many of the workers had invested their small savings in the industry. Three days before Polling Day, huge posters appeared on the Boardings—'Return National Government and Silk Mills will be Reopened.' This was followed on the eve of the Poll and during Polling Day itself with the lighting of certain fires, smoke being visible through the tall chimney stacks. One can appreciate the effect this might have had upon the voters in such a district where poverty had been widespread since the closing of the factory. On the Sunday before Polling Day, the Canvass Returns for the Constituency were available, and it was calculated that we had a majority of approximately 2,000. As Agent, I felt very uneasy about the situation. Information had been collected from Hendon, where the 'National' Candidate was connected with the Public Assistance Committee, and his record of voting upon that body was most useful. A leaflet was drafted, which I am certain would have had the effect of changing a large block of votes, had we been able to distribute it in some of the working class areas. Sir Stafford, however, would not approve of the leaflet, as he was not prepared to contest the election on anything other than Party Policy. However, in spite of a terrific barrage, he did increase his poll over that of the By-Election by 200 votes, and won by a majority of 429."

Thus Cripps was thrown yet further into the leadership, especially when Lansbury scandalized his back-bench colleagues by getting up in the House and defending the Anomalies Bill of the previous Government. Not even the physical representations of Lansbury's deputy, Cripps, who rushed into the House and clutched in vain at his coattails, would make him subside.

Beatrice Webb, Cripps's aunt, joked him after this occurrence: "I am afraid you must be feeling rather lonely on that opposition bench, though Lansbury seems to be doing well in his own way and creating a certain impression of directness and honesty as well as good humour. I am also afraid that you will find it rather difficult to combine a busy professional career with leadership in the House of Commons and that even solicitors may be frightened off by some aspects of your public work. However, that is the penalty of taking up the cause of the bottom dog—the upper dog will not love you!"

This electoral defeat, though in the main it must be attributed to the uniting of the political opposition forces into a single anti-Labour bloc, set up anew the currents of discussion and recrimination inside the Labour party. In this period of intellectual ferment the figures for the loan of boxes of books from the Fabian Society to local Labour branches was nearly twice as high as ever before or since. Yet these heart-searchings might be supposed to have taken place in a vacuum, with no millions-strong Labour movement fighting for its life, for all the leadership of the Labour and trade-union savants. The period of the richest spate of leftist and Socialist phrases was also the period of the greatest isolation of the Labour and trade-union movement from the workers they were supposed to be leading.

The bankers and industrialists who had presided at the formation of the National Government did not intend to follow in the faltering steps of the Labour leaders. If, as a prominent Conservative M. P. said later, the Labour party "made no attempt either to create a condition of things which would make it possible for private enterprise to function, or to take over the industries themselves to run them and manage them," the National Government did not propose to find itself in any such Hamlet-like dilemma. Labour might not be expected to run the country in the interests of capitalism, but the representatives of capital certainly could! The first move, the passage of the National Economy Bill, was an indication of what was ahead for the British working class. Two months after the formation of the National Government its economic implications were fully revealed.

The debate over the bill—more particularly Cripps's analysis of its consequences—laid bare the price which the workers would have to pay because of the capitulation of their leaders, and the prevailing tone of the Tory advocates of the National Economy Bill was symptomatic. The Minister of Pensions, Major Tryon, in a brush with Sir Stafford, suggested with more than casual accuracy that ". . . the Communists are the people who believe in Socialism and the Socialists are the people who sit on the Front Bench." He pointed out that ". . . the present situation of the nation is a position in which it has found itself after more than two years for which honorable members opposite are more responsible than we are." This is the sneering attack of a platform orator. The MacDonald Labour Government could not have prevented the world crisis. One suspects that Major Tryon was simply using the opportunity to taunt the Parliamentary Labour party with the timidity and cowardice of their erstwhile representatives. And he did so boldly, pointing out that the cuts proposed by the National Economy Bill—which Sir Stafford Cripps was now opposing for the Labour party—were the very same cuts in wages and unemployment relief which were first advanced with the approval of the MacDonald ministry.

It has already been suggested that the concealed purpose of the National Government was to salvage the position of the hitherto ruling groups at the expense of the working class. What evidence can be offered for this contention? First, as Sir Stafford pointed out, the National Economy Bill "was introduced into this House as an emergency measure to accomplish one purpose. That purpose was to save the gold standard," and the wage cuts were contemplated only as a last resort to keep the currency stable. But, Sir Stafford continued, between the introduction of the bill and this debate, *the gold standard had been abandoned by the National Government.* What justification could there be, then, for inflicting hardships on the unemployed and in reducing the salaries of the teachers and the army and navy? The answer, as Sir Stafford gave it, was clear and unequivocal—the bill was nothing more than a device to depress "the standard of living of the workers in this country while the going was good." This effort was to be accompanied by a provision which was an open move toward Fascism. No other phrase could describe the power which the bill gave the National Government to reduce expenditures from the Consolidated Fund without consulting Parliament. This was unprecedented, since it "puts into the uncontrolled power of Ministers a right to take from a large number of people in this country varying sums of money to which these people are in many cases entitled by statutory agreement. This House has no power whatever to control the amount of money so taken, or the person from whom it is taken. . . ." The only grounds on which the Tories could defend this provision was the same one which Hitler and Mussolini had used in attacking democracy—that it was inefficient to cling to democratic measures. Mr. R. J. G. Boothby, who rose to debate with Sir Stafford, expressed this point of view with naïve clarity: ". . . I do not think that we shall ever get through the troubles in which we find ourselves if we spend our time clinging to constitutional procedure which has become outworn, and is no longer efficient for the immediate purposes of this country."

Thus it can be clearly seen that the first step of the National Government was a step in the direction of Fascism.

By propaganda in the press and the radio, in what can only be called a hysterical effort to stampede the electorate, the National Government had returned a decisively Tory Parliament. Given their majority, and a free hand to "save the country" along the "doctor's mandate" lines, the Tories proceeded to sneak in tariffs; but "it had to be proved that protection was not a question of party politics but of national necessity." It was a national necessity, the Tories claimed, to check the dumping of goods into the country. They rushed through the Abnormal Importations Bill, which imposed duties up to one hundred per cent on commodities which were supposedly being dumped. Next came proposals for a duty up to one hundred per cent upon certain fruits, vegetables, and flowers; a move which was justly characterized by the Labour party as the first step in the taxation of food.

Neville Chamberlain, Chancellor of the Exchequer, on February 4, 1932, openly revealed the Government's policy on tariffs. He announced a general duty of ten per cent on all imports, with the significant exception of meat and wheat. He also announced the setting up of an Import Duties Advisory Committee, which could remove articles from the free list to the tariff list without Parliament's approval.

From the Import Duties Act to Empire Free Trade and the Ottawa Conference was only a short step. Four members of the Cabinet, the Samuelite Liberals and Snowden, were ready to resign over the issue of protection versus free trade: Mac-Donald, the Prime Minister, was too far gone for any assertion of integrity. It was imperative that the imposition of tariffs should *not* appear to come from the Tory party but from a National Government *above* parties. Hence the famous "agreement to differ" was put into operation. Dissenting members of the Cabinet were allowed to disagree publicly and in Parliament, while still remaining members of the Cabinet. This unprecedented plan was prompted by the fear of having to appeal to the electorate directly to sanction the tariffs. The resignation of four Cabinet members would have necessitated another election. A contest fought over the issue of tariffs might have been disastrous for the Tory advocates of protection.

But this device could not be used in the case of the Ottawa Conference, called to organize a protective system of Empire Free Trade (significant euphemism!). This was so flagrant a partisan policy that the Free Traders in the Cabinet did resign in September, 1932. At this time the National Government was participating in a conference at Lausanne which was designed to unsnarl the reparations tangle. It was impossible to participate honestly in both conferences, because the economic and political principles upon which they were based contradicted each other. The Lausanne Conference was designed to improve international relations by the modification of absurd and unjust reparations which had been placed upon Germany. It was conducted peacefully, around a conference table, in civilized fashion; and it had the wholehearted support of the British people. The Ottawa Conference, however, could only have one effect—an increased tension in international relations between Great Britain and those countries whose imports would be taxed in order to give preference to Dominion products; all this, furthermore, at the expense of the worker, whose cost of living would rise because of the tax on such food staples as wheat and meat.

The question of the "interrelation of the Ottawa Conference with that which is proceeding at Lausanne" was first raised by Stafford Cripps, in a discussion in the House. Mr. J. H. Thomas, Secretary of State for Dominion Affairs, gave the National Government's statement of policy at Ottawa, which was, as he admitted, "The first conference held for purely economic purposes." After outlining the almost insuperable difficulties which stood in the way of any settlement, i. e. the impossibility of gaining preferences for Great Britain without injuring colonial industry, he went on to mention "the factors that give us encouragement and hope." The general tariff of 10% had exempted imports from the Dominions pending the Ottawa Conference. Mr. Thomas cited this as a factor in obtaining the good will of the Dominions. But Sir Stafford gave it a different interpretation: "I was always under the impression that the somewhat curious date which was put in was in order that immediately after the Ottawa Conference, if there were no re-

sponse by the Dominions, the preferences might be withdrawn
. . . it is idle to say it is a gesture and that we do not ask
anything in return." Only that morning, Sir Stafford pointed
out, the Prime Minister had said at Lausanne: "There is nothing
smaller than a world, there is nothing less than a system, which
is crumbling at our feet." But if this were true, then how
justify Ottawa, which was concerned with considerably less
than the world? Ottawa was concerned with the British Empire, and would only further endanger the system which the
Prime Minister had seen crumbling. Sir Stafford asked for
assurances that "in the discussions at Ottawa the position of
this country vis-à-vis foreign countries will not be left out"; but
this was precisely the assurance which the National Government
could not and would not give. The rationale of Ottawa was the
effort to exclude foreign countries from Dominion markets, in
order to aid British capitalism at the expense of the working
class; the repercussions of such a move upon the international
plane had, therefore, of necessity to be disregarded. Further,
since the Dominions were mainly agricultural, a prerequisite to
any reciprocal system of Empire Free Trade was a willingness
on the part of Great Britain to tax meat and wheat. Mr. Thomas
refused to say whether these were to be included among the
items to be bargained over; but, when pressed by Sir Stafford,
Mr. Thomas was forced to admit that the Government "were
prepared to offer a meat quota." Also, as Sir Stafford hastened
to point out, "wheat and meat, which had been specifically put
on the Free List in the Import Duties Act, can now be removed from the Free List at the discretion of the Committee
of Three." The outcome was almost anticlimactic. Though not
on the tariff list, food was indirectly taxed even more viciously
by the rigid import quota scheme invented in 1932 and subsequently taken up by many other countries. The first quota

scheme on wheat was introduced by the Wheat Act of 1912, and, in the Ottawa agreement between the British and Australian governments, meat was made subject to rigid quotas benefiting the meat producing dominions.

The same tactic is seen in British international policy, and the same intention of placating the British electorate by a policy supposedly designed to foster and secure international co-operation, while at the same time a parallel policy is being pursued with the actual purpose of aiding British capitalism and further aggravating the resultant conditions of international anarchy. During the next year the National Government moved in two opposite directions. They attempted to use Japanese aggression in Manchuria as a means of safeguarding British imperial (ultimately capitalist) interests; but they also called a World Economic Conference. This Conference met eighteen months later than its original call owing to the desire of the National Government to postpone it till the conclusion of the Ottawa agreements.

Whatever chance the World Economic Conference might have had of arriving at any successful solution was blocked in advance by the policy of economic nationalism which had been accepted at Ottawa. "It is wholly impossible," Sir Stafford told the House, a month after the failure of the World Economic Conference, "to maintain a fiercely competitive system and at the same time to bring about international co-operation." There were others who saw the deception revealed by this simple statement, and they restated up and down the country Sir Stafford's claim that the economic policy of the National Government made it virtually impossible for the World Economic Conference to accomplish its purpose. The National Government could not find a single independent economist of repute who would go to the Preparatory Commission of this conference on its behalf. Hence the British found themselves represented in this key position by two officials of the Treasury.

It was Neville Chamberlain, Chancellor of the Exchequer and official spokesman for big business interests, who approached the World Economic Conference with the statement about "the economic warfare which has arisen between us and other countries." "We must maintain that warfare," he declared, "so long as it is the other countries who have taken the aggressive and are unwilling to make any sort of reparation or restitution for the wrongs they have done us." Such injured innocence, in this sophisticated age, can ónly be admired; but it was surely a little ungenerous of Mr. Chamberlain to identify virtue so completely with his own cause. The presupposition of all Mr. Chamberlain's divagations was, as Sir Stafford pointed out, "the absolute necessity for the maintenance of profits arising from productive industry." Hence the National Government was adopting the usual capitalist inference "that it is necessary to have a restrictive policy in order to decrease the amount of goods on the market, so that the price can be raised, profits may be higher, and a greater inducement may be offered to the manufacturer to produce the goods, or to the cultivator of the soil or the mine-owner to produce the various raw materials." This is, of course, one method of keeping the price level—and the rate of profit—stable; but it is hardly of much assistance in easing unemployment or bringing sorely needed commodities within reach of the working class. Sir Stafford suggested that the National Government pursue a policy such as President Roosevelt was then advocating in America, "to inject purchasing power in the system by means of forced expenditure of some sort or another, and it is by means of pumping in the consuming power to start with in order to meet production that a revival of the price level will be brought about." The suggestion made no headway. Sir Stafford was even interrupted by a member of the House naïve enough to ask whether he thought "that production will continue unless profits are made?" Such a policy would run counter to the interests of British capitalism, and was unthinkable to the National Government.

For our present purpose it is irrelevant whether or not the National Government expected fruitful consequences from the World Economic Conference. The postponing of the Conference to make way for Ottawa seemed to suggest that it was considered of secondary importance. Certainly any solution to the economic and political problems of the world crisis would involve some sacrifice of national interest; and, in the face of the offensive launched by resurgent British capitalism, such a desire is hardly plausible. It is just possible that the World Economic Conference, like the one at Lausanne, was another sop to the pacifist and international predilections of the British electorate. At any rate, simultaneously with these conferences the National Government was trying to safeguard British imperial interests by more efficacious methods. The technique is illustrated by its attitude toward the Japanese invasion of Manchuria.

A critic of British imperialism has written that in the early stages of the Japanese offensive on China in 1931, Britain supported Japan, not only in accordance with its general line of playing off Japan against the United States, but also as the strongest military force in the Far East against the national revolutionary movement in China. These statements are borne out by the Tories themselves. Sir Nair Stewart Sandeman of Sandeman's port and sherry, rose in the House to reply to Cripps and said with commendable honesty: "I frankly am pro-Japanese. . . . Frankly, I wish we were in closer touch with Japan and were prepared to say that we were going into the

Yangtze Valley. . . . I am certain that it would mean at once
peace in China, and the poor Chinese people would know that
the next day's livelihood was safe *and we could make goods and
export them to China.*" (Italics mine—E. E.) This is the commercial motive, nakedly, brutally revealed. In the face of this,
let us consider Sir Stafford's plea for an embargo against Japan,
based on the findings of the Lytton Commission in Manchuria.
The report of the Lytton Commission was unanimously accepted by the Assembly of the League of Nations, and, said Sir
Stafford in 1933, "It is important to notice that the findings of
the Assembly of the League of Nations are based upon a series
of breaches of faith by Japan." That is to say, there was no
longer any question of Japan's guilt as an aggressor in Manchuria. "Since this is true, the question now arises: What are
we to do as a sequel to Japan's action upon the League of
Nations' unanimous report? The Foreign Secretary at that time
announced, after the Lytton Commission's Report, the National
Government proposed to stop further export of arms to both
China and Japan. But no one can suppose that by means of an
arms embargo alone anything except a moral effect will be
brought to bear upon the Sino-Japanese position, because every-
body knows that there are large arsenals in the Far East; money,
on the other hand, is probably the most important factor and
might have a decisive effect far more rapidly than an embargo
on arms." And, further, if the intention of the National Government was to place an embargo on *both* China and Japan, of
what necessity was it then to wait for the League of Nations
Report proving that Japan was the aggressor? "If we are going
to put an embargo on both parties, that is a thing suitable to
be done before you have decided upon the aggressor." But,
though for himself he realized the contradiction and the inadequacy of placing an embargo on both countries, yet as repre-

sentative of the Parliamentary Labour party Sir Stafford did not oppose the imposition of an embargo. "It will not have any very great effect as regards stopping the war in the Far East," he said, "but, on the other hand, I think that it may have some effect on world sentiment, because a lead is a great thing, especially when it is a fine moral lead." The object of this lead would be to encourage other countries to follow with an embargo; and here, as Sir Stafford is careful to say, "When it comes to an agreement between the different nations . . . I hope . . . that that agreement will be based upon an embargo against Japan alone."

But this was not the most important question raised in that debate. With almost prophetic insight, Sir Stafford put his finger upon the policy which was adopted by the National Government in the following years. "A very serious question," he says, "has been raised by several of the speeches made this evening and, indeed, by the statement of the Foreign Secretary, Sir John Simon, that we will not become involved in this war in any event. Nobody wants to become involved in this war. . . . But does that statement mean—the Committee must face up to it—the abrogation of Article XVI of the Covenant? . . . Are we merely going to put ourselves into the position of performing what we would call the centuries-old ceremony of kowtowing to the bullies of the world, or are we going to say that the theory of sanctions is a real theory and is, indeed, a theory and a practice that was invented for the purpose of assisting in keeping peace, and are we going to apply it? Probably, the Foreign Secretary will not want to answer that question tonight, but sooner or later this House will have to come to a determination as to whether they are to treat Article XVI as a mere scrap of paper."

The unwillingness of the Foreign Secretary to make a clear

statement on that issue was later to enable the Labour party, over the opposition of Sir Stafford, to support the National Government, in the delusive hope that the National Government would effectively stop Italy from dismembering Abyssinia. It was to lead directly to that fatal series of concessions to Hitler which formed the prelude to war. These actions may be briefly indicated here in the words of the *Daily Telegraph,* which declared in October 1931 that Japan was "an old and proud friend and firm ally, who is rightly regarded as the main bulwark against Bolshevism in the Far East."

THE RIGHT REACTION

The failure of Labour's fighting policy to defeat the electoral tactics of the Tories led to a revival of the right and a plea for even greater moderation on the part of Labour than before. This was led by Messrs. Clifford Allen and Godfrey Elton, who both finally broke with the Labour party, and were both then elevated to the peerage. Mr. Allen, with considerable cogency, maintained that it was Mr. MacDonald, and not the remainder of the Cabinet, who had proved the most loyal to the traditional principles of the Labour party. For, whereas "the Labour Government cannot avoid the conclusion that their refusal to carry into effect their own Cabinet opinion in favor of economies meant that they deliberately decided to hand over the welfare of the workers to others, and abandon the control of world affairs," Mr. MacDonald had acted with "the courage and realism of Lenin, although, of course, in different circumstances. He saw he was confronted by a transitional menace, as Labour would often be again if it retains its faith in a peaceful transition from capitalism to socialism. He therefore decided to save the workers from as much suffering as he could, and the nation, too, even at the cost of a temporary retreat (as tragic and painful as retreats always are), and then once more to set his face to rebuilding his party and his nation on better socialist foundations."

The Labour party, on the other hand, according to Mr. Allen, acted crudely and indelicately. "By the tone of its opposition in Parliament," he wrote, "it helped finally to doom all efforts to save the gold standard, intensified the cleavage with its old leaders, struck terror into the hearts of a public which could have been so easily rallied to a true understanding of the failure of capitalism, and gave the impression that Labour was out for a revolutionary policy at one of the most sensitive moments of financial anxiety which has ever faced the British nation."

The polemical antics of Mr. Allen are important as presenting in caricature the outlines of all that is worst in Labour party outlook, now as then. Mr. Allen defended his attitude by an antithesis between "Socialism" and "Labour," advocating more Socialism and less Labour. How explain this? The answer is simple. The everyday demands of Labour were class demands, connected, however subconsciously, with that bitter reality so revolting to the pacifist soul, the class struggle. Unable to stomach the class struggle, Mr. Allen set up in opposition something sublime and utopian, emasculated of all class content—his own concept of Socialism, the watchwords of which are "justice" and "planning" but which has nothing to do with "the emancipation of the working class," still less with "workers' rule."

Mr. Allen was duly taken to task for his championship of the "treachery." Cripps himself performed this necessary duty in the columns of the *Daily Herald,* though he failed to comment on Mr. Allen's peculiar views of Socialism and Labour.

The immediate questions concerning Labour's Socialist policy which agitated the movement were not at first questions as to what form of Socialism was to be introduced. They were concerned, rather, with the pace at which it was to be introduced. The "gradualists" held the theory that Socialism could be introduced piecemeal, concession by concession, by taxation, state interference, and social services. The attack on this theory begins to figure frequently at this time in the speeches of Sir Stafford Cripps. He perceived that a Socialist Government was like an airplane—if it tried to go too slowly it would stall and crash. Only later in the development of the Socialist League did such questions as compensation and workers' control agitate the party conferences.

Predominant among the fashionable cries were those for "monetary reform" and "managed currency." The depth of the crisis of 1931 was attributed by Labour intellectuals to the artificial return to the gold standard and parity with the U. S. A., effected by Winston Churchill in 1925, and to the consequent elevation of the bank rate and the restriction of credit, together with the enormous burden of interest paid to the rentiers. The whole of the blame was laid by these theorists on the shoulders of the bankers. An attempt was even made to distinguish between the criminal and unpatriotic actions of the bankers and "speculators" and those of the "sound" industrialists and businessmen. Mr. A. L. Rowse, for example, wrote, "I want to emphasize the important point that there may at some time be a re-alignment of forces between industry and finance, and the working class movement in this country. . . . The old industry allied itself with finance, I will not say to its own destruction, but to its debilitation. . . . I would appeal to those people concerned in the direction of industry, and primarily to the younger men who are now arriving on the threshold of responsibility."

Essentially, Tory opinion was divided on monetary policy, and the Labour party theoreticians had focused on the facet of capitalist policy which seemed at the time to suit best their own apologia. The more conservative interests, closely connected with international finance and the imperialist rentiers—those who had been responsible for the 1925 restoration—desired to restore the balance of payments in favor of England. (She was in danger of losing her place to America and France.) "With a balance of payments in her favor, Great Britain would be in a position to make foreign loans again, and to resume her old place as the world's monetary center." For this purpose, they were prepared to contemplate a temporary abandonment of the gold standard as a weapon in the trade war. On the other hand, the more aggressive, purely industrial interests were willing to play with inflation recklessly, because for them the trade war was not a means to an end—the restoration of Britain's financial supremacy—but was an end in itself.

Another plank of the Labour "Socialist" platform was the increase of purchasing power—that "building up of the home market" that figures so largely in "The Great Britain," doubtless picked up by Sir Oswald in the far-off days when "Ford v. Marx" was the slogan of the I. L. P. Over and over again the Labour publicists, led by the *Daily Herald* editorials, exposed the pathetic short-sightedness of the National Government policy which maintained that economies, cuts, and rationalization were the cure for unemployment when the crisis was, in fact, one of overproduction and underconsumption. This was "the root fallacy," in the *Daily Herald's* phrase. They believed that if only the capitalists would have the common sense to return to the palmy days of Labour's social service expenditure, all their difficulties would be over.

Although this was undoubtedly true, it was a short-sighted view of the economic situation. No cognizance was taken of the fact that increased social service expenditures, including higher wages, would raise the price of commodities, naturally affecting the sale of British commodities in the competitive export market. Helping the working class solely through increased social service expenditures was ultimately self-defeating, for the consequent rise in the price of export commodities would decrease the sales and lead to further unemployment. How this problem was to be met without the wholesale abolition of the burdens of accumulated debt and parasitism by the expropriation of the capitalist industry was not answered by the Labour theoreticians of the time.

On the political side, the demand was raised for the reform of the inefficient and obstructive parliamentary procedure which, with a certain amount of justification, the Labour functionaries were blaming for their ineffectiveness of the past two years. In particular, it was determined to limit the power of the House of Lords, which had been responsible for throwing out most of the meager residue of progressive legislation that Labour had succeeded in forcing through the Commons. This question had never before appeared on the official Labour election manifesto. There is no doubt that its presence there was due in no small measure to the influence of Cripps, who had learned more thoroughly than any other Labour leader the true lessons of the 1931 debacle.

It remains to be asked why Stafford Cripps was entrusted with the leadership of the official leftward "swerve" (it scarcely merits the appellation "turn"), rather than the leaders of the I. L. P., from whose theoretical armory so many of the new weapons had been drawn. To answer this, we must briefly recount the evolutions of the I. L. P. from the days of 1930, when Margaret Bondfield rejected the amendment of Jenny Lee regarding the raising of the benefit for children of the unemployed. Thereafter the left-wing group of the I. L. P. sought to cut themselves off from the Labour party's more flagrant acts of capitulation before the "economic blizzard." Though they never went so far as to vote against their party on a motion on which the Government might be defeated, they sought in every possible way to dissociate themselves from the lethargic evasions of the Government, continually sniping at the Labour Ministers from their back-bench "mountain," to the acute resentment of the more "loyal" members of the party. A movement arose in the I. L. P. for a complete break with the Labour party, whose inveterate reformism was coming to be regarded by the more revolutionary members as incurable. The dissatisfaction of the I. L. P. with the Labour Government's attitude on the unemployment question led to a dispute over the constitutional right of members to oppose in debate and to vote against the Government in the House.

It was over this limited question that the official break in Parliament between the I. L. P. and the Labour party came about. But the differences separating the semi-purged Labour party from the ultra-purged I. L. P. were claimed to be much more fundamental. For while the Labour party, led by Cripps, was picking up the threads of the "Socialism in Our Time" propaganda of 1924, the I. L. P. was deciding, not without many hesitations and contradictions, to turn against Labour reformism for good and all. A "Revolutionary Policy Committee" was formed which agitated openly for disaffiliation from the Labour party, for a complete break with parliamentarianism and adoption of revolutionary methods. The official leadership of the I. L. P., James Maxton, Fenner Brockway, etc., also favored disaffiliation, but insisted on preserving their distinction from the Communists by retention of many of the traditional demands of the I. L. P. which were being adopted so eagerly by the Labour party.

Opposed to these two groups there was a third, consisting

mainly of Socialist intellectuals who took the view that the Labour party was still the only effective vehicle in Britain for a transition to Socialism, and who maintained that only by remaining inside the Labour party was there any hope of influencing it. It was out of the leaders of this third group that the Socialist League was largely formed. When the League finally assembled, it had within its ranks some of the best brains in the working class movement, including, besides Sir Stafford Cripps, its leader and chief spokesman, Sir Charles Trevelyan, Professor Harold Laski, William Mellor, E. F. Wise, H. N. Brailsford, G. R. Mitchison, Professor Richard H. Tawney, and G. D. H. Cole.

The preliminary conference of the Socialist League adopted a resolution which is extremely important, since it has formed the theoretical basis for whatever differences have existed and now exist between the policy of Sir Stafford Cripps and that of the official leadership of the Labour party. This resolution may be divided into five parts: (1) Industrial measures; (2) rejection of reformism; (3) recognition of the indivisibility between the political and industrial struggle; (4) the necessity of concentrated Labour action; (5) immediate measures to be taken.

The resolution began with a ringing affirmation of unconditional support to all working class struggles: "This conference of Labour, Trades-Unions, and co-operative organizations, held under the auspices of the Socialist League, pledges its full support to all workers, especially those now fighting for an improvement in wage conditions." But industrial struggle alone is not enough: "At the same time, this conference warns the working class of the dangers inherent in schemes for the reconstruction of capitalism, which, basing themselves on the need for private profit, not only intensify the bitter wage struggles internally, but accentuate the danger of war between competing capitalist powers." In other words, the industrial and the political struggles are indivisible. "The conference declares that today every economic struggle of the workers for higher wages or better conditions is in reality part of the struggle for political power." How, then, must the Labour movement organize to take cognizance of this indivisibility? "If the economic crisis of today is to be solved in the interests of the workers, there is needed a concentration of all the forces of the Labour Movement, not merely to aid workers engaged in wage struggles or in resistance to capitalist oppression, whether of workers or workless, but to create the political power and understanding necessary to bring down the National Government and to secure the election of a Labour Government, pledged to immediate fundamental measures of socialization of the means of production." Finally, the suggestion which was to earn the Socialist League and its leader, Sir Stafford Cripps, the undying enmity of the trade-union and Labour party bureaucracy was the demand for democratization within the Labour party itself. "In the effort to mobilize the forces of Labour on the political field it asks the Executive of the National Labour Party to prepare plans for giving greater weight and power in the governance of the Party to the Constituency Parties, on which falls in fact the day-to-day work without which victory is impossible, and to explore ways by which the essential bond with the Trade-Union movement may find expression increasingly through the local units of the National Party."

The conflict of these three groups worked itself out through the spring and summer of 1932. At a special conference held in July, the vote for disaffiliation was won by 241 votes to 142, but suggestions for a complete adoption of a revolutionary policy and an approach to the Third International were defeated.

The I. L. P. thus doomed itself to the role of a small propagandist body with ever-dwindling influence, torn between the then uncompromising armed revolutionism of the Communist party and the "constitutional revolutionism" of those of its members who still regarded it as possible to work inside the Labour party. When the two latter trends came together, in the Unity Campaign, the I. L. P. joined them.

IV

THE IMPACT OF FASCISM

THE VICTORY of German Fascism in 1933 demonstrated that Fascist methods were not to be confined to countries which were lagging industrially. Germany was one of the great mass-production countries; her technological resources were surpassed only by those of the United States, and in the manufacture of precision instruments she was unrivaled; her industrial techniques had reached such a pitch that Great Britain fought one of the most disastrous wars in history to eliminate her from competition for colonial markets.

Some part of this fact glimmered through to the Labour party, for at the Trades-Union Congress of that year, Sir Walter Citrine presented a document called *Dictatorship and the Trade-Union Movement,* which seemed to presage a new realization by the trade-union bureaucracy of the danger of Fascism. According to Sir Walter, "they (the trade-unions) had to expose Fascism and show how inimicable it was to everything based on humanity. They had to show that it meant not only slavery of intellect, but ultimate slavery of the working class people of this country."

How did the leaders of the trade-unions propose to demonstrate this? As shown in the manifesto issued by the National Council of Labour, *Democracy versus Dictatorship,* the leaders of the British Labour party declared themselves unalterably opposed to "all dictatorships whether of the Right or of the Left." But what did this actually mean? It meant that the leaders of the Labour party were confusing the economic nature of Fascism with the political mechanisms by which it foisted itself upon the people.

If this were true, the challenge of Fascism was not the challenge of the dictatorship in any sense but the challenge of capitalism itself. By shifting the issue from capitalism to dictatorship, the leaders of the trade-unions and the Labour party weakened the stand which might have been taken against the National Government. For, as Stafford Cripps later pointed out in his pamphlet of 1934 called *"National" Fascism in Britain,* it is not necessary for Fascism to change the political form of capitalism from parliamentary democracy to dictatorship. "The worker [in England]," he wrote, "is being and has been disciplined, not viciously and ruthlessly as in Germany and Italy, but gently and firmly as one would expect from a country-gentleman Fascism in England. Colored shirts are not necessary and are embarrassingly obvious; a special constable is much cheaper and attracts less attention. But do not let us be deluded because the signs are less obvious in this than in other countries, as to the direction Britain is following, politically and economically."

From its very inception the National Government had shown its Fascist tendencies. It was formed on the appeal to patriotism, asking the electorate to forget political parties and save the country. But saving the country, as shown in the last chapter, was to be accomplished by attacking the living standards of the workers. Not only that; the National Government moved slowly but steadily to organize country-gentleman Fascism. One of the most instructive examples of this tendency was the Police Force Act of 1933. This limited the membership of the Police Federation, restricted the period of service of ordinary constables to not more than ten years, and set up a special college for commissioned officers drawn mainly from the "public" schools and older universities. This was called Trenchardism, because it was based on a report by Lord Trenchard, then the Commissioner of Police for the Metropolitan Area (London). It bore close resemblance to the police system developed in Germany. The debate on this bill definitely revealed its Fascist tendencies. Seymour Cocks referred to the limitation of membership of the Federation as "essential to the Hitlerized and militarized police force which it was the intention of the Government to establish." Eleanor Rathbone said, "the idea is that if the democracy pushes reforms too far, then they, the upper class, will step in and pervert the constitution in order to serve their own privileges."

The Police Bill was shortly followed by the Sedition Bill, whose alleged purpose was to make better provision for the "punishment and prevention of endeavors to seduce members of His Majesty's Forces from their duty and allegiance." The Sedition Bill bore a striking resemblance to some of the decrees promulgated by the ill-fated Brüning Government in Germany. As drafted, the original bill provided for a reversal of traditional British legal procedure. It was a direct attack on freedom of speech and civil liberties. The assumption that a man is innocent until proven guilty was inverted in the original bill. Though it was not passed in its original form, it is instructive to note the effort to establish a precedent in the Duncan Case in 1934. Mrs. Duncan was charged with obstructing an officer by insisting on addressing a public meeting. The police officer admitted that the meeting was orderly, but said that Mrs. Duncan's arrest was justified on the grounds that she might have said something which would have led to a breach of the peace. According to the police, she might have said something which would, possibly, make the unemployed less contented! This is analogous to

Hitler's statement that he took Prague in order to preserve the peace. It is an excellent method by which freedom of speech can be curtailed. In America the technique was used by Mayor Frank Hague of Jersey City, to justify the forcible removal of Norman Thomas, the Socialist leader, in order, as he blandly explained, to preserve the peace. The tactics are similar, though the suavity with which they are executed may vary with the supply of country-gentlemen. These efforts of the National Government were carried forward in conjunction with the maneuvers at Ottawa, at the Disarmament Conference, and finally in relation to Japan. They present a picture of the National Government moving both internally and externally along the road to Fascism, playing a dual role in regard to its statements and its actions—a role which was to receive its first public display during the Italo-Ethiopian crisis of 1935.

THE ISSUE OF COLLECTIVE SECURITY

With remarkable accuracy Stafford Cripps foresaw all the consequences of the British failure to adopt a policy of collective security against Japan. The issue arose again in 1934. Speaking in the House on May 18, Sir Stafford put four straightforward questions to the National Government. "First: Does the country still stand by the report of the League of Nations of February, 1933, and regard Japan's position in Manchuria and Jehol as a breach of the Nine-Power Treaty? Secondly: Does this country repudiate its obligation to respect and preserve the territorial integrity and political independence of China, including Manchuria, under the Nine-Power Treaty and Article X of the Covenant? Thirdly: Is the Government prepared not to enter into any treaty, agreement, arrangement, or understanding with Japan in preservance of the provisions of Article II of the Nine-Power Treaty, or does it repudiate that Article as well? Lastly:

What attitude has the Government adopted toward the question of Security? Is it prepared to sacrifice any part of this country's independence of action or decision in order to attain international security?" These were the key questions. They never received a clear and unequivocal answer.

Indeed, what answer could there be? There was no denying that Japan's position was a breach of the Nine-Power Treaty. There was no denying that Great Britain had repudiated its international obligations to China. The very lame excuse made by Sir John Simon was that the Nine-Power Treaty did not bind the contracting countries to respect *and preserve* "the integrity of China, but only to respect the sovereignty, the independence, and the territorial and administrative integrity of China." By this ingenious if somewhat technical argument, Sir John concluded that Great Britain had not "pledged itself to use its Army, Navy, and Air Force for preserving the territorial integrity of another." A more ominous note was introduced by Mr. Stanley Baldwin. At the time it seemed obvious; but in the light of later events it looms as the first adumbration of a policy which was to have disastrous consequences for the Labour party. "If you go in for the collective maintenance of Peace," Mr. Baldwin said, "it is no good going in for it unless you are prepared to fight in will and also in material. Nothing could be a worse guarantee to the world or a more cruel deception of your own people than to say, 'We will guarantee peace by arms, but not be ready for it.' There is no doubt that if you are going to force a collective guarantee or a collective sanction, it means that you have to make this country a good deal stronger than she is today. *These remarks are perhaps not directly relevant to the matters we are discussing at this moment.*" But they are most certainly relevant to the Election of 1935, where this reflection of Mr. Baldwin's was elaborated into

a policy which defeated the Labour party on its own chief plank
—collective security.

Collective security had been debated pro and con all through
1934. For it was obvious that upon this issue depended the fate
of disarmament, peace, and whatever hope there might have
been of easing the economic tensions engendered by imperialism.
The Fascist countries were still comparatively weak. Any talk of
provoking war by a system of collective security was not only
nonsense but was quite openly an attempt to camouflage the real
situation. (There is an interesting analogy here to the pre-
Munich tactics of Neville Chamberlain, in distributing gas
masks, digging trenches, etc.) How did the National Government meet the issue? It did so by pretending that its program
of rearmament was only for the purpose of strengthening its
position as an advocate of collective security. Stafford Cripps has
analyzed the growth of this tactic in his book, *The Struggle for
Peace*. "It was Winston Churchill," he writes, "who first appreciated the political value of this phrase (collective security)
to reactionary conservatism. After Germany had left the League,
and as a consequence the League had fallen completely under
Anglo-French domination, he realized that adherence to the
doctrine of collective security would be tantamount to supporting a strong Anglo-French alliance, which could be built up
under the cloak of the League. Under this guise, the anti-German power grouping would earn the good will of many who
would otherwise be against it, and rearmament, professedly for
collective security, would be accepted by those who would never
consent to such a step for imperialist purposes."

Collective security as a political tactic has no intrinsic virtues;
it can be used for any purpose. The anti-Comintern Pact of
1936-37, ridiculous as it was on the surface, might be called a
move toward collective security—the collective security of the

Fascist Powers. Thus it is possible to apply the term to any effort at a general understanding between countries. The National Government, now under Mr. Baldwin, proceeded to take advantage of this ambiguity. The first glimmering of such an approach could be seen in his speech in the House quoted above. Its development had to wait on the growth of peace sentiment in Great Britain.

Before considering the crucial Italo-Abyssinian issue, it should be stressed, as has been done by Sir Stafford, that "in their dealings with Italy the major factor was not the saving of Abyssinia, or even the maintaining of the safety of British and French possessions in North Africa, but the maintenance of Italian capitalism. A second Communist state in Europe would have menaced gravely the stability of European capitalism; although it was desirable if possible to limit the growth of power of Italy in North Africa, it was even more important to avoid the overthrow of Italian capitalism." This was the line which, in spite of many inconveniences, British capitalism was subsequently to follow. It would be naïve to assume that the declaration of war against Germany in September 1939 indicated a reversal of this policy. What it did indicate was that Chamberlain was outmaneuvered by Stalin. Every concession which the National Government made to Hitler weakened the imperial interests of Great Britain at the same time that it made the position of Soviet Russia more precarious. Chamberlain and British capitalism were gambling on the hope that Hitler would be forced into conflict with Stalin. This hope was reinforced by Hitler's anti-Soviet declarations. Such a war would have been disastrous for both sides, and would have left British capitalism in an extremely strong position. The Russo-German nonaggression pact of August 1939 put an end to these plans. Appeasement now would serve no purpose except further to weaken the British Empire. With the hope of turning Hitler to the East gone, there was nothing to do except fight. That the Chamberlain Government had no antipathy to Fascism as such was shown by their continual flirtations with Mussolini until the Norwegian fiasco drove Chamberlain out and put Churchill in.

The Sino-Japanese affair had shown that the National Government had no intention of supporting the Socialist conception of collective security as an alternative to imperialist powers, whether new or old. Mr. Baldwin, speaking at Glasgow on November 23, 1934, said: "It is curious that there is growing among the Labour Party support for what is called a collective peace system. Well, now, a collective peace system in my view is perfectly impractical in view of the fact that the United States is not yet, to our unbounded regret, a member of the League of Nations, and that in the last two or three years two great Powers, Germany and Japan, have both retired from it. It is hardly worth considering when these be the facts." Lord Swinton, Secretary of State for Air, said in February, 1935: "Collective Security is the policy of the Socialist Party, and it will sooner or later lead this country into a war."

Mr. Baldwin reversed himself on May 27, 1935, when he said: "The League of Nations is the sheet anchor of British foreign policy." What caused this startling shift? First, British calculations as to the possibility of controlling Japanese imperialism in the Far East had received a severe setback. After receiving British support in her Manchurian adventure, Japan proceeded to clamp down on the Open Door. Mr. Hirosi Saito, the Japanese Ambassador to the United States, said: "Japan does not desire to interfere with legitimate foreign business in China, but it wishes to be consulted by those who want to deal with China before concluding any transactions." What would happen, Mr. Saito was asked, if the foreign governments were to ignore this request? The answer is significant: The Japanese Government would consider it an unfriendly act. The Federation of British Industries sent a mission to Manchukuo and Tokyo, but it soon became clear that Japan had no intention of relinquishing its colonial markets for the blandishments of the British. Manchukuo was to be effectively closed to all non-Japanese enterprises, including British. The Japanese economic invasion, especially in respect of textiles, was pressing British interests hard throughout the Far East, in India, in all the markets of the world. Britain consequently began to put up heavy duties in its colonies against Japanese goods. Thus the British attempt to utilize Japanese imperial ambitions for British ends—to stamp out Chinese nationalism and threaten Soviet Russia—backfired economically.

In the Italo-Abyssinian situation British action was complicated by this first failure. Furthermore, Italian imperial ambitions were this time dangerously close to Britain's Empire line of defense. The Mediterranean and the Red Sea were Britain's vital line of communication with its Empire in Africa, the Near and Middle East, India, and Australia. Italian dominance in the regions of the Red Sea, on the basis of control of a solid block of Eritrea, Abyssinia, and Somaliland, as well as Yemen on the other shore, meant a deadly peril to that line of communication, and was also the starting point for an ultimate converging attack, from Libya on the west and Abyssinia on the south, for the conquest of the Sudan and Egypt. On the other hand, under peaceful conditions the Italian conquest of Abyssinia would entail certain advantages for Great Britain. According to the inter-Departmental report of Sir John Maffey, Permanent Under-Secretary of the Colonial Office, "whereas in case of war . . . an efficient Italian control over Abyssinia would be a menace to neighboring British possessions, it would be a boon in normal everyday administration. . . ."

Thus the National Government was faced with the necessity of adopting a dual policy, geared to fit ambiguities. It was necessary to bolster the League to checkmate the demands of Italian imperialism—but only if it became too insistent. It was also necessary to soft-pedal a genuine system of collective security, which would weaken the Fascist powers and decrease their effectiveness as the vanguard of capitalism's assault upon Soviet Russia. The Hoare-Laval sell-out of late 1935 was simply the rational compromise which would have resolved these mutually contradictory possibilities. A further point which had considerable weight was that the National Government had to meet the growing sentiment in Britain for a collective security policy.

Speaking in the House on the day that Hoare resigned, Sir Stafford Cripps analyzed the difference between the Italo-Abyssinian crisis and the Sino-Japanese crisis. "The Sino-Japanese dispute had to be dealt with in the early days of the National Government," he said, "when the prospects of a General Election were still a long way off, and when the sentiment in the country was still comparatively unstirred upon the great issues of peace and war." But since that time the conditions had altered: ". . . when the Italo-Abyssinian crisis became publicly acute, the prospect of an electoral appeal was very much closer and the foreign policy of the National Government had become a very live issue in the domestic forum of our politics." As a result, "The Prime Minister realized that the peace sentiment might be needed electorally by the National Government, provided that for a time it was made to appear to the people that the liberal sentiment was in the ascendancy in the Government. The true imperialistic basis of their policy was soft-pedaled very gently, while the liberal sentiments were blocked from every platform all over the country." Thus, before the election, the National Government issued a manifesto which said, in part:

"The League of Nations will remain as heretofore the keystone of British policy. . . . We shall continue to do all in our power to uphold the Covenant and to maintain and exercise the efficiency of the League." Anthony Eden also gave expression to similar sentiments: "It is clear that our part should be to pursue a foreign policy that is frank, stalwart, and above all firm in support of the League of Nations and of the collective peace system. . . . We shall always be found ranged on the side of the collective system against any government or people who seek by a return to prewar politics to break up the peace which by that system we are seeking to create."

The leadership of the trade-unions and the Labour party failed to recognize this sudden shift of policy for the masterly political maneuver which it was. They accepted the National Government at its word, and endorsed the pious terminology. At Brighton in October a sharp clash occurred between the Socialist League, led by Sir Stafford, and the protagonists of the official line. The Socialist League opposed the official policy as clearly an effort to utilize anti-imperialistic sentiment in favor of imperialistic ends.

In one of the most momentous debates of his career, Sir Stafford upheld his position with eloquence and foresight. The resolution which he opposed was moved by Hugh Dalton, on behalf of the National Executive Committee. "This Conference," the resolution read, "pledges its firm support of any action consistent with the principles and statutes of the League to restrain the Italian Government and to uphold the authority of the League in enforcing Peace." The ambiguous words could easily be construed to give complete approbation to anything the National Government did which was "consistent" with the League. The dangers of such unconditional approbation were clearly drawn by Sir Stafford: "To me the central factor in our decision must turn, not so much upon what we as a country should, or should not, do, but upon who is in control of our actions. I cannot rid my mind of the sordid history of capitalist deception. The empty and hollow excuses of 1914, which I was then fool enough to believe, echo through the arguments of today, the 'war to end war,' the need to fight to save democracy, the cry to crush the foul autocracy of Prussian militarism, all have their counterparts in today's arguments. Throughout the history not only of British imperialism, but of every other imperialism, these have always been fine and patriotic excuses, acts full of useless suffering and tragedy to the workers, acts that brought with them not the promised light of salvation, but only a dimmer and more horrid chaos. Can we trust the Conservative Party, that Party whose criminal record has been . . . backed by the great industrialists and capitalists who today control the 'National' Government—can we trust them with the lives of British workers?"

To those who accused him of inconsistency, Sir Stafford had this to say: "I have been accused of changing my views on this topic. I have changed them, because events have satisfied me that now the League of Nations, with three major powers outside, has become nothing but the tool of the satiated imperialist powers." This analysis, however, was based not only on "the sordid history of capitalist deception" in the past, but the recognition that the political situation necessitated another deception in the near future. An examination of the general political situation in which the election was fought will bear out this conclusion.

Writing to his son, Lord Parmoor commented that, "If the League of Nations had been adopted as a guide of peace, disarmament would deprive the present Tory party of the happy hunting grounds for their sons and relations; and the Foreign

Office, instead of being a world authority, would sink into a quiet insignificance. This would be a great advantage to true Socialism, and in my view a true preliminary step. It is a very crucial matter in my opinion, and of the utmost importance. You know that I am a believer in the League of Nations Covenant, but I found out at Geneva that Tories and officials of the Service departments and of the Foreign Office, although issuing any number of softly worded peace suggestions, yet always desired to put the Geneva Protocol as far away as possible and to diminish its influence. Their one desire was to keep the complete independence of our foreign policy, and to enforce our views by force rather than by common co-operation."

"It was not long," wrote Sir Stafford in 1936, "before the result of the Peace Ballot in this country, with its overwhelming majority in favor of collective action, made the Government realize that they must base their rearmament program on collective security if it was to have any hope of electoral success. They therefore performed a quick-change turn and came before the electors as the protagonists of the very collective security which they had so recently derided. With an almost sickening reiteration of the words they called upon the country to support a program of British imperialistic rearmament in the sacred cause of world peace."

In that stormy debate which we have quoted, this analysis was anticipated. With bitter sarcasm he lashed out at the deceit and treachery of the National Government. "We will put on sanctions . . . they must only be reasonable; they must be such sanctions as will really have no effect, and then we will offer to settle the matter by giving her [Italy] half Abyssinia. That is untold generosity on the part of Imperialism. What other instance is there in the history of Imperialism where a backward race has been allowed to keep half of its territory? So the

Prime Minister . . . said: 'Why, they are allowing Abyssinia to keep half her territory; that is a very good and fair settlement to all the parties, Italy, Abyssinia, and the League of Nations.' " But it was hardly a good settlement for those voters who had returned the National Government to office, under the mistaken impression that the foreign policy of the National Government was one of collective security. Since the large majority of the voters had been in favor of collective security, as was shown by the Peace Ballot early in 1935, the official endorsement of the National Government given by the leadership of the Labour party considerably diminished the chance of a Labour victory at the elections. Hence the issue in the elections narrowed down to one of personality. Sir Stafford deals with this point in *The Struggle for Peace:* "Once the people are allowed to believe that a League of Nations and collective security can be operated to bring peace in an imperialistic world, there is really no fundamental distinction between Labour, Liberal, and Conservative foreign policy. The Conservatives are no doubt recognized as more thorough-going in their professions of imperialism, and therefore they are perhaps the most competent party to put through an imperialistic policy. The question then resolves itself into one of the good or bad intentions of individuals who form the government, and a man with a reputation for honesty, such as Mr. Baldwin once had, is more likely to be trusted than any other leader who professes that peace can come within capitalism."

The truth of this contention is clearly seen if we consider the error of the Labour party leadership. Their error was twofold. First, they set their faces rigidly against their potential allies of the Communist party and the Independent Labour party; and second, they fell headlong into the trap laid for them by Mr. Baldwin. They failed to see any significance in the

Silver Jubilee other than a becoming gesture of loyalty to a well-loved monarch. They failed to see through the hoax of sanctions, and genuinely believed the Government had undergone a death-bed repentance. At the Trades-Union Congress, Sir Walter Citrine said:

"The National Government can be abused and is abused every day in the week by individual delegates, but we do not propose to bring forward to you in every one of our resolutions we submit some new expletive, some new opprobium of the latest misdeed of the capitalist government of this country or any other country. As for Mr. Rowlands, he said in his well-meditated speech that what we have to do is to expose the war policy of our own government. He failed to give any evidence of that policy in respect to Abyssinia."

This was said after the newspapers had been full of details regarding the attempt of Eden to fix up an imperialist bargain with Mussolini, and his attempts to conclude a deal with Baron Aloisi at Paris. For weeks before Citrine spoke pamphlets on Abyssinia were on sale describing the secret treaties between the imperialists of Britain, France, and Italy in respect of that country.

In the *Daily Herald* of October 15th we see how completely the Labour party had been taken in by Baldwin:

"The General Election will be fought on domestic issues and not exclusively on foreign policy.

"Six months ago it looked as if foreign policy would dominate the election. Between Labour and Tories there was a gulf that seemed unbridgeable on foreign policy. Now, incredible as it would have seemed six months ago, the Government is supporting the League."

Again, in a *Daily Herald* editorial of August 29th: "There still seems to be a belief that the British attitude is determined only partly by the League. It is shaped also, it is said, by imperial interests. If France really believes this, she is making a great mistake."

And in September: "Irrespective of party, irrespective of domestic conflicts, the overwhelming majority of the nation stands firmly behind the Government."

The war resolution at the Trades-Union Congress and the Labour Party Conference was carried through without any section criticizing the National Government. At this point the National Government chose to hold a general election. Certainly it was an unfair "snap" election; but the Labour party Executive can hardly complain, since they all but went down on their knees and begged for it through their blind and childish acceptance of any inconsistent story the National Government threw together for them.

This complete failure to understand the situation meant that the Labour party had an extraordinarily weak platform. While the eyes of the whole country were fixed on foreign policy, the Labour Government could muster no arguments against their opponents except on domestic issues. The popular appeal of domestic issues was at a lower ebb than almost ever before, both because of the fact that Great Britain was then enjoying the upward grade of the boom-slump cycle, and because of the dramatic events in the international sphere. The meager Labour platform encouraged a defeatist outlook which went far to damp down any remaining enthusiasm felt by the rank and file. A. J. Cummings, the able political editor, wrote in the *Liberal News Chronicle:*

"One must deplore the shameful spirit of political defeatism which has overtaken the Labour Party in this country. One day last week a group of Labour leaders in London were discussing with an air of patient resignation the prospect of returning 170

Labour representatives to the next Parliament. That was the maximum calculation. I should have thought that the mere normal operation of the Party machine, coupled with the narrowest swing of the political pendulum, would ensure a Labour representation of at least two hundred."

All the battle cries were on the depressing theme of possible increases in the representation of the party. Morrison, on November 2nd, made the stirring announcement: "We are going to do very well in this election; if our people go on as they are and make the supreme effort that is necessary, the Party will do very well."

As the crowning touch, the leaders of the party in their election pamphlet proudly quoted Mr. Baldwin:

"The Labour Party as a whole has helped to keep the flag of Parliamentary Government flying in the world through the difficult periods through which we have passed. I want to say that, partly because I think it is due, and partly because I know that they, as I, stand in their heart of hearts for our constitution and for our free Parliament, and what has been preserved against all difficulties and all dangers."

The pamphlet goes on to quote The Times's gracious assent to this statement as a "moving and well-deserved tribute to the Labour Opposition." Well-deserved it was indeed. But the services for which the tribute was paid were hardly such as it was tactful to recall to those who were genuinely seeking socialism.

Palme Dutt summed up with biting accuracy in Labour Monthly of December 1935:

"They entered the Election denouncing unity, denouncing the class struggle, denouncing Communism, vowing that they were as devoted to the Constitution as Baldwin, and quoting Baldwin's contemptuous pat of praise to the Labour Party as their best testimonial, vowing that they would maintain armaments

as efficiently as the National Government, vowing that they
would maintain the National finances as efficiently as the National Government, protesting that the existing economic recovery was not the special merit of the National Government
and would not be injured by their coming to power, and in
every respect appearing, not as the leaders of a rising class
proclaiming war without truce on the National Government
and the whole capitalist order for which it stood, but as pale
and ineffectual counterparts of the National Government, seeking to carry forward the same type of policy with a slightly
more progressive color."

Cripps must have full credit for his far clearer understanding
of the machinations of the National Government than any of his
colleagues. He was under no illusion as to the real meaning of
the Jubilee. In his speech at Caxton Hall in September he said:

"The new phenomenon in our national life of a 25-year Jubilee
has been sedulously surrounded by the politicians with a well-
cultivated ballyhoo from which they hope and indeed boast that
they will derive electoral benefit. In this I believe they will be
disappointed. . . . It is not only understandable but reasonable
that the people should express their loyalty to their nation
through the medium of a titular sovereign on appropriate occasions.

"Apart from that aspect of the question, there is every reason
in the tragic and depressed circumstances of the workers today
why they should accept an opportunity for the relief and escape
of a national jollification.

"But neither of these matters offer justification for a ruling
class utilizing the loyalty of the People, for the purpose of assisting them in an electoral campaign. The organized expenditure of large sums of public money up and down the country
to this end cannot be justified.

"The Conservative Party have claimed as their own the National Flag and the National Anthem, and they desire to monopolize for their own purpose the national loyalty."

He realized, too, that the Government fully intended to go ahead with an enormous armament program as soon as the election was safely over. Speaking again at Bristol on the Jubilee, he said:

"There is another aspect of the same matter which is likely to prove even more dangerous. The cry of false patriotism that is raised to support a policy of large armaments has always been a trick of the militarist and capitalist imperialist. . . . The big navy scares of 1910-1914 are now being repeated in the big Air Force scares of the present year."

In another speech just before the election he referred to the same trick in respect to the Navy:

"It is rather a novel thing to hear the Conservative Party going about crying 'stinking fish' with regard to the Navy. There was a time when they were always proud to say what a marvelous navy it was. Now, because it suited them, they were willing to decry it and say it is a lot of scrap iron, and that its admirals' knees are shaking at the mere threat that Mussolini might do something in the Mediterranean. Mr. Baldwin has said that we have only three capital ships built since the War. He did not tell them that no other country had any, nor did he say that the First Lord, who came before Parliament every year to report on the state of the Navy, has said each year during the National Government's rule that the Navy had been maintained at the highest state of efficiency.

"Why has this red herring been drawn across the trail? Perhaps one of the reasons might be found in the attitude of the City of London to the rearmament program. From that program up to date a profit of 29,630,000 pounds has been made, and doubtless the mouths of the financiers are watering at the prospect of an unlimited loan for the purpose of rearmament."

Nor did the significance of the Cabinet changes in the summer of 1935, when Ramsay MacDonald retired from the Premiership, escape him:

"A reshuffle of posts has taken place—to make quite certain that the Government shall be completely Tory in policy. The last shreds of pretense as to its national character have been blown away. The three most important posts of Prime Minister, Foreign Secretary, and Chancellor of the Exchequer are all now in the hands of whole-hearted Tories."

He fully appreciated the tricks by which the Tories had achieved electoral successes at previous elections: the Red Letter scare of 1924, and the Gold Standard scare of 1931. He foresaw that some such trick was going to be played on this occasion too, and there was every sign that collective security was going to be the main feature. In a speech at Birmingham he laid bare the projected hoax with regard to collective security and Abyssinia:

"Why is it that the Government have rushed the present election upon the country, right on top of the municipal elections? Because the Government are afraid that if it took place any later the crooked bargain which is going to be made with Mussolini whereby a 'sphere of influence' over Abyssinia will be given to the Italians, will be flung back in the Government's own face. The acid test of the Government's sincerity will be whether Ethiopian independence emerges from this scuffle as untouched as it was last January."

THE CLEVER MR. BALDWIN

The outlook for the British Labour movement was more hopeful at the beginning of 1935 than it had been for a very long time. An impressive victory had been won by the working class on the question of cuts in the relief scales. These reductions, of from two to nine shillings per week, raised a storm of protest. Demonstrations, protests, and strikes such as had not been seen since 1926 threw the capitalist class into what Mr. Baldwin described as a "curious state of hysteria and panic." On February 5th an announcement was issued that the new scales would be suspended at the end of a further week, and reduced payments under the scales would be made up. The next day, orders for immediate cancellation of the new scales were sent to the principal towns. The victory for the working class in this battle was complete.

This spectacular success was like new life to the movement. A few weeks later, by-elections at Wavertree and Norwood emphasized the new hope by startling Labour successes. At the same time there was a growing belief among the people at large, in the system of collective security through the League of Nations, and a genuine desire for disarmament and a constructive international effort to discover and root out the economic cause of war.

How was it then that with all these growing forces in their favor the Labour party failed so lamentably in the autumn election?

The answer once more lies in the rigid determination of the leaders of the Labour party to keep out of their ranks anything savoring of militancy. They had taken no part in the spectacular victory of February 6th; they had indeed done all they could to damp down the enthusiasm and militant spirit of workers all over the country that had led to it. In the struggles of the miners that followed, they gave no assistance other than one or two rather vague declarations of theoretical agreement; any sign of strike action to enforce the demands was met by official frowns and portentous warnings about the wicked Communists who were trying to foment strikes. On March 25th the Black Circular, directed against any sort of co-operation with Communists, was adopted by the General Council. From this moment dated the decline of Labour support. Had the leaders of the Labour party followed up the victories won by the rank and file that winter, an electoral victory in the autumn would have been almost certain. For the first time in many years, the capitalist class was on the run; victory for Labour was in sight. And a victory for Labour in that autumn of 1935 would have meant a different fate not only for Abyssinia but for the whole of Europe.

At the same time as this attack upon allies of the left came gestures of friendship toward the right. Instructions were sent from Labour headquarters to all local Labour parties and Labour councils to participate in the Jubilee celebrations got up by the National Government for their own purposes. Honors were bestowed upon prominent Labour leaders—in token of their services, present and to come, to the National Government. This collaboration with the National Government had an immediate effect all over the country, reflected in the by-elections of the ensuing summer, when the Labour vote fell to low levels. It is impossible not to see the contrast of the two periods—the period of the rising united front struggle and the rising Labour electoral vote; the period when the Labour party leadership openly collaborated with the National Government to strangle the United Front and its reflection in the setback of the Labour electoral advance.

While the Labour party Executive was driving the party to its defeat, the National Government was laying its plans with great efficiency. Mr. Baldwin contrived the celebration of the Royal Silver Jubilee (a celebration which has no precedent in

British history) as a gigantic piece of "national unity" propaganda, designed to reawaken in the public mind the spirit of militant nationalism which the Peace Ballot had showed to be so lamentably lacking. The Peace Ballot had indeed presented the Government with a very difficult problem. In the interests of international capitalism an immense rearmament program in the near future was essential. Yet here were eleven millions of the electorate going out of their way to express their desire for disarmament and collective security. Something had to be done—and quickly—to liquidate this contradiction, for there was barely a year to run before the next general election was due. Clearly, the Government would not stand a chance if it let either rearmament or its true policy with regard to the League of Nations come before the public notice. So Mr. Baldwin set to work to mislead the electorate on these two vital points.

His various statements about rearmament make interesting reading in the light of the free hand demanded little more than a year later by the National Government for their rearmament schemes. Here are a few of them. In a broadcast, October 25, 1935:

"We do not want and no one will propose huge forces for this country."

On October 28:

"There has not been, there is not, and there will not be any question of huge armaments or materially increased forces."

On October 30:

"I will never stand for a policy of great armaments."

On October 31, in a speech to the International Peace Society:

"I give you my word that there will be no great armaments."

The wholly cynical spirit in which these promises were made is established beyond doubt by the statements made by Baldwin himself in the House of Commons after the election. First he showed that he was under no illusion as to the real state of public opinion:

"There was probably a stronger pacifist feeling running through this country than at any time since the War."

"At the election of Fulham, a seat which the National Government held was lost by about 7,000 votes on no other issue but the pacifist."

"The National Government candidate who made a most guarded reference to defense was mobbed for it."

Then comes his famous confession. In the full concourse of the House of Commons he said:

"I put before the whole House my views with appalling frankness. My position as the leader of a great party was not altogether a comfortable one. I asked myself what chance was there —when that feeling that was given expression to in Fulham was common throughout the country—what chance was there within the next year or two of that feeling being so changed that the country would give a mandate for rearmament? . . . I cannot think of anything that would have made the loss of the election, from my point of view, more certain."

The Italo-Abyssinian war was now over and in the forefront of politics was the Franco rebellion. It was therefore on this particular issue that he must express his enthusiasm for peace and collective security. The story of the betrayal by which he achieved this is too well known to be worth repeating in detail: how the British Government seemed to change quite suddenly from a policy of aloof indifference to the fate of Abyssinia to one of active support for League of Nations action against Italy; how Sir Samuel Hoare roused breathless hope and excitement both at Geneva and among his countrymen at home by his famous speech on September 11 in support of collective security; how the election was hurried through while the glory of this speech was still unsullied in the eyes of the British public and the world; and how, after the election was over, the betrayal was brought to light, and it was seen that the sanctions were a mere mockery and intended only to tide over the period of the election.

Writing a short time later in an article called "If I Were Foreign Secretary" (*World Review of Reviews*), Cripps predicted the betrayal of Munich and the inevitability of war: "The world will get tired of *'perfide Albion'* and we shall be set upon one day and left an isolated carcase to be picked by the new imperialistic vultures. Robbed of our Empire and with no socialist confederation to take its place we shall indeed be the victims of a most unhappy end."

V

SPAIN

THE PRESTIGE AND INFLUENCE of the Labour party were at a very low ebb. The leaders were inactive; the rank and file disillusioned and apathetic. The defeat and betrayal of the Executive Committee in the election by the National Government seemed to have crushed the spirit of the Labour party once and for all— even though the party, with 159 seats, had trebled its seats in the House of Commons; a minor dent, indeed, into the National Government majority of 432 seats out of a total of 615.

The trade-unions were failing to take advantage of the boom which was quite clearly setting in and which should have given them the opportunity for substantial gains both in wages and organization. For industry in 1936 was doing far better than in any year since 1929. Imports of raw materials were larger by 15% than in the previous year, and industrial profits had risen from under 6% in 1932 to almost 10%. The building boom had actually been on since early 1933 and reached a peak in 1936-7. Altogether the stage seemed set for a militant trade-union policy which would greatly improve the conditions of many workers. But nothing was done. The boom was allowed to take its course without any attempt by the leaders of the working class to secure for their followers a fair share of the national prosperity.

The electoral field was equally discouraging. The municipal elections resulted in a net loss of eighty-one seats. In by-elections important seats which had been won by Labour in 1929 were not regained. At Preston the Government candidate went up by

3,500 votes compared with 1929, while the Labour candidate went down by nearly 7,000. The gloom and disillusionment felt throughout the Labour movement were well reflected in the Edinburgh Conference, one of the most discouraging that had ever been held. Here are some comments from persons of various political views who attended it:

"The Edinburgh Conference was by no means so good as it might have been. The Party is passing through an intellectual crisis on foreign policy and armaments." (Herbert Morrison, M.P. for South Hackney and head of the London County Council.)

"This Party of ours at the present time is making practically no headway in the Country. If anything, we are going back." (Dr. Alfred Salter, M.P. for West Bermondsey)

"Whether or not it was the most important Conference the Labour Party has ever held, it was certainly the queerest up to date. If variety is the spice of life, then that condiment was abundantly present. Stupidity, ambiguity, credulity, gullibility, obstinacy, were in evidence, blunders were clamant, betrayal was hinted at, and there was more than once the quite unfair whisper of treachery.

"No doubt the issues were critical. Delegates, many of them uninstructed by their affiliated organizations, many of them obviously ignorant and uninformed upon the questions upon which they had to make momentous and far-reaching decisions, many of them wielding a block trade-union vote that steam rollered all oppositions, showed themselves childishly credulous and quite incapable of doing what above all they were assembled to do—to determine and announce the political, social, and economic policy of the Labour Party in home and foreign affairs." (L. MacNeill Weir, M.P. for Clackmanan and East)

"In my opinion the Labour Party, apart from wholly unpredictable contingencies, stands little or no chance of getting a clear majority at the next General Election, or at the next but one." (G. D. H. Cole)

"It is possible that another conference of the same kind would destroy the Party as an effective force for a long time to come." (Lord Addison)

"The worst annual conference in the postwar history of the party." (Harold Laski)

"It was not a good conference." (Dr. Hugh Dalton, M.P. for Bishop Auckland)

The malaise and discontent that spread throughout the rank were not the result of a psychological trend, as some would have us believe; it was the result of certain quite definite and distinguishable defects in the structure and leadership of the party. These defects, however, which were to be gloriously revealed by the Spanish crisis—as they had been previously by the Abyssinian crisis—were temporarily obscured by encouraging aspects of the internal situation.

There were hunger marches against the Means Test, signifying concerted action on the part of the workers which, for a moment at least, seemed as though it would lead to the much-coveted unity of the British working class. The hunger marchers reached London on November 8, 1936, and were received by a reception committee representing all the various Labour organizations. Wal Hannington, the Communist leader of the unemployed, and C. R. Attlee, the leader of the Parliamentary Labour party, appeared on the same platform. The temper of the National Government was illustrated by the fact that they refused to receive delegations of the hunger marchers; and two days after the entrance of the marchers, a very interesting debate took place in the House. According to Mr. Baldwin, he had refused to receive the marchers because their main aim was "to cause trouble, to cause fights with the police, with the guardians of law and order. . . . That is the way civil strife begins—civil strife that may not end until it is civil war." Why? Because "for many years and certainly this year, everyone who came on these marches knew what the practice had been, and what the position of the Government was. If every man did not know it, the organizers did, and one does not feel a great deal of sympathy with men who may be encouraged to embark on these marches under the supposition, possibly, on the part of some of them, that something will happen which you know will not happen." In other words, it was useless for the hunger marchers to present their grievances to the Government, simply because the Government had already decided *in advance* that nothing could be done to relieve their condition. Strange procedure indeed for a so-called democracy! And even stranger in view of the fact that, as Sir Stafford proceeded to point out, "Many manufacturers' groups, coming in their cars to Downing Street, are received by Ministers of the Crown, and consulted on problems that face the Government." In contradistinction to this, "at no time have the Government given opportunity to these people, who are peculiarly affected by the Means Test, to put their first-hand point of view before the Government, and one is not surprised at hearing speeches . . . when they said that the only possible reason why the Prime Minister and the Cabinet would not meet them was because they were afraid of them. . . ."

So far as the possibility of civil strife is concerned, Sir Stafford raised the question which the Prime Minister's insinuations had attempted to confuse. It was not by receiving them that the Prime Minister might foment civil strife, but rather by *not* receiving them. There were nearly 250,000 marchers, including a large number of definitely middle-class men and women, especially young men and women, joining in the demonstrations in Hyde Park—one of the most orderly demonstrations which had ever been seen. If the Prime Minister refused to receive these marchers because of the danger of civil war, then the result would be, Sir Stafford continued, "to make them think there is no use in peaceful demonstrations. It is to give the very handle he does not want to give to those who say: 'What is the good of your marching peacefully and behaving yourselves if the Cabinet pay no attention to it?' and, therefore, suggest to them that they should use other methods. If the Prime Minister wants to maintain democracy in this country, and the constitutional forms of this country, I suggest to him that when there is a deep-seated evil, and people who are suffering from it, even though they be poor, take the trouble to march—some of them 200 miles—to London, in order that they may be received and put their case before either Parliament or Ministers, the Government should say, 'We are just as prepared to listen to the case put up by the poor people outside the House of Commons as we are to listen to the case put up by the rich people who want some advantage from the Government.' "

The Tory spokesman following Sir Stafford dragged one of the Labour party's ghosts from the closet, and held it up to the light for all to see. He remembered that in 1930 there had also been a huge march: "There were over a million more people out of work than there are now . . . one might have thought . . . that they would have received an enthusiastic welcome here and in Downing Street as well. But what happened? They were not told that they were welcome to come and put their case before Labour's Ministers . . . instead, they were treated, according to their own leaders, not only with indifference, but with positive rudeness."

The unity displayed at the reception of the marchers, and the solid support evoked from all branches of the Labour movement might, in a superficial view, seem to indicate an advance in the movement since the days of 1930, when the disgraceful incident referred to above occurred. But had it really? The crucial test came in the Spanish issue. In the light of the available evidence it is hard to believe that it was met with any tactical advance over what might have been done by the leaders of the party in 1930.

THE SPANISH INVASION

On July 4th the League of Nations raised its sanctions against Italy, and in the same month, on the 18th, a Spanish revolt broke loose. Obviously, there was more than a casual connection between the two. The result in Spain was actually, as everyone except the National Government seemed to know, a planned invasion of Spain by Italian Fascists and German Nazis. Because of Mussolini's interest in making the Mediterranean an Italian lake, the Italians bore the major share of the fighting. The fact that the Spanish revolt was planned by the Fascists long before it broke out is amply supported by documentary evidence collected by impartial observers. An article by "Pertinax," the diplomatic correspondent of the *Echo de Paris,* a Catholic Conservative newspaper, will provide sufficient illustration. "It is too easily forgotten," he writes, "that in July 1936, four Caproni airplanes staffed with officers and noncommissioned officers of the Italian Army, had the bad luck to land or be wrecked on the wrong side of the border between Algeria and Spanish Morocco. M. Peyrouton, the High Commissioner in Rabat, personally cross-examined those men, whose names and military ranks were indicated on papers found on board. They all declared that they had been recruited from various units of the Italian Air Forces at the beginning of July, and had received their final instructions on the 15th, that is, three days before the outbreak of the counterrevolution, and in fact played a large part in its instigation. The lifting of sanctions—themselves a measure without any effect, because applied too late—enabled the Fascists to embark upon another conquest." It may be interesting to recall that about this time Chamberlain was referring to sanctions as "mid-summer madness."

In the early days of the Spanish war British policy was somewhat obscure. In view of the necessity of keeping the Mediterranean sea lanes free, one would have expected close co-operation with France. The Mediterranean problem affects both countries equally, and their interests in checking Fascist supremacy on the Moroccan coast, in the Balearic Islands, and elsewhere would seem to be identical. A typical statement of this position is found in the *Daily Telegraph,* where Sir Abe Bailey, the South African multi-millionaire, wrote: "I am afraid that the success of General Franco would bring nearer Mussolini's dream of transforming the Mediterranean into an Italian lake and might also give Germany that foothold in Morocco for the realization of which she nearly plunged the world into war in 1911." However, the exigencies of the international situation made such a nineteenth-century attitude inadmissable to the National Government. Over and above Great Britain's imperial interest was the interest of capitalism as an economic system. In the nineteenth century capitalism was assumed to be permanent. But the revolutionary aftermath of the first World War, and the rise of the Soviet Union, had illustrated the dangers of dissension among capitalist states. Fascism could be regarded as essentially friendly to capitalism because it was based on the defense of private property and was financed by large industrialists whose property was anything but "private." The best contemporary evidence available as to the workings of the Fascist economic system maintain that the Fascist appeal to large capitalists is mainly the appeal of consummate and unprincipled propagandists in search of funds. The demands of the Fascist bureaucracy have encroached on the "inalienable" rights of private property almost as drastically as would a Communist system. Private property under Fascism is as much of a myth as political democracy under Communism. For this reason, Great Britain was forced to play a double game: popular sympathy was with the Loyalist Government, but the National Government found it expedient to help Fascism by helping General Franco. Because of popular opinion this could not be done openly. It was necessary to camouflage British aid to Franco with the excuse that it was actually a means of preventing a European conflict.

The National Government had the audacity to maintain that the famous "nonintervention proposal" originated in France, where the Popular Front Government of Leon Blum was in office. The Tories in the National Government pointed triumphantly to the fact that their policy was first propounded by the Socialist Premier of France. This falsehood was exposed by the veteran French Socialist, Jean Longuet, who headed a delegation of representatives of the Popular Front who "came to London with the express knowledge and approval of Leon Blum, to see whether British opinion could be mobilized in support of a French denunciation of the nonintervention agreement that was now seen by all to be a cruel mockery." British justification for the charge that France had originally proposed "nonintervention" lay solely in the fact that France announced her decision on July 26th, while Britain's acceptance of the proposal was officially announced later. However, Yvon Delbos of the French Cabinet has confirmed what is common knowledge: that Great Britain pressed France into declaring a policy of nonintervention. That such a policy was not in any way concerned with preventing a European war by the preservation

of neutrality—as was claimed by the National Government—
is proven by the fact that the embargo on the export of arms
to Spain was applied unilaterally by Britain and France, before
the Fascist Powers even consented on paper to follow such a
course. This can hardly be called neutrality in any sense of the
word. A further proof of the ignominious role of Great Britain
in the Spanish affair can be inferred from the fact that France,
in the person of Leon Blum, felt impelled on August 2nd to
issue an appeal for guaranteed nonintervention—this at a time
when the policy was supposed to have been already in force.

Not content with shutting off the flow of arms to Spain in
complete disregard of its international obligations as a member
of the League of Nations, the National Government sabotaged
every effort of the Spanish government to get a fair hearing
before the League and the Nonintervention Committee. Numerous instances can be cited, but one in each case will be enough.
The Spanish Government accused Portugal, Germany, and Italy
of violating nonintervention. According to usage, these accusations had to go to the countries concerned, all of which said
that the accusations were "entirely without foundation." Without further investigation, Great Britain chose to accept the
answers. At Geneva Señor Del Vayo, the Spanish representative, under pressure from Anthony Eden, abstained from officially bringing the Spanish question before the League in the
early days. Sir Stafford Cripps tells us in a speech that "the
secretariat of the League refused to publish documents handed
to M. Avernol by Señor Del Vayo enumerating cases of violation
of the nonintervention agreement because of pressure from
Great Britain." There can be no doubt that the National Government was actively on the side of Fascism, holding the diplomatic fort for France while Hitler and Mussolini poured troops

and munitions into Spain to help crush a constitutionally elected
government with a mildly liberal social policy of reform.

LABOUR'S FOREIGN POLICY

In this crisis, what was the policy of the British Labour movement? We have already seen how the Labour party reacted in
the Abyssinian crisis, supporting the collective-security platform which the National Government had advanced as an election tactic to win the general election. But this was not an
isolated phenomenon. The policy of supporting the National
Government had a historical development. Since the continued
capitulations of the Labour party helped to impel Sir Stafford
Cripps to join the Unity Campaign, it is well to trace Labour's
foreign policy in some detail.

The rise of Fascism was the force which necessitated the
abandonment of traditional Labour party foreign policy—disarmament, war resistance, compulsory arbitration of disputes,
adherence to the League of Nations. As Nazism and Fascism
grew more powerful, however, these stand-bys were gradually
invested with a new—and extremely significant—meaning. It
had been quite compatible, before, to link up the League of
Nation's policy with absolute pacifism—with the hope that all
nations could settle their disputes amicably, under the guidance
of reason and international law. Indeed, at the 1933 Labour
Party Conference, two resolutions were passed which illustrated
this assumed linkage—one resolution calling for joint industrial action to prevent war, and another resolution supporting
the League of Nations. From 1933 onward, however, this link
was no longer congruous with the realities of the international
situation. To stand for the League, it was increasingly realized,
meant to be ready in case of necessity to fight a war. Slowly but

surely the orientation of the League had changed from a pacifist idea into an armed alliance under Anglo-French domination, threatening, and threatened by, Nazi Germany. Labour only gradually became aware of the full implications of this change.

At the Southport Conference (1934) it was evident that the Executive Committee had sensed the necessity for a new statement of policy. The Annual Report stated: "In view of recent events on the continent . . . there might be occasions when the movement would assist only defensive action taken to preserve the nation and its democratic institutions." The effect of this was somewhat counteracted by the policy statement of the National Executive entitled: "War and Peace." Clearly this document was influenced by the traditional aversion of British Labour to the foreign policy of a capitalist government. This aversion previously found expression in resolutions favoring a general strike in the event of war; and this aversion caused "War and Peace" to be cluttered up with schemes for an international air and police force and for a Peace Act of Parliament. The most important aspect of this document, however, was the imputation that a League of Nations policy might conceivably involve war and the support of the Government. It was necessary, "War and Peace" declared, "to distinguish between a war of an aggressive character and a war undertaken in defense of the collective peace system. . . . Labour policy recognizes . . . the duty unflinchingly to support our government in all the risks and consequences of fulfilling its duty to take part in collective action against a peace-breaker."

Obviously this last sentence obliterates the distinction between Labour's foreign policy and the Government's foreign policy. For in the light of this statement what could it mean to expose the Government's real motives in foreign policy and the real causes of war ("the chaotic conditions arising out of production for profit"); and to what purpose was it to threaten to oppose the Government if it acted according to its real motives? A general strike to prevent war was sidetracked; the burden of responsibility for taking a stand against war was shifted from the shoulders of the Labour movement, for it was declared that "the responsibility for stopping war ought not to be placed on the Trade-Union movement alone. Every citizen who wants peace . . . must share the responsibility." This line was drawn further at the Brighton Conference (1935), where Hugh Dalton moved the Executive's resolution on "Italy and Abyssinia" which condemned Italy; appealed to her to abide by her pledges to the League; called upon the British Government with the other nations to take all necessary measures to restrain the Italian Government; and—calling into play an old Labour panacea—advocated the convening of a world economic conference. Labour pledged "its firm support of any action [i. e. of the Government] consistent with the principles of the League."

This change in Labour's foreign policy, from one of opposition to the Government to qualified support, was accompanied by sharp conflicts within the party itself. Cripps resigned from the National Executive shortly before the Brighton Conference, and came out in full opposition to the new line. His attack consisted partly of a criticism of the Labour party's extreme eagerness to trust the Government's word; in effect he prophesied the Hoare-Laval sell-out.

Cripps had a slight intellectual tiff with his father on this very subject. Writing on September 16, 1935, he said: "I agree with you that we should not support the National Government in sanctions, though not from entirely the same point of view. The Party as a whole seems to be in a first-class muddle as to its views. . . . It is a pity that there should be these acute differences but I don't think it can be helped." Parmoor replied the following day: "You say that you agree with me that we should not support the National Government in regard to sanctions, although our reasons for this differ. I think that this puts my view rather too high. My objection was intended to be leveled against military sanctions because I believe myself that the difficulty can be overcome without them, and that if it comes to a question of military sanctions there will be considerable difference of opinion. I stated this view quite frankly at Geneva in 1924 in my public speeches and I have not altered it. But the chief point is to try and rally to the main lines of the League Covenant and to see what can be done." Addressing himself to Parmoor on the following day as "My dearest Pa" (Cripps's favorite salutation to his father), Cripps replied: "When I was referring to sanctions I was really meaning military sanctions. I quite understood the view that you took up, but I don't think really that you can separate economic and military sanctions, as the former are so liable or likely to lead to the latter."

Most of the criticism launched against Sir Stafford was based on the fact that constructively he had little to offer. "It is unfortunate, tragic, but inescapably true," he said, "that the British workers cannot at this moment be effective in the international political field." These words have been so often used against Sir Stafford that it is well to point out their metaphorical nature. All that Sir Stafford is saying is that a shift in emphasis is required on the part of the Labour party. Of course British workers could play a part in international politics. But how? By supporting a reactionary imperialist Government whose partiality toward Fascism was established? No: what Sir Stafford advocates is internal opposition at home to the National Government as the best method of functioning effectively in international politics. Altruism should begin at home; but the bureaucracy of the Labour party chose support of the National Government. The result was that British reactionaries, rather than the British workers, were effective in the international field.

This struggle within the Labour party indicated that drastic changes were taking place in Labour's traditional alignments. The National Executive was committing itself with open eyes to the support of an alliance of capitalist powers against Fascist aggression. Although the National Government had pretended to advocate this policy in 1935, its deception was soon revealed. The main point of difference was that the Labour party precluded deals with Fascist countries. But, if it supported the supposed policy of the National Government, what was to prevent a Hoare-Laval sell-out? Labour had a clear and concrete policy of its own, but it was a long way from being a truly independent policy. The Labour party was clearly confused by the new situation; it was only too eager to accept the Government's word that it was in agreement with the Labour party; it was ready to accept without question the assurance that the National Government, too, had shifted its foreign policy. Worst of all, it surrendered its only chance of using its influence by refusing to demand guarantees. It literally begged the Government to allow Labour to give its support.

All these contentions are clearly illustrated in the handling of the Spanish invasion by the National Government of Mr. Chamberlain. Here was a genuine class division over foreign policy. Chamberlain was prepared to sacrifice the imperialist interests of Great Britain in order to avert what he considered the greater threat of working class movements in Europe. Hence the Labour party was in an extremely advantageous position, for it could fight Fascism by pointing out that Fascism endangered imperial interests. Here was a genuine basis for a united front of all parties definitely opposed to Fascism. Such a united front, based on this specific and limited issue, offered genuine hopes for an electoral victory which would turn out the Chamberlain ministry; and, in the realm of international affairs, at least, such a government could play a constructive role.

The shibboleths and slogans of abstract theorists could not obscure the important reality: that, for the moment at least, the interests of British imperialism and the interests of the working class coincided. This had not been so to the same extent in any previous situation. Strengthening Fascism previously had not involved a direct threat to British supremacy—though it is true that the Manchurian and Abyssinian adventures had struck close to British spheres of influence. Failure to share in the Japanese spoils had seriously alarmed British capital. This, combined with the fact that Spain controlled the entrance to the Mediterranean, made the support of the National Government to France seem suicidal to old-fashioned imperialists. So strong was the natural tendency of the Labour party, however, to support the Government's policy, that the obvious farcical policy of nonintervention was followed supinely for a whole year. The National Executive of the Labour party swallowed the line of the National Government hook, line, and sinker.

THE BANKRUPTCY OF THE EXECUTIVE

Thus, in a resolution sent to Anthony Eden, asking the National Government to investigate charges of nonintervention, the National Executive committed itself to the view "that the French Government initiated the policy of nonintervention." Nonintervention, the National Executive admitted, had been placed in danger "by Nazi Germany, which had already established a vast system of espionage, corruption, and intrigue in Spain. Fascist Portugal has aided and abetted the rebellion, and its territory has been used as a base." In spite of this fact, which was apparently accepted as true, the resolution went on to say that "nonintervention agreements may . . . lessen international tension, *provided they are applied immediately, are loyally observed by all parties, and their execution is effectively co-ordinated and supervised."* (Italics mine—E. E.) These last conditions were, of course, dependent for their execution upon the good will of the National Government; they could only be enforced if the National Government were genuinely interested in maintaining neutrality and preserving peace. Could the leadership of the Labour party truthfully assume that it was? On the basis of past experience it is difficult to see how responsible leaders of a great working class party, supposedly alive to the economic basis of politics and the class interests of the ruling group, could follow such an obviously disastrous policy.

At any rate, the impassioned speeches of the two Spanish representatives at the Edinburgh Conference left no doubt in the mind of anyone that there had been decided intervention on the side of General Franco. What was the response of the National Executive? Mr. Attlee introduced their resolution, which endorsed the demand which had been made for "the investigation of the alleged breaches of the Nonintervention Agreement." Something of the temper of the National Executive may be illustrated by the fact that Mr. Attlee used the following speech to reassure his comrades: "Yesterday Mr. Greenwood and I visited Neville Chamberlain, and we laid before him the views of this conference as to the urgency of this matter; that it was not a matter that could wait; that time was the essence of the situation, and you know from the statement that has been published in the press that Mr. Chamberlain assured us that the British representatives were fully conscious of the dangers which would be incurred if the situation were not cleared up without delay."

This was apparently enough for Mr. Attlee, but when Ben Smith, a Labour M. P., asked him to repeat the substance of his conversation with Chamberlain, Mr. Attlee refused to do so. "We had," he said, "not been instructed to report to this conference. We reported to the body that sent us there—that was the National Council of Labour [i. e. the body which approved the resolutions just quoted from]. . . . We went there, we pressed for immediate action; we, of course, had discussion, and you had in the press the response of Mr. Chamberlain to them."

The tragic fallacy of this well-intentioned but academic stand was revealed by Mr. Philip Noel Baker:

"The leader [Mr. Attlee] tells us we must have proof. I agree, but I believe, with great respect, we have it. Our Spanish colleagues said we could not ask for Law Court proof. If we did I think it is there. I have seen the Spanish 'White Book' to the Assembly; I have seen Miss Rathbone's Report; I have seen the actual photostat production of rebel newspapers, talking of Count Rossi in September taking part in celebration of rebel victories. I have seen a photostat of a Fascist paper speaking of 'our National Junker airplanes' which were doing such magnificent work for the rebel cause. I believe those documents are proof. Now if you want Law Court proof can you claim that this Foreign Office Committee is like a Law Court? Any honest diplomat will admit that a Diplomatic Committee is the least well-adapted committee of any for dealing with a question like this, and I am afraid that they will drag it on and drag it on, and when the result comes out there will be a Minority Report, with powerful arguments from the Fascist Powers, which the Governments will use as an excuse for doing nothing.

"Even if you were to accept the necessity of Law Court proof, even if you admitted the committee was a Law Court, you ought still to apply the principles of law, and the fundamental principle of law is that while a crime is going on there shall be an injunction to restrain it—that before the verdict is produced, the wrong-doers shall not face the Court with a *fait accompli*. If this Court cannot give us a verdict within a week, let it give us an injunction. What injunction is possible? It is no good passing resolutions asking General Franco to be a gentleman and not to attack Madrid. The only effective injunction would be to suspend the operations of the embargo and let the Spaniards buy rifles and ammunition in this country."

To this Mr. Ernest Bevin could only reply: "We understand this statement (the resolution of the National Executive) to mean . . . that from the moment we leave this conference, our officers will be on the doorstep [of No. 10 Downing Street], not in a week, but every day, putting pressure on to get results." And while the indomitable spirit of the Spanish workers was slowly being crushed by the superior arms and equipment of Franco's foreign allies, all that the Labour party could do was to bring "pressure" upon the National Government to enforce the nonintervention act on both sides. Something was salvaged from the fiasco of this debate, however, by Sir Stafford Cripps, who introduced an amendment to the resolution to the effect that the Labour party *knew* that the Fascist powers had abrogated the nonintervention agreement. Although this destroyed Mr. Attlee's reason for asking for an *investigation* of the situation, Mr. Attlee accepted it as an "obvious statement of fact," and the amendment and the resolution were both carried unanimously.

Even granting the view of the National Executive, that it was possible to alleviate the situation by bringing "pressure" to bear upon the National Government, one must inquire how this pressure is to be made effective. By sitting on the doorstep of the Foreign Office? As practical politicians it is difficult to imagine that the members of the National Executive could believe so. However, this was the only form of action which the National Executive pledged itself to take. Even after the National Executive had issued a denunciation of nonintervention, the steps proposed were far from clear. Speaking at the Trades-Union Congress at Norwich (1937), Sir Walter Citrine expressed his abhorrence of the fact "that the British and other Governments continue to deny the legal Government of Spain the right under international law to purchase necessary arms and equipment, thus affording support to the Fascist rebels." Therefore, Sir Walter said, "the problem before the Labour movement was to find a practical course to carry out their objective to help the Spanish workers." But how was this to be done? Outside of recommending that "the Council of the League of Nations . . . examine this problem in all its aspects and . . . propose measures, including the withdrawal of foreign troops from Spain, which will effectively safeguard the peace of nations and enable the Spanish people to recover their political and territorial independence," Sir Walter had nothing to offer. This was the constructive policy of the leadership of the Labour party! But it is significant that Sir Walter *did* find something to say about another policy. "If this Government refused to move," he asked, facing the issue boldly, "what was the alternative? Were they thinking of a general strike? That, or anything like it, would be utterly futile and only divide Labour's ranks."

What more need be said about the pathetic inadequacy of the leadership of the British Labour party? Only what Sir Stafford wrote in *The New Statesman and Nation:* "The tragedy in Edinburgh was the 'tight-rope walking' by the platform on both sides, and the failure of the movement to accept the challenge of events in Spain. To the ordinary man and woman the Party gives the appearance of such doubt and hesitancy that it is not recognized (as it should be) as the only and inevitable leader of the workers against the National Government's drive for war."

Obviously the only practical answer to the question posed by Sir Walter Citrine was the unification of the working class, the fusion of all working class and anti-Fascist parties on a specific, limited program, whose immediate objective would be to turn out the Chamberlain Government. With such a movement gaining momentum—as it surely would—the "doorstep pressure" tactics of the National Executive might have some effect. Without such evidences of mass support, their complaints—as was the case—would be politely received, politely promised consideration, and politely forgotten. Besides the necessity for this tactical basis, there was also the fact, already mentioned, that the anti-Fascist objectives of the working class and the imperialist objectives of a section of the Tories coincided. Thus an effort to achieve a United Front would merely be to take advantage of a favorable opportunity, and to respond to the pressing needs of the moment. Beyond this, there were other (equally good) reasons for advocating a campaign to achieve working class and anti-Fascist unity.

Speaking to his constituents in Bristol in 1936, Sir Stafford said: "Up and down the country all kinds of joint committees are now in operation on which Labour Parties and the Trade Councils are combining with Communists and members of the Independent Labour Party for the purpose of working for peace and civil liberty and against such evils as the Means Test and war and Fascism. This unity has arisen out of the necessity for militant opposition by the workers and the failure of the Labour party to take the lead in such opposition." Perhaps even more important is the truth of the statement by G. D. H. Cole, previously quoted, to the effect that the Labour party stood "little or no chance of getting a clear majority at the next General Election, or at the next but one." This statement must be linked with that of Cripps, a month later, that "the decay and apathy within the political Labour movement cannot be cured until there exists for its members a truly democratic way, not only of electing their leaders, but of registering their opinions and directives."

It is important to recognize that the drive for unity was not only the response to the external international situation, but was tied up with a steadily increasing discontent in the rank and file of the Labour party itself. The trend toward unity was, in essence, an effort to break the domination of the National Executive—a domination which, after the Edinburgh Conference, was seen to be a stranglehold which might well suffocate the life of the British Labour movement. The bitterness with which the Executive conducted the fight against the Unity Campaign can only be explained by the fact that the Unity Campaign was linked up with the constituency issue; and the fight of the constituency parties was avowedly an attempt to wrest control of the movement from the block vote controlled by the National Executive. With this in mind, we can approach the fight of the constituencies and the history of the Unity Campaign—not to speak of the personal hostility to Sir Stafford Cripps—with a clear idea of their significance.

VI

UNITY

Iɴ ᴛʜᴇ ꜰᴀʟʟ of 1937, Stafford Cripps said: "In the face of the world situation, both in the Fascist countries and in those countries where democracy still survives, there can be no doubt that, whatever view you may take, the issue of working class unity is one of supreme importance, and one that, however much we may try and get rid of it from our councils, will constantly be forced to our attention by the developments of the class struggle nationally and internationally in the world."

It was because of his very deep conviction, he said, that "in unity lay the hope of the accomplishment of the objective of power for the working class, that I, in common with others in the Party, took the steps that we did in January last." His reference was to the highly important, and controversial, Unity Campaign.

The domination of Labour party conferences by the trade-union "block vote" has long been a familiar grievance within the British Labour party. In itself this is undemocratic, for it signifies the suppression of minorities (which may be considerable inside the various trade-unions). Although the practice falsifies the voting somewhat, it would not be important if the trade-union vote were itself democratically cast. Unfortunately this is not the case. On many issues—Spain, for example—one receives the unmistakable impression that the vote of the annual conference was actually contrary to the sentiments of the majority of members. In practice, this has meant that trade-union leaders like Ernest Bevin and Sir Walter Citrine could act to the detriment of a more decisively Socialist policy within the Labour party.

Very few of the workers, supposedly represented by the trade-union votes, are aware of the divisions of the Trade-Union Congress, of the date of meeting, or of the delegates who attend it. It is a rare thing for the agenda of the congresses, on whose decisions depend the line of the unions at the Labour party conferences, to be considered even by the higher committees in a union; and the agenda certainly never comes up before the union members in the branches for discussion and amendment. Resolutions for the next Congress usually have to be passed by annual conferences of the affiliated unions, customarily seven to ten months before the Congress. Only a few weeks before the Congress, the General Council issues a report containing very important proposals on policy; and, if the workers adhere to the usual union routine for sending amendments, it is physically impossible to discuss them with any adequacy before the Congress meets. Furthermore, practically no reports are made by the delegates or unions at the end of the Congress to branches or members.

Under these circumstances, the plea of the Constituency Labour parties (the non-trade-union membership of the Labour party) for a larger share of representation becomes fully understandable. For there can be no doubt that the Constituency parties, unlike the unions, do discuss very fully the agenda of the party conference—especially when, as is often the case, the Constituencies dissent from the line of the National Executive. Yet the five largest unions—the Miners' Federation, the Transport and General Workers Union, the G. & M. W. U., the Railwaymen, and the Textile Workers—have more than 1,-

300,000 votes, whereas the total strength of all the Constituency Labour parties comes to not more than 450,000 votes.

The second grievance of the Constituency parties was financial. Many of them are unable to send delegates to the conference, for lack of funds. In addition, it is difficult in some parties to find competent delegates who are able to leave their jobs during the conference period.

Bound up with finance, also, was the question of the selection of parliamentary candidates. Even Mr. Attlee has admitted that "the finance of the big Unions has enabled them in the past to secure for the Trade-Union nominees many of the safest seats in the country, and in the selection of candidates up to recently they had a considerable pull, owing to the fact that they were able to take responsibility for all expenses."

Lastly, the Constituency parties maintained that the unions were enabled to keep this grip on parliamentary candidates only by having their members pay the political levy, not into the local divisional party, but into the central political fund of the union. The political levy—in theory at least—is a contribution to the Labour party funds, and it is ridiculous that it should be taken out of a constituency in urgent need of funds for political propaganda in order to swell the election expenditure of some trade-union official fighting an absolutely safe Labour seat.

The position becomes even worse when we consider the role of the National Executive. Of the resolutions, motions, and amendments on the final agenda to the party conference, between eighty-five per cent and ninety-five per cent are presented by the local Labour parties. About ten per cent of these reach the floor of the conference and about three per cent are actually passed. The Executive, in fact, exerts an enormous clandestine control over the actual work of the conference. A motion or amendment may be dropped from the agenda of the conference for a number of technical reasons, or, as sometimes happens, for no explicit reason at all. The result of these tactics has been that in the six conferences from 1932 to 1937 the Executive was defeated only ten times. (These rare occasions on which the Executive has had to give way to the wishes of the rank and file have included, however, such important issues as the nationalization of the joint stock banks, a resolution requiring the next Labour Government to stand or fall on definite Socialist legislation, and a resolution for workers' participation in the management of the socialized industries.)

After the 1935 Conference, matters came to a head. A group of members set to work on a certain Wednesday night; they hired a hall for the following evening, and called a meeting of all constituency delegates to consider what action should be taken to make the Constituency parties an effective force in conference.

At this meeting, Sir Stafford Cripps took the chair. Delegate after delegate voiced not only the Constituency parties' sense of frustration and futility, but their determination to find a way out of an intolerable situation. Cripps was appointed Chairman, Mr. Ben Greene, of the Home Counties Labour Association, Secretary, and Mr. Aneurin Bevan, M. P., and Mr. St. John Reade represented two of the ten divisions on the Provisional Committee.

From the start they made clear their stand in regard to the trade-unions. Their argument was that, because of the preponderant influence of the trade-unions, the party became a purely "class" or "sectional" party, instead of a "national" party appealing both to "investors" and "managers" as well as mere "horny-handed sons of toil." "The Constituency Parties," wrote St. John Reade in the *Bristol Labour Weekly,* "do not resent control by the Trade-Unions, provided control is exercised through the democratic machinery of the political movement; what they complain of is control by a group of Trade-Union officials exercised through the highly decentralized machinery of the 'block vote' and the 'political levy'."

Various proposals were put forward for the democratization of the party constitution. The more far-reaching involved the cancellation of the political activities of trade-unionists in the Constituency parties, by making the Constituency parties the one unit of political organization. The trade-unions, co-operative and Socialist societies, now affiliated nationally, would be invited to affiliate their members locally with the appropriate Constituency parties. All affiliation fees would be paid to local parties, which would retain a considerable proportion and forward the remainder to the central office.

Mr. St. John Reade summed up the advantages of this change under four heads: "First, it would provide divisional Labour Parties with the steady income between elections which is essential for adequate organization and propaganda. Second, it would mobilize the full weight and power of the politically minded trade-unionists inside each division in the struggle to attain a parliamentary majority. Third, it would rid the Labour Party of the charge that it is not a democratic movement in the true sense of the word, but a bureaucratic 'caucus' of officials. Fourth, it would end the scandal of the 'adoption market,' by placing divisional Labour Parties in a strong financial position and enabling them to choose as their candidate the individual whom they consider best qualified to carry the Labour standard and most likely to appeal to the electorate."

The essential difficulty confronting this proposal lay in the immense organization and reconstruction involved, and the inevitable opposition of the union caucuses to any diminution of their powers over the political movement.

The only result of the agitation was a grudging concession of the National Executive to the Constituency parties. At the Bournemouth Conference (1937) proposals with regard to changes in the Constitution were discussed, the principal item being an increase in the membership of the National Executive Committee giving two additional seats to the Constituency Labour parties. This, of course, was by no means an adequate answer to the Constituency proposals; for the main point of the Constituency demands—the right of Constituency parties to elect their own panel, which would function as a group, to the National Executive—was not taken into account. The proposals of the National Executive provided simply for the addition of two more individual members of the Constituency parties to the National Executive; but they, too, were only individual members, whose proposals could be treated as individual foibles, with no basis of mass support. The fact that the National Executive was aware of danger, however, can be seen from a consideration of the remarks of Mr. George Dallas, who presented the resolution for the National Executive. In moving the adoption of the proposals he said, in effect, that the local Labour parties were growing in power, and that there had been a feeling of frustration—that, no matter how many of them put their strength together, they could not possibly get on the Executive the people they wanted. The committee, he said, wished to take that feeling away, and had no fear that any disaster would come from changes of this kind. This meant that the National Executive had decided to grant a minor concession in order to quell a dangerously rebellious feeling; but they were at the same time assuring the trade-union bureaucracy that this concession would not in any way endanger their domination. Accepting this logic, the proposal was passed by the conference; and on October 6, 1937, four new members were elected to the National Executive by the Constituency party—Harold Laski, Philip Noel-Baker, Sir Stafford Cripps, and D. N. Pritt—two of whom were the members newly added to the Executive. But it is important to note that this concession, minor as it was, came only after the Unity Campaign had been initiated. This is additional proof, if proof were needed, that the National Executive considered the fight of the Constituency parties and the Unity Campaign as one issue. And it is also significant that the four new members of the National Executive were all, with the exception of Philip Noel Baker, members of the Socialist League, who had been in the forefront of the fight for Unity.

The first public intimation that something was afoot appeared on January 12, 1937. On that date the Labour party Executive issued its appeal to party loyalty. This document called the attention of members to the fact that there was a large amount of current discussion on the subject of a "united front," and that: "Members of the Party were continually being urged to support various special organizations promoted under Communist auspices for immediate purposes, but in the main intended to secure united activity between Communists, Socialists, and Trade Unionists for particular Communist objects and to further the 'United Front' policy." Members were urged to take no part in such activities on the grounds that: "Apart from the elementary principle of loyalty to the Party directly challenged by these various proposals, the diffusion of effort and finance involved could not fail to weaken Labour organization throughout the country." The appeal called attention to the fact that the Southport Conference of 1934 had rejected the proposal for affiliation of the Communist party in the following terms:

"That united action with the Communist Party or organizations ancillary or subsidiary thereto, without the sanction of the

National Executive Committee, is incompatible with membership of the Labour Party, and that the National Executive Committee seek full disciplinary powers from the next Annual Party
Conference to deal with any case or cases that may arise."

The appeal continues as follows:

"In these circumstances the National Executive Committee
is of the opinion that association with the following organizations is in direct conflict with Annual Conference decisions, and
that the support of Party members should be definitely withheld
from them:

(a) Organizations which are clearly formed to pursue 'United
Front' or 'Popular Front' activities;

(b) Organizations which are being promoted to weaken the
Party's organizations and electoral power by association
with other political bodies which do not share the Party's
determination to achieve our democratic Socialist objectives."

This document was a forewarning of what was to come. The
Labour party Executive, knowing of the movement that was
on foot, naturally wanted to make their own views on the matter
as widely known as possible and therefore enlisted the sympathy
and support of the movement *before* the Unity campaign had
been able to put forward its case.

This appeal roused considerable excitement. Everyone realized
that there was something in the air, and awaited further developments with interest. For nearly a week nothing happened. Then,
on January 18th, the Unity Campaign was launched.

The first step was the issue of a joint manifesto from the
Socialist League, the I. L. P., and the Communist party announcing that these three bodies had decided to unite to fight for

certain immediate objectives on which they were all agreed. The general objectives were outlined as follows:

"Unity of all sections of the working class movement.

"Unity in the struggle against Fascism, reaction, and war, and against the National Government.

"Unity in the struggle for immediate demands, and the return of a Labour Government as the next stage in the advance of the working class to power.

"Unity through the removal of all barriers between sections of the working class movement, through the strengthening of Trade-Unionism and Co-operation, through the adoption of a fighting program of mass struggle, through the democratization of the Labour Party and the Trade-Union Movement.

"Unity within the framework of the Labour Party and the Trade-Unions."

Note here the emphasis on loyal support of the Labour party and the trade-unions, and on the necessity for working *within* the party. This is important because of the accusations that were later hurled at the Unity campaign as being a disruptive breakaway movement from the ranks of the Labour party.

The Manifesto goes on to elaborate its immediate program as follows:

"Let the Movement not wait for General Elections but now by active demonstration win and organize support for:

Abolition of the Means Test.
T. U. C. scales of unemployment benefit.
National work of social value for Distressed Areas.
Forty-hour week for industry and the Public Services.
Paid holiday [vacation] for all workers.
The abolition of tied cottages for agricultural workers.

Co-ordinated Trade-Union action for higher wages in industry,
   especially in mining, cotton, and sweated trades.
Non-contributory pensions of 1 pound at 60.
Immediate rehousing of workers in town and country.
Power to get back the land for the People.
Nationalization of the mining industry.
Effective control of the banks, the Stock Exchanges with their
   gambling, and private profiteering—profiteering accentuated
   by the armament boom.
Making the rich pay for social amelioration."

The Manifesto was signed by Stafford Cripps, William Mellor,
and G. R. Mitchison for the Socialist League; by James Maxton,
Fred W. Jowett, and Fenner Brockway for the I. L. P.; and by
Harry Pollitt, William Gallacher, and R. Palme Dutte for the
Communist party.

The alliance between these three parties naturally caused
something of a sensation. Before we go further, we must pause
to examine the differences between these parties and the difficulties they had in coming together. This will give some clue
to the inherent weakness of the Campaign which helped to
bring about its utimate failure.

In the first place their relations to the Labour party were
different. The Socialist League was within the party. The Communist party was outside, but was ready to enter without special
conditions—had in fact made repeated applications for affiliation.
The I. L. P. was outside, and was prepared to enter only on the
following conditions:

(1) The I. L. P. should remain as an organization.
(2) The I. L. P. should retain its own newspaper and its right
   to publish its own literature.

(3) The I. L. P. should have the right to voice its own policy on the platform.

(4) The I. L. P. should have the right to criticize in a comradely spirit the official policy of the Labour Party and the policy of other sections of the party.

At the beginning of the negotiations the I. L. P. representatives had also insisted that before the I. L. P. would apply for affiliation the constitution of the Labour party would have to be democratized and the right of I. L. P. representatives in Parliament to vote according to their own principles would have to be recognized. During the discussions these demands were modified, however, and the I. L. P. agreed to regard a reasonable promise that these changes would be made as a sufficient ground for application for affiliation, without waiting for these changes actually to take place.

Now as to the actual program of the Campaign, there were very serious differences indeed on some of the most urgent questions of the day, particularly questions of foreign policy.

On the question of Spain the Communist party and the Socialist League were in complete agreement. Both wanted an immediate active policy of assisting the Spanish Government in every way practicable. The I. L. P., on the other hand believed that the Spanish Government, no less than France, was a bulwark of capitalism; and that though it was fighting for democracy against Fascism, nevertheless this democracy was a capitalist democracy, and thus a victory for the Government would be essentially a capitalist victory; whether Franco or the Government was victorious, the workers of Spain would be equally the losers. Sincerely holding this belief, the I. L. P. naturally could not favor any scheme for active support of the Spanish Government. It is to their credit, however, that they were prepared to subordinate this difference in the cause of unity. A few days after the Campaign was launched, the following Four Points were published as representing the views of the Unity Campaign Committee on the subject of Spain.

(1) The immediate raising of the embargo on the supply of arms to the Spanish Government.

(2) The immediate raising of the ban imposed by the National Government on volunteers for the Spanish Government.

(3) Full support by the National Council of Labour for the sending of volunteers, and for providing the necessary funds for their dependents.

(4) Action by the National Council of Labour to raise money to provide adequate medical supplies for the Government troops, food supplies and assistance for the victims of Fascist aggression in Spain.

This resolution was passed with great enthusiasm at every Unity Campaign demonstration. It was a very great pity that a third of the promoters of the Campaign, due to the nature of the case, could do no more than pay lip service to the demands on this vital and urgent issue.

There was also the question of pacts with other countries. The Communist party was in favor of an immediate pact between the Soviet Union, France, Great Britain, and other democratic countries. The Socialist League was in favor of such a pact only after a Labour Government had come to power in Britain, while the I. L. P. went even further, and would advocate a pact only between countries with working class governments. This last policy, of course, amounted, in the circumstances, to the rejection of all pacts for the time being.

The outcome of this disagreement was on the whole favorable

to the peace alliance and League of Nations policy, and was expressed in Clause 3 of the Unity Campaign Agreement as follows:

"Advocacy and action to save the peoples of the world from the growing menace of Fascist aggression, by mobilizing the maximum effective opposition to such aggression and for the maintenance of peace, for the defense of the Soviet Union and support of its fight for peace, and for a pact between Great Britain, the Soviet Union, France, and all other states in which the working class has political freedom, to secure peace."

An Addendum to the Agreement stated:

"With regard to the proposed pact, we recognize that the Communist Party is free to demand that the Government shall immediately adopt such a pact . . . and that the other two organizations are free in advocating the pact to place their emphasis on the necessity of a change of Government in order to realize the pact."

The question of the attitude of the campaign toward the Soviet Union presented another difficulty. Here was very dangerous ground indeed, for while the Communist party and the Socialist League were in general agreement as to the achievements of the Soviet Union, the I. L. P. believed that the present Soviet Government had betrayed the cause of Socialism. Clearly some kind of agreement had to be found as to the best way of preventing these very real differences from forcing themselves into the forefront, thereby ruining the aspect of unity essential to the cause of the Campaign. It was, therefore, suggested by the Communist representatives that the I. L. P.'s reservation to the clause urging support for Russia's foreign policy should not be included in the actual agreement, but should be put in a letter to Sir Stafford Cripps, chairman of the Committee, and that both the Socialist League and the Communist party should indicate that they concurred with the I. L. P. in making reservation. The object of this was to enable the I. L. P. to remain true to the beliefs which they sincerely held, without making this a matter for public controversy at a moment when unity was all important. For the same reason the following Addendum was added to the Agreement:

"All parties agree to abstain from any general criticism of the policy of the Soviet Union or its government, and in the event of any party considering it necessary in a particular case to criticise them, before any such criticism is made, the three parties will meet to discuss the matter with a view to preventing any break in unity."

Another important point of disagreement was the question of the Popular Front. Both I. L. P. and Socialist League were against an alliance with Liberals and left-wing Conservatives on any issue however urgent, while the Communist party advocated such an alliance as the most effective way of mobilizing the country against the National Government. This disagreement was amicably settled by the decision to allow all parties to express their views on the point publicly without making the issue a part of the campaign itself.

Thus the Unity Campaign was launched. Its first great public meeting was held in the Free Trade Hall at Manchester, and it was an impressive success. Even papers such as *The Times* remarked on the enthusiasm that the meeting aroused. The speakers at this meeting were Cripps, Maxton, and Pollitt, and all three speeches were remarkable for their clearness and moderation. Cripps's opening paragraphs in particular are worth quoting, for here is a memorable expression of unwavering loyalty to the Labour party: it was not much later that bitter attacks were being launched against him as being a disruptor of the movement and a traitor to his party. Here are some significant sentences from the opening of his speech:

"Let it be clear that the object of this demonstration is to show our unflinching determination to defeat the National Government and all that it stands for, and to urge the vital necessity at this critical moment in our history, for presenting a United Front within the Labour Movement, to oppose the United Front of capitalism which has been brought into being under the leadership of the Tories within the National Government.

"There are those in this country who are only too anxious by their words and through the Press to represent this Unity Campaign as designed or destined to create splits and disunity within the movement.

"Nothing is further from the truth. Such a result would defeat our whole purpose, which is to unite those elements of the working class which are at this moment dangerously and tragically disunited.

"It takes two to make a quarrel, and we do not intend to be one of the two.

"Whatever may be done or threatened by the official control of the Labour movement, we shall continue to do our best to bring about that Unity within the movement which we regard as the essential precursor to the winning of political power by the working class of Britain."

The emphasis on the necessity for working *within* the framework of the Labour party was then underlined by Harry Pollitt:

"I believe that the whole experience of the last few months proves the absolute need and the desire of a very large number of the workers for Unity, but Unity *within the Labour Party* [my italics—E.E.]. Therefore the Unity Campaign, in placing working class unity within the Labour Party as its central aim, really corresponds to something vital in the outlook of the working class at the present time.

"Every form of breakaway, of split, or talk of the formation of new organizations, must be and will be vigorously opposed. What we aim at is the strengthening of the Labour Party by bringing into it all sections of the Labour Movement and making it in that way all-embracing and all-powerful."

After this beginning, the movement grew with extraordinary rapidity for a few weeks. By February 5th, there had been seven mass meetings, and five thousand pledge cards had been signed, mostly by trade-unionists. By February 19th, additional pledge cards had been signed (6,000 of them by members of the Labour party) and £600 had been taken in collections. By March 5th, 13,000 pledge cards had been signed at public demonstrations, and collections amounted to over £800. The gains represented by these figures had been further consolidated by the formation of fifty-two permanent Unity committees all over the country, and another sixteen were in process of formation. By May 21st, 36,000 pledge cards had been received, and collections at meetings amounted to £1,673. Side by side with this growth of members and money came letters and resolutions of support from all over the country.

Development such as this belied the prophecy that the Unity Campaign would meet with no mass support. It was received all over the country with an enthusiasm that surprised even its promoters. But unfortunately, mass support was not enough. The savage and ultimately successful attempts made by the Labour party Executive to crush this new movement constitute a sordid story. Nevertheless, it is a story that should be told, in order that the downfall of the Unity Campaign will not remain inexplicable.

The first step in the offensive of the Labour party Executive against the Unity Campaign was a skillful misrepresentation of the aims of the Campaign. It made the issue not one of disagreement as to the methods by which certain ends could be achieved, but one of loyalty *per se*. The appeal to loyalty was issued as if the party was defending itself against disloyalty among its members. In the appeal issued on January 13, five days before the Unity Campaign was launched, the last paragraph reads:

"We therefore urge all our members to place their Party loyalty in the forefront of their political activities, to discuss differences regarding matters of organizations or of policy within the Party itself, and to exert their full influence so as to consolidate the Party strength in the Constituencies, in the Municipalities, and in Parliament."

It was in this document also that the Executive quoted the vote against united action with the Communist party given at the Southport Conference in 1934. The figures on this occasion were 1,820,000 to 89,000. But it did not quote the more recent vote at the Edinburgh Conference of 1936 which was 1,728,000 to 592,000. The *Daily Herald* also took part in this shabby trick by describing this defeat as "a material and moral rout; the majority was overwhelming"; whereas in describing the vote on Spain, where the minority was even smaller (519,000 against 1,836,000) is said: "The size of the minority was evidence that approval is given with misgiving and with a heavy mind."

These introductory misrepresentations were followed up. A leading article in the *Daily Herald* described the initiation of the Unity Campaign as follows:

"The three-party agreement between the Communists, the Socialist League, and the I. L. P. will come as no surprise to loyal members of the Labour Movement.

"Discussions have, in fact, been proceeding for many months in secret, and the leaders of the Socialist League, while professing loyal observance of Labour policy, have been quietly preparing to associate themselves with the two parties which have, to their credit, at least attempted to disguise of their opposition to the Labour Party. . . . For months the three bodies have been criticizing the Labour Party, its policy, the decisions of its annual conference, in very nearly identical terms.

"The only difference was that the Communists and the I. L. P. were under no obligation not to do so. By virtue of its affiliation, the Socialist League was so obliged. But the obligation sat lightly, and the doctrine and policy of its leaders have for some time been indistinguishable from that of the Communist Party. . . ."

These insinuations about the clandestine and dishonest behavior of the Socialist League in coming to terms with the Communist party were reinforced by a press campaign against Communism in general.

After a few days representing the Unity Campaign as "A triple alliance which lines up against Labour" and so forth, and likening Cripps himself to Sir Oswald Mosley as a traitor to the party, matters came to a head with the threat to disaffiliate the Socialist League.

On January 30th, the Executive issued the following statement: "The National Executive Committee of the Labour Party regrets that the Socialist League has taken action which its National Council must have known would be contrary to the cause of unity in the ranks of Labour, and would render the League ineligible for continued affiliation to the Labour Party, especially having regard to the statement of Party Loyalty issued by the Executive, on January 12th.

"The National Executive Committee resolves that the Socialist League, having acted at a special conference on January 16 to 17, 1937, on the recommendation of its National Council, in direct defiance of Labour Party Conference decisions, be disaffiliated from the Labour Party, nationally and locally."

The reaction of the public to this ultimatum was varied. The general feeling was one of sympathy with the Socialist League, qualified by the belief that the Executive were within their legal rights. And undeniably they were. Unfortunately the campaign of misrepresentation put over by the Executive had done its work. Even some sympathizers had been led to believe that the Unity Campaign was in reality a breakaway movement. Indeed, Cripps received several letters congratulating him on this supposed fact, as well as letters blaming him for it. The Executive had successfully sown the seeds of confusion in the public mind.

The legal situation too added to the confusion. The Executive were within the letter of the law in disaffiliating a body which indulged in joint activities with the Communist party. The legal position was clear, but this ruling was one which had hitherto not been put into force. As the Socialist League pointed out in their reply to the ultimatum, "Members of the Labour Party, prominent as well as rank and file, have repeatedly appeared on platforms in joint activity with the Communist Party and the Independent Labour Party, without any action being taken by the Labour Party Executive."

A case in point was that of the University Labour Federation. Arthur Greenwood was president of this organization and Hugh Dalton was closely associated with it. In January of the previous year the Federation had united with the Federation of Student Societies led by Communists to form one University Labour Federation affiliated with the Labour party. Not a murmur of protest to this amalgamation had been raised, and it seemed reasonable to inquire how Arthur Greenwood could reconcile his public denunciation of the Unity Campaign with his presidency of a body containing a large proportion of the proscribed elements. Some degree of publicity was given to this matter, the result of which was that the secretary of the University Labour Federation received a notice from the Labour party Executive instructing them to dissociate themselves from these Communist elements. It is, however, evident that the application of the rule had been previously left to the discretion of the Executive. Rigid application of the rule in the case of the Socialist League amounted, therefore, to deliberate discrimination against them.

The Unity Campaign Committee discussed at length the best course to adopt in this situation. The I. L. P. representatives urged the Socialist League to stand firm and thus become a breakaway party, on the grounds that if the Socialist League dissolved itself it would be surrendering in advance the claims made by the I. L. P. and the Communist party for the right to enter the Labour party as independent parties.

Not all agreed with the I. L. P. representatives. Others argued to the effect that disaffiliation would put the League outside the Labour party and that its position would then be no different from that of the I. L. P. and the Communist party. Now the value of the Socialist League to the Unity Campaign consisted largely in the fact that it formed part of the Labour party, and therefore brought the I. L. P. and the Communist party into co-operation with the Labour party itself. Thus it made it possible for thousands of people to associate themselves with the Campaign without concern that they were breaking away from their own party. The disaffiliation of the Socialist League meant that its value to the Unity Campaign was practically destroyed; and the only question that remained was whether it had other value sufficiently great to justify its continued existence. It seemed clear that it had not.

The fact of disaffiliation in itself was not of great importance so long as membership of the Socialist League was not incompatible with membership of the Labour party. But when (March

12th) there came the ultimatum stating that from June 1st members of the League would no longer be eligible for membership in the party, the position was clearly untenable. It was therefore urged very strongly both by the Communist party representatives and most of the Socialist League representatives that the League should be voluntarily dissolved. This would give the individual members the opportunity of continuing the Unity Campaign as individuals within the Labour party, though no longer as members of an organization. The alternative: the Socialist League could be a fellow outcast with the I. L. P. and the Unity Campaign would then be forced to abandon its fundamental principle of achieving unity within the framework of the Labour party.

The former viewpoint carried the day. Of course, in a sense it was surrender, and, as such, a blow to the pride of some of the League leaders. Cripps himself felt this strongly, but he had to think not only of the above general considerations, but also of the fact that should he take a rigid stand and by doing so allow himself to be expelled from the party, his colleagues would be placed in a most difficult position.

"It is rumored that action is to be taken against myself and others this week to turn us out of the Labour Party. I am anxious to remain in it. I believe there are many people in the party who are anxious that this heresy hunt should not take place. Let me make it clear that I am not concerned in the slightest degrees with my personal position. Individuals do not count compared with the movement, but I am concerned to prove that the idea of unity is something that the rank and file want."

Thus it was for the sake of unity in the Labour party that Cripps refused to be driven by pride into what would have been a quite futile gesture. It was largely due to his wisdom on this point that it was possible for the Unity Campaign to proceed as

it did with undiminished energy for several more weeks—weeks
of lasting significance to the whole Labour movement in spite
of the apparent defeat with which they concluded. For it was
Cripps who did perhaps more than any of the other leaders to
preserve the vitality of the movement in spite of this first rebuff.
Of the twenty speeches he made at mass meetings in the course
of the campaign, fourteen were delivered after the ultimatum
of March 30th announcing members of the Socialist League to
be ineligible for membership of the Labour party. This redoubled
energy that he displayed in the face of the prevailing atmosphere
of defeatism in this period is a thing for which he deserves the
lasting gratitude of the Labour movement.

Cripps's decision to remain within the party met with general
approval among his supporters. His own East Bristol constituents declared their support of his conduct in spite of rather
strenuous attempts of certain influential opponents in the local
party to secure a different decision.

Meanwhile a deliberate campaign of mud-slinging and misrepresentation was well under way in the official organs of the
Labour party. The Socialist League was represented as weak,
treacherous, and torn by internal dissensions. The public were
reminded of the original discussions within the League concerning the wisdom of embarking on the Unity Campaign. The
protest lodged by certain London members of the League on
the inception of the Campaign were magnified out of all proportion. There were also a series of insinuations about the sources
of the Campaign's finances. Early in April a statement by the
Executive spoke of "large sums of money, the sources of which
are not disclosed," being spent on the Campaign. Dr. Hugh
Dalton was reported in the *Daily Herald* as follows:

"The so-called Unity Campaign was being financed by one
or two rich men who were using their private wealth in constant

attacks on the policy and leadership of the Party to which they still nominally belonged, and setting at defiance decisions of the Labour Party's annual conference regarding joint action with the Communists. If it [the Unity Campaign] were deprived of these plutocratic props, the whole agitation would speedily collapse."

These insinuations were publicly repudiated by Mr. Mellor, and a full statement of the Campaign's accounts was published. This did not seem to be enough, however, for a flood of letters appeared forthwith in the *Daily Herald* making the most fantastic suggestions about the finances of the Campaign. Predominant was the "Moscow Gold" theory.

In the meanwhile, the "heresy hunt" had begun. The first victim was William Mellor. He was the prospective Labour candidate for Coventry; but the Executive refused to endorse his candidature. This incident took place on January 30th, when membership of the League had not yet been declared incompatible with either membership or official position in the Labour party, and there was no question of Mellor having been nominated by the League, since there was no branch of the League in Coventry.

This attack was followed up by many others. A group of Councillors of the Sheffield Trades and Labour Council, for example, declared their support for the Unity Campaign, and forthwith steps were taken to make them withdraw, and to mobilize the members against the president, newly elected by a large majority.

Then early in March, George Strauss, M. P. for North Lambeth and one of the ablest administrators on the L. C. C., was dismissed by Herbert Morrison from his position as chairman of the Highways Committee and vice-chairman of the Finance Committee. The reason for this was nothing else than his activity in the Unity Campaign. Not long after this the Labour candidate for Kingston was informed that the Executive would not endorse his candidacy in view of his support of the Unity Campaign and membership of the Socialist League. From Scotland and Wales came news of action by party organizers designed to prevent the question of Unity from being discussed by women's sections and local Labour organizations. In some cases membership of the party was being refused to applicants whose husbands were Communists.

The heresy hunt culminated on June 6th. George Strauss was announced to speak at a Unity meeting at Hull with James Maxton and Harry Pollitt. He received a letter from the Labour party saying that if he spoke on the same platform with these two he would be expelled from the party.

The Unity Campaign committee met to discuss this development. It was clear that this attack was to be the precursor of others, and that the policy of the Executive would be to expel one by one all the leaders of the Unity Campaign. This would mean the death blow to the Campaign. With all its promoters and supporters outside the Labour party its claim to represent unity of the working class forces would be grotesque. There was no alternative. The only thing to be done was to submit to the ruling that members of the Labour party should not appear on the same platform as members of the I. L. P. or Communist party. Members of the Labour party were henceforth to speak at meetings and serve on Unity committees with members of their own party only. The Unity Campaign would in fact be divided, one part run by the Labour party members, and the other by Communist and I. L. P. members.

The I. L. P. representatives were very critical of the surrender. But, just as in the earlier case of the disaffiliation of the League, no useful purpose would have been served by ineffectual gestures of defiance. The Executive had won, and the only sensible and practical thing to do was to retreat with as few losses as possible, and prepare for future campaigns.

In his speeches at Hull at this time, Sir Stafford said: "Nothing will ever induce me after my experiences in the last six months to regard the Communists or the I. L. P. or any Socialist working class organization as the political opponents of the Labour Party . . . .

"Let the National Executive not only call off the heresy hunt but instruct the Transport House officials that as long as an individual is accepted as a member of the Labour Party, it is not their function to inquire into his particular political views. He is entitled, whether Left or Right wing, to the same consideration, the same encouragement, and the same advantages or disadvantages. If the policy of excluding the Left—whether it be the Socialists within the Party or the Socialists or Communists outside the Party—is allowed to determine the actions of the Labour Party organization and organizers, then there will be one inevitable and fatal consequence. Deprived of such elements throughout the country the Labour Party will not be strong enough to defeat the National Government.

"The only hope of working class power and control is to continue all working class parties and sections upon the common basis of the class struggle. If the Labour Party controls are allowed to continue with their policy of excluding the Left, then the workers' cause in Great Britain will be as disastrously lost as it was by a similar tactic in Germany. It is for the rank and file to decide this great issue, and they can decide it—if they wish—so as to change the whole face of British and world politics, and they can change it by revising the decisions of Edinburgh at the next Labour Party Conference."

"Since then," Stafford Cripps went on to say, "my views have not altered." Briefly Sir Stafford reviewed the history of the opposition of the National Executive to the Unity Campaign: "Objection was taken by the National Executive to the Socialist League, as an organization, embarking upon the course which it took. With the single aim of preserving the maximum amount of unity within the working class ranks, the Socialist League was dissolved at the behest of the National Executive. Objection was then taken to individuals associating with members of the Communist Party and the I. L. P.—an objection, I may state which was not extended to those who associated themselves with members of the opposing capitalist parties—the Conservatives and the Liberals. But to meet this, and again in an attempt to preserve the unity of the Party, that association was brought to an end."

After continuing in this vein, Sir Stafford pointed out the singular fact that "Lord Cecil, Mr. Winston Churchill, and the Archbishop of Canterbury are three as bitter opponents of the working class as you could find in Great Britain, and yet eminent members of the Labour Party in high and influential positions have shared and are sharing platforms with them today. Why is it, I ask, that only the Left of the movement are forbidden this right of Association which passes unchallenged when indulged in by the Right?" And finally, Sir Stafford alluded to the desire of the National Executive to retain their bureaucratic domination, when he asked: "Is it a distrust of the political judgment of the rank and file of the Movement that leads to this anxiety to crush out all unorthodox propaganda in the Party?" Put there was no answer except the personal abuse of Mr. J. McGurk, who suggested that Sir Stafford left the National Executive because "the members are not high-brow enough for him." "Sir Stafford," Mr. McGurk continued, "is a rich man with rich pals around him, and they are the biggest

danger to the Labour Party in this country. . . You will find
those chaps where Mosley is before much longer," Mr. McGurk
prophesied darkly. "I am expressing an opinion that is shared
by many people in this conference. Mosley did exactly the same
thing." Coming after Mr. McGurk's effusion the speech of
George R. Strauss was a decided relief, especially since Mr.
Strauss very acutely put his finger on the crux of the question;
"Why is it," he asked, "that they [the National Executive] have
taken such fierce action against us and against us alone? I believe they realize that this movement of the Unity Campaign
was in fact, as it was meant to be, a real challenge against the
whole spirit of the present leadership. It was a manifestation of
the discontent that existed in the rank and file of the Party up
and down the country with the inaction and compromise of the
leaders on all important matters that were taking place."

Once again, however, the block vote of the trades-union won
the day, and the fate of the Unity Campaign may be inferred
from the following letter of Sir Stafford Cripps and William
Mellor, written in 1937: "The Labour Unity Committee has
given full consideration to the future of the Unity Campaign, in
the light of the decisions at the Bournemouth Conference of
the Labour Party, and has come to the conclusion that the further independent existence of the National Committee and the
local committees would damage and not aid the objectives that
have been pursued in the campaign.

"It has therefore decided that the National Committee shall
be dissolved as from today, and asks you to take immediate
action to dissolve your local committee likewise."

VII

THE CALL FOR A PEOPLE'S FRONT

IN 1932, CRIPPS was an ardent supporter of "no collaboration with the class enemy." In 1937 he advocated a United Front of working class parties. In 1939 he was an equally ardent supporter of a People's Front which should include any elements—Liberal, Imperialist, Conservative, etc.—who were prepared, for whatever reason, to adopt a policy of resistance to Fascist aggression.

Was this a *volte face* on Cripps's part? Did it represent a lamentable abandonment of principle, or could it be justified as a necessary tactic in the face of a rapidly shifting political picture? Before attempting to answer this question in terms of the political situation existing at that time, it is interesting to record some of Cripps's old statements which were dragged out and used against him by his political opponents, both Right and Left.

In his pamphlet, *The Choice for Britain* (1934), he repudiated the idea of a Popular Front in these words: "Nothing in my view is more dangerous than the idea that some temporary alliance of pro-democratic forces should be brought about not based on the achievement of socialism. Such an alliance, like the Labour Government of 1929-31, would find itself incapable of doing anything except deepening the crisis of capitalism, with the inevitable consequence of the bankruptcy of democracy and its elimination in favor of some sort of dictatorship which would come from the Right, and not the Left." These words were of course seized on eagerly; and along with them, others, like the following: "These coalitions or groupings may be considered effective for the immediate purpose of opposition to reaction, especially when the forces of reaction are in power, but they carry within them the seeds of their own disintegration unless the working class parties are prepared to abandon the class struggle as the basis of their political action.

"Once power is gained, if it can be gained by such an alliance, the working class movement is either condemned to the futility of reformism or the coalition naturally splits down the line of cleavage of class interests."

If these statements are true, they constitute a perfect argument against the Popular Front for which Cripps was agitating, and, taken absolutely, would seem to confirm the view that Cripps is an unprincipled political adventurer. But what his opponents invariably omitted was the context in which these remarks were made. It is not generally recognized that to posit an end which is manifestly incapable of practical realization is just as unprincipled—if not more so—as shifting ends to align them with more accurate observation of the situation at hand. These statements were made at a time when the primary need of the Labour movement in England was recognition of its exclusively Socialist basis; but when the most pressing question before the British Labour party was not foreign policy but the question of the ultimate ends of the movement.

Though MacDonald had left the party many of the men who stayed with it supported the MacDonald policies which were almost indistinguishable from the policies of the National Government. They stayed with the movement through traditional loyalty rather than through any deep-rooted Socialist conviction. Recognizing this, Sir Stafford and his fellow members of the Socialist League felt that what the movement as a whole needed most was recognition of its specifically Socialist character—a recognition oriented toward the problems arising from the transition from capitalism to Socialism within Great Britain itself. Consequently the Socialist League concentrated all its efforts upon this aspect, continually agitating for more definitely Socialist measures and pronouncements by the Labour party and insisting that the party could achieve its purpose only by becoming conscious of its Socialist heritage and purpose. At such a time collaboration with other parties could only seem a betrayal. "Collaboration" in the past had meant Mondism and MacDonaldism—collaboration with the Right, capitulation to the purely reformist policies of MacDonald which included, it should be remembered, cuts in unemployment relief. The main foe, clearly, was the antiquated leadership of the Labour party, whose vested interests had made them afraid to move in almost any direction.

At that time, too, there was still hope of easing the international situation. Conditions had not become as desperate as they did later. It was assumed that there would be sufficient time to convert enough voters to Socialism to insure a Labour majority in the House of Commons. Problems of method were broached— would it be possible to achieve Socialism peacefully? and if so, how?—but there was no feeling that the very structure of democracy would be threatened if some action were not taken *now*—if the proposals of the Socialist League, for instance, were not put into immediate action. This was precisely the feeling throughout Great Britain as the international tension increased. A brief summary of the developments in the international situation at that time may help in clarifying Sir Stafford's stand.

THE RESIGNATION OF ANTHONY EDEN

Perhaps the most significant event of that period was the resignation in February 1938 of Anthony Eden as Foreign Secretary.

This act gave credence to the reports of a split between two groups in the Conservative party, which seemed to take the Popular Front to the realm of realistic and practicable political tactics. Eden, as Herbert Morrison said, was "one of those younger men of the Conservative Party who had ideals, who had vision, who had aims which commanded support outside the strict political circles within which he moved." If one disregards Mr. Morrison's penchant for vaguely inspirational rhetoric, this means that Eden was felt to have an interest in the preservation of the British Empire, while Chamberlain's interest seemed to be the preservation of the capitalist system and its presumed supporters—the Fascists. Eden's resignation came, significantly enough, over the question of opening negotiations with Italy for an Anglo-Italian agreement; and the main point of the negotiations revolved around the willingness of Mussolini to *take action* to show his good will—not merely to accept "in principle" the verbal formula proposed by Mr. Chamberlain.

Mr. Chamberlain, following his line of "appeasement," had been trying to initiate conversations with Italy for a long while. Italy did not seem to be in a receptive mood; and it was not until February 10, 1938, that—to quote Mr. Chamberlain—"a fresh opportunity arose to break out of this vicious circle." The Italian Ambassador, after speaking with Anthony Eden, had called upon Mr. Chamberlain with instructions to say that his government "were ready at any time to open conversations." The Italian Government blandly requested that the conversations should be as wide as possible, embracing, of course, the question of the formal recognition of the conquest of Abyssinia." Although Great Britain was still a member of the League, Mr. Chamberlain, delighted at this turn of events, said that, "Formal recognition of the Italian position [?] in Abyssinia was one that could . . . be morally justified if it was found to be a

factor, and an essential factor, in a general appeasement." Astute
politician that he was, however, Mr. Chamberlain informed the
Italian Ambassador that Great Britain would not recognize
Italy's Abyssinian adventure without getting something in return. He said: "I told him [the Italian Ambassador] that the
British Government regarded a settlement of the Spanish question as an essential feature of any agreement at which we might
arrive." He also asked the Italian Government to spare Great
Britain any possible embarrassment: "I said it was essential that
it should not be possible, if we went to the League to recommend the approval of the agreement, for it to be said that the
situation in Spain during the conversations had been materially
altered by Italy, either by sending fresh reinforcements to Franco
or by failing to implement the arrangements contemplated by
the British formula." Mr. Chamberlain's language betrays him
once again—note that he speaks of Italy sending *fresh* reinforcements. So Italy *had* been sending reinforcements? What becomes
of nonintervention then? Mr. Chamberlain immediately indicated that this plea was only to save Great Britain's face before
the League, and was not an actual criticism of Italy's previous
actions—to which, of course, he had been accessory. "I did not
believe these intimations would occasion his Government a moment's anxiety, since I was confident that his Government would
approach the negotiations in the same spirit as we do, namely, in
perfect good faith and with a sincere desire to reach agreement."

It should be remembered that the period directly preceding
the Anglo-Italian negotiations was one in which, as Mr. Attlee
said in a reply to Mr. Chamberlain, "Signor Mussolini has been
insulting the Prime Minister's colleagues for months and months,
is fomenting discontent all through the Near East, including
Palestine and Egypt and everywhere else, is carrying on an
abusive campaign against this country, and his friend, with

weapons which he supplies, attacks our ships and kills our sailors." It was these facts which Eden considered before he chose to resign. In a personal explanation to the House of Commons on the day after his resignation he said: "The immediate issue is as to whether . . . conversations should be opened in Rome now. It is my conviction that the attitude of the Italian Government to international problems in general, and to this country in particular, is not yet such as to justify this course. The ground has been in no respect prepared. Propaganda against this country is rife throughout the world." Eden then went on to say that it was the duty of the British Government especially in relation to Spain to "show the world not only promise but achievement." The import of this was that the Italian Government should be forced to show, by *action*, that it intended to reach a peaceful solution to these questions. Eden's thoughts were stated even more strongly, with some important amplifications, by Viscount Cranborne, Under-Secretary of State for Foreign Affairs, who resigned along with him. There are many ways, Viscount Cranborne pointed out, by which the Italian Government could show its good will: "They could stop their anti-British propaganda in the Near East; they could bring back some of their troops from Libya, which can present a threat to nobody but ourselves; they could, finally and most important, withdraw some of their forces from Spain. Any such evidence—not formulas, not promises but concrete achievements—would be welcomed by us . . . in default of such evidence I am afraid that for His Majesty's Government to enter on official conversations would be regarded not as a contribution to peace, but as a surrender to blackmail." This was, indeed, the general interpretation put upon the opening of Anglo-Italian conversations, and the conclusion of the Anglo-Italian Agreement fully justified the fears of those who saw in these conversations further aid from the National Government to the Fascist Powers. But before that date—presumably striking while the iron was hot, for Mr. Chamberlain was obviously in a conciliatory mood—Hitler effected the long-anticipated Austrian Anschluss.

ANSCHLUSS

The events leading up to the Austrian Anschluss are well known. One month before the *Reichswehr* marched, Mr. Chamberlain was solemnly assuring Arthur Henderson that, according to his authoritative information, the conversations which had taken place in Berchtesgaden between Hitler and Schuschnigg on February 12, 1938, resulted in a renewal of Germany's "assurances of nonintervention in Austrian domestic affairs." The well-informed foreign correspondent, M. W. Fodor, tells a different story. According to him, "The last chapter of the story that is Austria began in November when Viscount Halifax, then Lord Privy Seal, visited Berlin and Berchtesgaden and told Hitler that Great Britain was not interested in Central Europe." Already Viscount Halifax, successor to Eden as Foreign Secretary, was being employed by Chamberlain to do his political dirty work. Is it too much to assume that Mr. Eden was aware of the implications of such a move, and resented this division of authority? This may be pure supposition, but one recalls Eden's words in his personal explanation to the House of Commons: ". . . . I should not be frank with the House if I were to pretend that it is an isolated issue as between the Prime Minister and myself. It is not. Within the last few weeks upon one most important decision of foreign policy which did not concern Italy at all, the difference was fundamental." What that issue was has never been revealed. At any rate it is clear that Hitler was given *carte blanche* in Central Europe by Chamberlain. Mr. Fodor is even more explicit later in an article in which he writes: "The visit of Lord Halifax to Berchtesgaden November 17, 1937, left Hitler with the impression that England would not interfere if Germany occupied Austria, and that she would dissuade France from going to the help of Austria." Thereafter events moved rapidly. The first official hint of impending action was given by Baron Von Neurath to the French Ambassador to Berlin, at Christmas. According to Mr. Fodor, he said: "I must add that Germany cannot any longer watch idly the sufferings of our co-nationalists in Austria." Three months later, on March 11, Dr. Schuschnigg, the Austrian Chancellor, was presented with a German ultimatum asking him to postpone the proposed Austrian plebiscite. He agreed, specifying, however, that the Nazis should in the future refrain from interference in Austrian affairs. Hitler, using his now well-known method of allowing no mercy to the smaller nations, handed to Dr. Schuschnigg a second ultimatum demanding that he resign the Chancellorship in favor of Dr. Seyss-Inquart—an avowed Nazi. Hitler also demanded that two thirds of the seats in the cabinet should be handed over to the Nazis and that the National Socialist party in Austria be given full and unrestricted liberty. Schuschnigg was given one hour to reply; shortly after the time limit elapsed he announced over the radio that the Austrian people had yielded to force. The Anschluss had been consummated.

It is interesting to recall the British position on the Austrian Anschluss in the light of the actions taken by the League of Nations in 1939-40 arising out of the Russian invasion of Finland and wholeheartedly supported by Mr. Chamberlain's Government. Chamberlain, speaking in the House on March 14, 1938, took pains to outline the British position, stressing the history of British notices, protests, formulas, etc. But a closer examination of his remarks, and those of Lord Halifax, reveal some significant facts. Mr. Chamberlain felt called upon "to refute rumors that

His Majesty's Government had given consent if not encouragement to the idea of the absorption of Austria by Germany."
Immediately following this statement, for some reason Mr.
Chamberlain hastened to reassure the Czechs: "I am informed
that Field-Marshal Göring, on March 11th, gave a general assurance to the Czech Minister in Berlin—an assurance which
he expressly renewed later on behalf of Herr Hitler—that it
would be the earnest endeavor of the German Government to
improve German-Czech relations." Mr. Chamberlain denied
once again that Great Britain had ever encouraged the Austrian
Anschluss, but qualified his statement to some extent by adding:
"We had, indeed, never refused to recognize the special interest
that Germany had in the development of relations between Austria and herself, having regard to the close affinities existing between the two countries." He went on, ". . . . it has always been
made plain that His Majesty's Government would strongly dis-
approve of the application to the solution of these problems
of violent methods." What Mr. Chamberlain stressed was the
violent methods. This—not the Anschluss itself—formed the
larger part of his criticism. Nor did he mention the fact that
Hitler had given assurances to Austria, just as he had given them
now to Czechoslovakia.

Even more significant were the remarks of Lord Halifax in
the House of Lords on March 16th: "Whatever may have passed
between General Göring and myself, or other German leaders
and myself in Germany—which was and must remain confidential—I have never in any conversations that I have had with German leaders taken any other line but this: That, *while I did not
suppose that anyone in this country was concerned to maintain
the status quo in Europe for all time,* what they were concerned
to see was that no changes should be made in Europe *by violence."* Once again the stress is not upon the action itself but

the method; later, this was to be one of the loopholes through which the Prime Minister wriggled over Czechoslovakia. As regards the League of Nations, at the time of Eden's resignation Mr. Chamberlain had asked: "Does anybody believe that the League, as it is constituted today, can afford collective security? . . . . We must not try to delude small weak nations into think-ing that they will be protected by the League." Lord Halifax echoed, ". . . . nothing that the League can do can undo what has been done. . . . I confess that I can see no good to be gained at this juncture for the League or for any of the great purposes which the League represents, by bringing this matter before the League Tribunal." If this were true, then the British action on Russia was open to the same objection. The answer is obvious: Britain wished to mobilize world opinion against Russia, but not against Hitler.

The next move was revealed only a few days later by Mr. H. T. Lennox-Boyd, Parlimentary Secretary to the Ministry of Labour, who said: "I can countenance nothing more ridiculous than a guarantee that the frontiers of Czechoslovakia should not be violated when half the people in that country cannot be relied upon to be loyal to the Government of the day; and, from what I knew of Mr. Chamberlain, I did not think he would make a move to give a guarantee of that kind."

CRIPPS AND THE MINORITY MANIFESTO

The situation was obviously going from bad to worse.

Early in 1938, with the annexation of Austria and the resigna-tion of Eden, the Tory ruling class were compelled to come out in the open and place themselves in full public view on one or other of the two horns of their dilemma—Chamberlain and his capitalist friends on one; Eden, Churchill, and their imperialist friends on the other.

Cripps's speeches during this period present his perception of the forces at work. The week after the annexation of Austria he expressed the following views:

"Everything that has happened in the last three weeks is the inevitable outcome of the foreign policy of the Government over the last seven years. . . . The National Government have done all they could to build up Hitler's power, as the alternative to Hitler was a working class government in Germany, because Hitler was regarded as the bulwark against Bolshevism. The result of that policy is that in every part of the world they have endangered British Imperialism. . . . That is why Churchill has been opposed to the Government for so long. Churchill is a Liberal Imperialist; he would have done anything to protect the British Empire, and would have no qualms about working with Russia if it would achieve this. Churchill has always wanted the biggest force to protect the Empire, and has never wanted to play with Hitler, Mussolini, or Japan, because he realized that they were a great danger to the Empire.

"Churchill has been less concerned with the danger of working class power than the safety of the British Empire. That is the fundamental difference between Chamberlain and Churchill."

The policy of the Popular Front was in disfavor in left-wing British circles not because of abstract moral principles involved in co-operating with someone who had other ideals than your own, but because of a marked lack of elasticity in the average British Socialist's way of thinking. Refusing to co-operate with any section of the capitalist class may have been a very sound tactic so long as the capitalist class was homogeneous, with identical interests and no major disagreements about methods for furthering those interests. So long as that was the case, to co-operate with any section of this class was to co-operate with the whole class; hence the tactic of nonco-operation was the only logical one for a Socialist to adopt. But what was forgotten by many Socialists is that this tactic was only a tactic, not a principle. It was suitable only in certain circumstances and in answer to a certain type of attack. But these circumstances and this type of attack lasted for such a long time that the particular tactic for dealing with it became a tradition; it was elevated from a tactic to a principle, and is even now sometimes quoted like an eleventh commandment; an injunction that holds good in all circumstances and in the face of every type of attack.

Cripps's change of view on this question was due to his growing realization of the nature of his opponents. But the change was a gradual one, as was the development of his appreciation of the capitalist dilemma. It is significant, however, that as early as August, 1936, he had put forward in *The Socialist* proposals for a short program of action suitable for adoption by a Popular Front Government:

"The cardinal point, therefore, in our policy must be the challenge to and overthrow of capitalism. This, we admit, cannot be accomplished in a day, or a year, if democracy is to survive. We must, therefore, examine the situation with a view to seeing how we can best arrange our short-term program to achieve simultaneously three things.

"First, the decisive challenge to capitalism and imperialism put forward in unmistakable form;

"Second, the gaining of the largest area of support among the workers; and

"Third, the carrying through of the change we desire within democracy and without the violence of revolution.

"In the transition which we thus envisage there must, too, be immediate steps of ambulance work to relieve suffering and want and to improve conditions in the home and the working place.

"The program thus falls into two parts, the positive measures of advance to socialism on the one hand, and the relief work within the transition on the other. These two parts will have to be carried through simultaneously, so that it is not possible to allot them any priority.

"The main challenge to capitalism must be through the control of finance and the land. The joint stock banks in addition to the Bank of England, must be brought under National ownership and control. If these two big points of capitalist power are attacked and won there need be no fear that the Government carrying through such a policy will hesitate to go forward with a Socialist program. From the international point of view, a monopoly control of external trade in the chief exporting industries will be necessary in order to achieve economic co-operation with other Socialist states as a foundation for the nucelus of a peaceful world confederation.

"As measures of amelioration, the problem of the unemployed and the abolition of the Means Test, of mining conditions, of working hours, and of housing, will need to be dealt with on an imaginative scale, and full power must be returned to the Trade-Unions by the repeal of the iniquitous Act of 1927.

"A great works program financed by the nationalized credit of the country will not need fresh legislation except in finance, but will make its immediate impact upon unemployment during the transition period.

"This is a minimum program, but if honest agreement could be arived at upon it, and the promise to carry it through at all costs was a real promise, then I should be satisfied that any government which acted upon that promise would be a Socialist Government."

It is interesting to compare this with the measures which

Liberals favor, according to Mr. Elliott, writing in *Reynold News* in June, 1938:

"Liberals favor the control of arms profits, the establishment of minimum wages, holidays with pay, a national attack on malnutrition and on the problem of the Distressed Areas. They want to break the land monopoly, to extend the principle of public control to the Bank of England, to found a National Investment Board, and to exercise public powers in relation to public services like power and transport."

The only measure in Cripps's program with which Liberals would be likely to disagree seriously would be that for the monopoly control even temporarily, of export trade; and it should not be difficult to overcome this. Thus in 1936 Cripps was putting forward a minimum Popular Front program almost identical with what the Liberals in 1938 would have been willing to accept.

In the meanwhile, what was the Labour party doing—besides issuing pamphlets regretting this and that, and asking the National Government to adopt an international policy based on the League of Nations? The Labour movement as a whole, in these increasingly troubled times, felt an immediate need for constructive action. Ordinarily such constructive action would —and did—take the form of increased agitation for Labour votes. But such agitation could only make sense if there were any possibility of Labour gaining an electoral majority at the next general election. All calculations, however, seemed to indicate that this possibility was out of the question.

Any strategy based on a straight Labour victory at the next election was foredoomed to failure. But what to do? One answer was trade-union action. The response of the Labour party bureaucracy to such a suggestion was indicative of the actions which drove genuine Socialists to despair.

On April 23, 1938, an All-Party Emergency National Conference on Spain was held at Queens Hall, London. Present at the meeting were 1,806 delegates representing 1,203 trade-union, working-class, and Liberal organizations. A resolution was passed unanimously:

"The members of this Conference record their inflexible determination, by immediate action through their respective organizations, to secure freedom for the Spanish Government to purchase arms in defense of its people.

"Believing that not only the strategic safety of France, Great Britain, and the British Commonwealth of Nations, but the salvation of democracy itself depends upon victory for the Spanish Government, we pledge ourselves:

"(1) To use every means at our disposal to rouse public opinion in support of the demands of the Spanish Government to be placed before the League of Nations on May 9.

"(2) To give and secure support for every effort to supply food, transport, medical equipment, coal, and antiaircraft guns or for any other financial and material assistance necessary to secure the victory of the Spanish Government.

"(3) To support any political, economic, and industrial action which may be taken in support of these objects.

"Among the means to this end, we decide to send from this conference delegations to the Trades-Union Congress, the Liberal and Labour parties, the National Government, and the French Government, to bring to their attention the unanimous demands of this conference."

Statements from representatives of all anti-Fascist parties and trade-union executives gave some idea of the temper of the British working class. Mr. Wilfred Roberts, M. P. (Opp. Lib.), said that the conference represented 10,000,000 people. They could compel the Government to act by pressure of public opinion. He was a Liberal and regarded Socialists—red and pale pink—as equally dangerous, but he was prepared to co-operate with them in regard to helping Spain.

Mr. D. N. Pritt, M. P. (Labour Party), said:

"If the Government can be fairly and squarely faced with the realization that if they want millions of armaments here they must allow thousands of armaments for Spain, it will not be too late to save Spain and save Britain."

Mr. John James, of South Wales Miners' Federation, said: "If the Government has to have the support of the British Workers to make arms, they must be made to let the Spanish Government get arms and munitions.

"I say definitely on behalf of the South Wales Miners' Federation that we are prepared to do everything and anything jointly with our comrades of the other Trade-Unions.

"Let us call our Council of the Trades-Union Congress and organize united action."

Mr. James Griffiths, M. P. (Labour Party), appealed to all trade-unionists in the new and the old trade-union centers of Britain to combine their strength so as to be able successfully to go to Chamberlain and say: "If you want arms, we have the right to have our demands granted before we give them.

"We ought to go to our unions and demand an immediate special conference of Trade-Union Executives to consider action on Spain.

"I know the risks involved in industrial action, but I believe that the organized industrial might of the trade-union movement may yet save Spain, Great Britain, and the world."

Sir Charles Trevelyan, Labourite ex-president of the Board of Education, suggested an alliance between Great Britain, France, and Russia, working together as a League of Nations.

Mr. T. Schofield, of the Aircraft Shop Stewards' National

Council, said that this union was prepared to agitate for strike action to compel the Government to send arms to Spain. He added:

"We cannot separate the fight for arms for Spain from the fight against the National Government.

"We in the aircraft industry support the policy of the A. E. U. We are not prepared to co-operate with the Government. We demand a National Trade-Union Conference on these issues."

Mr. Geoffrey Mander, M. P. (Opp. Lib.), said:

"The trade-unions have the power now, and nobody has greater power, to swing this country back to the right track." He added: "Those who want the same thing should take common action to secure it."

Sir Stafford Cripps said: "I believe in the power and necessity of industrial action." He added that the key to the Spanish situation could be made to turn only when the workers of Great Britain made it clear to the Government that they were not prepared to enter into any bargains or make any concessions for a foreign policy for which they had no desire and which was "sacrificing their brothers and sisters in Spain."

So strong was the feeling displayed at this conference that a special meeting of trade-union representatives was called to consider united trade-union action on Spain. A delegation was chosen to ask Sir Walter Citrine, the general secretary of the Trades-Union Congress, to call an immediate conference of all trade-union executives. When the members of the delegation came to the office at the Trades-Union Congress, however—an office which had been built with their dues—Sir Walter declined to meet them on the ground that they came from an unofficial body. And this was the man who led the working class movement of Great Britain at one of the crucial moments of its history!

There was only one thing left to do. Four members of the National Executive—Sir Stafford Cripps, Harold Laski, D. N. Pritt, and Ellen Wilkinson—composed a confidential memorandum, setting forth the need for a Popular Front, which was submitted to the National Executive at a special meeting on May 5th. This memorandum was never distributed to the rank and file of the Labour party, and—so far as is known to the present writer—was never reprinted. It was rejected by the National Executive, and the only notice of its existence was the publication of an attack on the Popular Front, issued by the Labour party within a week of the submission of the minority memorandum. The document itself is a brilliantly incisive report on the international situation and the position of the Labour party; it summarizes all the issues which have been outlined in the present chapter and will receive more extended treatment in the next. Hence the memorandum is printed in full.

THE INTERNATIONAL SITUATION

It is unnecessary to dwell upon the depth of the crisis in which we are involved. No one in the Labour movement denies the urgency of defeating the Chamberlain Government at the earliest possible moment. Every day it remains in power increases the danger not merely to English, but to world democracy.

We cannot measure the crisis by comparison even with the immediate past. Its tempo is too rapid and intense. To judge our chances in the light of 1929, 1931, or even 1935, is, in our opinion, gravely to misread the situation. For its difficulties and dangers have so increased in these last weeks that the basis of past experience has been rendered obsolete.

What are the main elements in the new crisis?

(1) The continued maintenance of nonintervention, which means in practice that the supply of arms to the Spanish Government is gravely hampered whilst Franco is freely supplied. The effect of this is:

(a) Greatly to diminish the power of the Spanish democracy to maintain its hold upon its territory.

(b) To impair the morale of the democratic countries, both large and small, by its enhancement of Fascist prestige; it also gradually eliminates the democratic government of Spain from the forces opposed to Fascism;

(c) This, in its turn, weakens France as a force against Fascism by establishing a hostile frontier on the Pyrenees and by rendering insecure her Atlantic and Mediterranean sea routes;

(d) Beyond this, the working class movement in Great Britain is discouraged, and the country's strategic position is involved by the threat to the Empire routes and her naval position;

(e) Possible allies of democracy, above all the U. S. A., are isolated and estranged by the sense that Great Britain has abandoned the struggle to maintain the democratic principle and is acquiescing in its conquest by aggression.

(II) A further danger results from the occupation of Austria by Hitler. This is clearly intended as a new base for aggression in both Central and Southeastern Europe; for—

(1) It has greatly increased the prestige and striking power of Fascism not only in those areas, but over all Western civilization.

(2) It threatens Czechoslovakia and other free States in this area with internal disruption and a consequent loss of their freedom and independence.

(3) It acquires for Hitler new and important resources for his larger and later aggression both in the East and the West.

(4) It intimidates the smaller countries neighboring on Germany and thus forces them into the orbit of Fascist influence.

(5) It threatens the break-up of the Franco-Soviet-Czech pact, and thus endangers one of the main possible safeguards for world peace.

(6) It encourages the British Government to accept the results of Fascist aggression as a basis for negotiation with Hitler and Mussolini. It has aided the National Government in its effort to disrupt the Popular Front in France and to replace it by

a government less determined upon the defense of democracy and more ready to be persuaded into deals with the Fascist Powers on the basis of their aggressive conquests.

The Drift of the National Government

The policy of the National Government, as exemplified by its attitude to Spain and Abyssinia in the Anglo-Italian Treaty, and by its acquiesence in the Austrian coup, is on its external side effectively pro-Fascist. It rejects alliance with any group of anti-Fascist Powers, as it rejects, also, any return to the League of Nations and any attempt to build up collective security. The necessary implication of this outlook is, inevitably, a drift which will become increasingly rapid as Chamberlain's policy is followed through toward Fascist methods and ideology in Great Britain.

The National Government, moreover, is, as its propaganda in connection with the acceleration of rearmament and A. R. P. schemes makes clear, deliberately creating a war crisis atmosphere. It is doing so largely in order to be able to appeal to the country at the moment it considers most appropriate with the cry of "National Unity in face of the danger of War!"—a cry even more likely to be effective than the slogan—"National Unity in face of the danger of financial collapse!" which was used so effectively in 1931.

If the National Government should win the next Election, and thus secure another five years of life, we must, if we believe in our own propaganda, hold that within those five years we should drift either into another Imperialist war or into a definite alliance for concerted action with the Fascist Powers. Either alternative would greatly intensify the restriction of political and industrial freedom, and the more such restriction grows, the greater will be the tendency of the National Government—always under its assumed "mandate" of "National Unity"—to borrow the methods of suppression now in vogue in totalitarian countries. The area of democracy will shrink still further, and our ability to maintain it here will be proportionately jeopardized. It is, indeed, probable that, with or without a war, another six years of such a Government as the present, will see the process of the destruction of democracy and the establishment of capitalist totalitarianism both in Europe and Great Britain carried a long way toward completion—at least far enough to render the chances of successfully defeating the Government in power very much smaller than they are today.

The Need for Immediate Change of Government

The only alternative to the National Government and the disastrous results of its foreign policy as outlined above, is a Socialist reconstruction of Great Britain. For this, the overthrow of the National Government is an essential prerequisite, and all agree that that must now be our primary and vital objective. But the fundamental factor is that of time and the extreme urgency of this overthrow. In normal circumstances there could be no question but that it would be right to wait and work for the time when we could form a Government with a clear working majority whose immediate objective would be a full Socialist program. But the times are not normal. We cannot now afford to wait for that working majority upon the assumption that the situation will remain static until our access to power. To do so would be to risk losing for a generation—and perhaps forever— the chance of establishing the only conditions under which we can hope effectively to start the process of socialization. We would all agree that we have no right to imperil the working class movement and the institutions which it has built up in this country—to say nothing of the lives and future of our comrades in Spain, Czechoslovakia and other still free countries—by neglecting any political device that would increase the prospects of an early overthrow of the National Government. The question that presents itself is whether there is any such political device outside the strict confines of our own movement.

It is clearly imperative to take whatever steps are available to minimize the hazard of the next General Election. We cannot afford on any terms a Chamberlain victory. We owe this to Spain; we owe it to Czechoslovakia; we owe it to the remaining free countries all over the world. We believe that the attainment of the Socialist objective of our Party depends upon an immediate reversal of the National Government's foreign policy. The only condition for such a reversal is the defeat of Chamberlain at the next General Election.

The Present Facts of the Electoral Situation

How can the Labour Party best accomplish the overthrow of the National Government in the existing political circumstances?

We put forward the following propositions, which, we believe, will be accepted by members of every shade of opinion in the Party:

(1) The Labour Party can, at the present time, rely upon the support of the working class *at least* to the extent that this support was given at the last Election, unless, of course, the next Election is conducted under panic conditions similar to or worse than those of 1931.

(2) The growing strength of Trade-Unionism should lead to an increase in the political strength of our movement.

(3) A large number of unattached voters are definitely anti-Chamberlain at the moment, either vaguely or with conviction. There is widespread uneasiness in the Electorate as to the Government's policy, both Home and Foreign.

(4) A number of nonpolitical—e.g. religious, cultural, etc.—organizations are sentimentally pro-Peace, anti-War, and anti-Fascist, and therefore inclined to be critical of the National Government.

(5) Amongst political parties the Liberal Party, the Communist Party, the I. L. P., and the Co-operative Party are definitely anti-Chamberlain and broadly support the foreign policy of the Labour Party. They do not, however, accept our domestic policy except in part.

(6) At a time, like the present, of grave crisis in foreign affairs, the most powerful weapon of propaganda to win the unattached voter is the call to "National Unity for National Safety." At the moment, the danger of war, the composition and history of this Government, and the fact that it is the Government in power, place this vital weapon potentially in its hands.

We believe, as we have said, that the above propositions will command general acceptance. Those which follow are open to dispute, since they are necessarily built upon observations and estimates which differ with the experience of different individuals. We set them out because we believe, from our recent experience, that they are accurate conclusions:

(1) There is a considerable volume of opinion within the movement which has grown through the pressure of recent events

in favour of co-operation with other political elements hostile to the Chamberlain Government.

(2) The great number of persons who hold an indeterminate anti-Chamberlain opinion, although many of them might vote Labour, are not joining the Labour Party as members.

(3) The greater part of the Electorate is still politically unconscious. It is likely to be moved by some simple slogan such as a call to National Unity. This is of especial importance since the Government is in a position to call an election at the moment when such a slogan can be used to its greatest advantage.

(4) There is no such wave of *pro-Labour* sympathy or feeling in the country today as to alarm the Government seriously. There is a mass of opinion swinging against the Government, but it is not aligned definitely behind the Labour Party, and there is no reason to suppose that a General Election upon orthodox lines in the near future would lead to any sweeping change of representation.

(5) At recent by-elections in which the Party has been successful, every attempt has been made to win Liberal and other outside support. The main stress in these elections has been laid upon foreign policy—as to which there is a wide agreement —and ameliorative measures of domestic reform upon which there is little or no disagreement. None of these elections has been fought on the definite issue of Socialism v. Capitalism. In the present Lichfield by-Election, for example, the Labour Party is definitely encouraging and assisting such bodies as the Council of Action to take part in the campaign on our behalf, and the expenses of such participation will form part of the Labour candidate's election expenses. We believe that the reason for such electoral policy is clear and that it is right in the present circumstances.

(6) The present organization of the Party is defective in many industrial areas of which Lancashire and the Midlands are examples, and is practically nonexistent in a number of rural areas such as the South and West Counties. This does not give promise of any remarkable electoral results being forth-

coming from these areas upon the basis of present Party activity.

What Strategy Should the Labour Party Adopt?

In these conditions what is the strategy best calculated to secure the rapid defeat of the National Government?

Clearly, we must arouse a much more intense feeling in the country than at present exists. This must not only be anti-Government; it must also be definitely pro-Opposition. For this we must offer the country what the electors feel to be a practicable and effective alternative government with a majority behind it, and we must so define the objectives of that alternative government as to command the maximum possible support from every element that is anti-Chamberlain. Success in this strategy will depend to a large extent on the way in which the issue is presented to the country.

Clearly, the main issue, upon which all else turns, is Labour's foreign policy as against the Government's foreign policy. That is the issue which will command the maximum volume of support beyond the ordinary adherents of the Party. It provides the most effective counter to the propaganda of the National Government for National Unity. It is, in our view, inconceivable that any opposition could turn out a government in such times as these except upon the ground of a fundamental difference of policy in Foreign Affairs and upon the issue of Peace versus War, or Democracy versus Fascism.

The Democratic Alliance for Peace

We have given this question the best consideration we can. In the light of our experience, and bearing in mind especially the difficulty of winning over large numbers of the middle class, and all classes in the rural areas, we have come to the conclusion that an effective victory by the Labour Party alone is highly improbable at the next Election. We do not think this conclusion is controverted by any examination of past electoral results. Calculations of what might be done in this constituency or that by a combination of Liberal and Labour votes do not, in our view, enable any accurate forecast to be arrived at, since the next General Election is bound to be held in a crisis atmosphere and not in any normal political conditions. The way to overthrow the Chamberlain Government is, in our judgment, to rally the unattached and politically unconscious voters of all shades of progressive opinion and of all classes by the demand for the formation of a *new and more real National Unity*. We believe that supporters could be detached wholesale from the present spurious National Government in this way and in no other. Such persons, who form a large percentage of the Electorate, are more responsive to the emotional ideal of National Unity than to any considered and detailed program.

We illustrate our point by taking the case of Aylesbury. Here, a mere addition of the Liberal and Labour votes as cast in 1935 would still leave a National Government majority of 5,390. In our view, a fight between Labour and Liberal candidates in that Election will tend to decrease the strength of both by stressing a confusion of aims and a partisanship that will be emphasized by the Government candidate to his great advantage. A combined fight, on the other hand, would, in our judgment, have a good chance of registering another Government defeat. It would emphasize to the whole country the unity of the anti-Chamberlain forces in the most dramatic way. It would rally anti-Chamberlain opinion in many other areas. It would show the intensity of our view that the National Government is a National menace and must be defeated at all costs. It would also make certain that the desired support of Liberal and progressive elements would continue to be given to our candidates in the vast majority of the coming by-Elections.

It is essential to bear in mind the fact that any government which results from the next general Election will find itself plunged in problems of the greatest difficulty, and that to cope with those problems a clear working majority of not less than 40-50 seats will be essential. A government with a smaller majority would find it almost impossible to carry on and would gravely endanger the cause of democracy in this country. When calculating the chances of success, we are, therefore, dealing with the chances of winning a majority of 40-50 seats and nothing less.

Regretfully, therefore, because we view with reluctance the idea of allying ourselves with non-Socialists, we have come to the conclusion that the only chance, in the existing political circumstances, of replacing the National Government within a reasonable period of time by a government which will be strong enough to uphold democracy in this country in the face of European perils, is to co-operate with other anti-Government political Parties. It is better to join forces with anti-Socialist democrats than to see both Socialism and Democracy perish. We would base such co-operation upon a National Unity of the people against the vested interests of Conservatism and reaction. We believe that the call for such Unity should come from the leaders of the Labour Party, the Trade-Unions, and the Co-operative Movement, and that coming from them it would have an overwhelming effect upon the Nation.

The Basis for Co-operation

We suggest that the basis for such a call should be a short program on the following lines:

(1) The Foreign Policy of the Party as it has already been declared;

(2) Such items of the Short Term program as will be acceptable to the Parties responding to the call. In our view, these items would, perforce, include some considerable measures of Socialization. We believe that agreement upon a very considerable part of our Short Term program, including substantially all the ameliorative measures, would be attainable by negotiation in advance with the political bodies likely to co-operate.

We propose that such a call be made by the Labour movement, and that those likely to co-operate be sounded in advance through their leaders. We are convinced that a demand by the Labour Party for National Unity of the people in the face of the Fascist and War dangers represented by the National Government, would win an immediate response from the country. We believe that it would give the anti-Government forces a rallying cry that would transform the political situation. We believe it would force an issue and create a challenge that the National Government could not ignore. We are convinced that the one effective chance of that immediate victory which is essential for the salvation of democracy and peace lies along this road.

We do not attempt here to formulate the details of such co-operation. At the moment, the vital question is that of principle. We emphasize only our view that the party, by offering co-operation, will be in no danger of losing its own entity and organization, or of injuring the socialist cause for which it stands. It will in our view add to its general prestige amongst a number of people because it will be considered by them to have waived mere party advantage in favor of more vital issues.

We stress, again, that the major danger confronting the Party at the next Election is the certain use by the National Government of the call for National Unity against the foreign enemy. We see no other practicable means of countering that propaganda which is otherwise likely to prove successful save by creating ourselves the counter-cry of National Unity against the enemy of democracy at Home and Abroad. In the present grave emergency it is, in our view, the duty of Labour to organize that unity and to create the spirit of resistance to Fascism and War by seizing the initiative at this moment of supreme danger to the liberties of the workers by whom and for whose protection our movement was created.

We beg the National Executive, with all the emphasis at our command, to realize the gravity and urgency of the crisis. What is in jeopardy now is the whole future of our Movement as part of a democratic society. Capitalist reaction is sweeping us into the stream of Fascist tendency. We think that our proposal still leaves us a chance of fighting successfully against its current. But the tide is running fast. There is still the prospect that the Labour Party may give the lead to a national unity against Fascism for which we believe the people is waiting. The evidence daily accumulates of the impatience with which such a lead is looked for. We think it imperative to act before our opportunity is snatched from us by the National Government. We believe that action now on the lines we propose will give us a real assurance of a momentous victory.

STAFFORD CRIPPS
HAROLD J. LASKI
D. N. PRITT
ELLEN WILKINSON

VIII

MUNICH AND THE PETITION CAMPAIGN

WITH GREAT BRITAIN now fighting Nazi Germany, and assuring the victims of German expansion that their freedom is a prerequisite to any peace, the events of Munich have receded into the background. It has seemed uncharitable (to say the least) to recall that surrender to Nazi bluff and bluster, now that British soldiers, sailors, and airmen are calling that bluff with their lives. But it should not be forgotten that the policies of the Chamberlain Government were in large part responsible for the present war. The stand against Hitler is being made because the possibility of using him as a lever to overthrow Stalin vanished. Mr. Chamberlain declared war on Hitler because the Russo-German alliance meant one thing: that Hitler had betrayed the British Government.

The long series of surrenders which Great Britain had made to Fascist intimidation, the aid to Fascist expansion which had been given for years by the British ruling class, were given with one purpose in view, to strengthen the Fascists sufficiently to allow them to attack Russia. Fascism was also a threat to the British Empire; but the interests of Empire were subordinated to those of class. The Nazis represented themselves as the western bulwark against Communism, publicly announcing their plan to attack the Russian Ukraine. Reassured by these announcements, Mr. Chamberlain and the National Government aided and abetted the Fascists at every turn, weakening the British Empire as the strength of Fascism grew. When the Russo-

German pact was signed, the Tories realized that they had been tricked; the present war is a consequence of that realization.

The ignominy of Munich remains, however, to the everlasting disgrace of both Great Britain and France. The betrayal of a courageous and democratic people to the unspeakable brutalities of Hitler's perverted barbarians is an act so terrible as to be almost incomprehensible. There have been reports enough of the consequences of that betrayal in human terms. A book like G. E. R. Gedye's *Betrayal in Central Europe* with its eyewitness accounts of Nazi outrages in Austria and Czechoslovakia, says all that can be said about the horrors of Nazi *Kultur*. Here we are concerned only with the act itself, as a political and historical event; but its full horror should be kept in mind. For only by realizing the full impact of these events upon a man like Sir Stafford Cripps will his reaction become clear. The mind, after a time, becomes dulled at the repetitious monotony of stories about Fascist cruelty; the senses no longer react, after they have been assaulted without respite. The repercussions echo faintly in America, for distance serves as a cushion. But to those in England, watching the refugees arrive—that pitiful handful who were allowed admittance—the word "civilization" had a hollow sound. The very structure of their world seemed to be collapsing, and there was no time to wait for a Socialist majority in order to oust the man who had actually aided the perpetration of this foulest of crimes. Such was the attitude of all decent English men and women in those tragic days.

MUNICH

The assurance given to Czechoslovakia by Göring, at the time of the Austrian Anschluss, was the assurance which Mr. Chamberlain gave to the House of Commons, whose fear over the fate of Czechoslovakia was evident. Mr. Attlee pointed out that Germany had consummated the Anschluss at the very time when Great Britain was holding friendly conversations with Germany. Mr. Leopold S. Amery asked in the strongest terms for a clear statement from the Government; his request was repeated by Winston Churchill. But all that the Government did was to repeat a statement made by Sir John Simon on February 21st: "The obligations of His Majesty's Government toward Austria and Czechoslovakia are those which every member of the League of Nations assumes toward all its fellow-members. Apart from these, His Majesty's Government has given no special guarantees toward either country." This was tantamount to *carte blanche* for Hitler.

The Czech crisis is an excellent instance of Hitler's tactics. Czechoslovakia was founded in 1918 through the emancipation of Bohemia, Moravia, and Slovakia from Austro-Hungarian rule. These three provinces were part of a kingdom which had disappeared during the Middle Ages. At no time had the German-speaking population of these provinces been under German rule. Consequently, Germany had no historical right to interfere with the affairs of Czechoslovakia; and she did so only on the basis of a fantastic and unscientific racial theory which, if consistently applied, would justify interference in the internal affairs of the United States, which has—according to German calculations—twelve million Germans. The issue of the Sudeten Germans was nothing but an unscrupulous ruse of Hitler's employed to justify his aggressions. Actually the Sudeten Germans had greater rights and liberties than any other minority in Europe, with the possible exception of the small German-speaking minority in Denmark. The whole Sudeten question was nothing but a red herring; the real issue was German expansionist ambition.

That there was Sudeten discontent cannot be denied. But

this discontent was in no way a consequence of Czech suppression. It was, rather, due to the world industrial crisis. The Sudeten areas were the most highly industrialized in Czechoslovakia, producing mainly consumers' goods and luxuries. They were the very first to be curtailed by the crisis; and the tariff walls which sprang up then cut off many of the Sudeten markets in Central Europe. The economic autarchy established by the Nazis themselves was in large part responsible for the Sudeten unemployment, for Czech exports to Germany were reduced from 20% of the total in 1929 to 14% in 1936. Twenty thousand workers were thrown out of employment in the frontier districts alone by the refusal of Nazi authorities to allow them to continue working across the border in Germany, as they had previously done. It was essentially in response to this economic difficulty that the Henlein party was formed after the dissolution of the Czechoslovakian Nazi party in 1932. The *Daily Telegraph* reported a Sudeten German reservist as saying: "I and my family all voted for Henlein at the last election because we believed he would help us to get more employment. But never did we want to be torn away from the Republic." The same correspondent reported a conversation with a big Sudeten manufacturer as follows: "I am a good German patriot and voted for Henlein. But like all those, except the wild youths, who voted for him, we gave him a mandate only to serve our autonomy, to give the German language full equality with that of the Czechs in all branches of public life and to open the way to fuller state employment. Never was the question of our annexation by Germany put before us. . . ."

But Henlein did not confine himself to grievances which could be legitimately rectified by the Czechoslovak government. He rejected the idea of the equality of all citizens before the law, irrespective of race, creed, or religion—a principle which was basic in the Czechoslovak constitution—and demanded the reorganization of the country on racial lines. The Henleinists wanted government by racial leaders, local *führers* not responsible to Parliament. These proposals were openly intended to destroy Czech democracy internally, paving the way for the partition of the country by Germany.

International events were obviously coming to a head. But no clear and unequivocal statement of British policy had yet been given. Some hint of what that would be, however, could be inferred from the fact that *The Times* had sounded out public opinion by writing twice (June 3rd and June 14th) that the possibility of handing the Sudeten areas over to Germany should not be excluded. On June 27th, Mr. Chamberlain was asked whether he would seek any assurances from the Nazi Government, in view of the fact that Goebbels, six days before, had plainly intimated that Germany planned to annex the Sudeten areas. But the Government spokesman confined himself to saying that the statement supposedly made by Goebbels (it was given from a verbatim report of the speech in *The Times*) did not appear in the official version of the speech. Hence, the Government concluded, nothing was really meant. Parliament rose at the end of July, leaving the country in the hands of an inner Cabinet whose pro-Fascist leanings were common knowledge.

Meanwhile sundry important Nazis had been making mysterious visits to London. Henlein himself had come in May, and was introduced to men like Winston Churchill and Sir Robert Vansittart—both anti-Nazis—who were led to believe that his demands were really only to help the poor, unemployed Sudetens. Harold Nicolson says of this incident: "He paid me the honor of coming to my own Chambers in the Temple. I invited a few fellow members of Parliament (from every party) to meet him. We told him that although the mass of British opinion was in sympathy with his demand for local autonomy, we could not agree with the two last points in his Karlsbad program. He assured us that these two points had been 'mistranslated'; he had not the slightest intention of suppressing freedom of speech and action in the Sudetenland; he had no personal prejudice against the Jews or the Socialists. The autonomous area which he envisaged would be run on completely democratic lines. Nor had he ever intended to suggest that this small German minority would attempt to dictate the foreign policy of the whole Czechoslovak state. All he had meant by that point was that they would always oppose any anti-German policy on the part of Czechoslovakia. But, of course, they would oppose it only as a dissident minority, employing constitutional methods. We warned him that if he created a movement such as might lead Germany to violate Czechoslovak independence, Great Britain would go to war. *We imagined, at the time, that in so warning him we were expressing the views of the Government and the country. He was assured in other British quarters that these warnings were merely the ravings of the 'warmongers.'"* Here, in the words of an authority on British diplomacy, is the evidence that there were "other British quarters" who encouraged Henlein to believe that Great Britain would aid Germany to dismember Czechoslovakia. It is not difficult to infer which these quarters were.

The effect of these meetings was to encourage Hitler in his plans. Later in the same month German army corps were massed upon the Czech border. But quick action on the part of President Benes, who mobilized the Czech army, and the assurances of the French government that invasion would mean war, made Hitler think twice. "Mutual appeasement was assayed," as Mr. Nicolson puts it. Hitler sent his confidential envoy, Captain

Wiedemann, to visit London for private conversations with Chamberlain and Lord Halifax. Lord Runciman, according to Harold Nicolson, was sent to Prague as "mediator" as a gesture of good will to Hitler, although Chamberlain stated in the House that he was being sent at the request of the Czech Government. Just what powers Lord Runciman possessed was not clear. Mr. Chamberlain said that "Such an investigator and mediator would, of course, be independent of His Majesty's Government—in fact, he would be independent of all Governments." Apparently Lord Runciman was to subsist in some metaphysical realm of his own, beyond the reach of ordinary Governments. Or as Sir John Simon was later to put it in a speech at Lanark: "He is at Prague at this moment in no sense as the representative of the British Government, but as the representative of all men everywhere who desire justice and love peace." What this was to mean in political terms, however, remains to be clarified.

The Czech plan in answer to the Carlsbad proposals was rejected by the Henlein party on the eve of Lord Runciman's arrival. Lord Runciman's status was immediately defined by his choice of companions: "The English week end has been regularly spent hobnobbing with German aristocrats who are sore with the Czech Government because of its land reforms, while he has made the worst impression by being seen on a number of occasions in company with the Princess Hohenlohe, who is reputed to be a favorite emissary of Hitler. He has not accepted Czech invitations."

"Under pressure from the French and British governments," the Czech government proposed two further plans, the last on August 21st. After an interview with Hitler, however, Henlein left no doubt that he was not interested in arriving at a peaceable solution. Nothing less than the Carlsbad points would satisfy the Sudeten Germans, he said; and it was at this point that the hand of the British Government was revealed. *The Times* printed its famous editorial which went far beyond anything that the Sudeten leaders had yet demanded. It read, in part: "It might be worth while for the Czech government to consider the project which has found favor in some quarters, of making Czechoslovakia a more homogeneous state by the secession of that fringe of alien populations who are contiguous to the nation with which they are united by race." "This article," writes Harold Nicolson, "encouraged Hitler and Henlein to increase their demands. . . . Henlein broadcast an appeal for assistance against 'the reign of terror of the Bolshevist Hussite criminals in Prague' and declared the hour of liberation to be near. The crisis was drawing toward its climax."

Hitler's Nuremberg speech on September 12th was the signal for an outbreak of what were obviously prearranged riots in the Sudeten districts. *The Times* reported on September 22nd: "Every German account of the frontier incidents is refuted by eyewitnesses here . . . storm troopers who were masquerading as Sudeten Germans had come over the frontier at several points and what terror there was was their work." The riots, however, produced a revulsion of feeling among Sudetens which was further aggravated by Henlein's demand, made on September 15th, for the cession of the Sudeten areas. The Czechoslovak cabinet met on the same day, taking strong measures. Martial law was extended to sixteen districts; Henlein was declared subject to arrest; the Sudeten party was ordered to dissolve. A joint proclamation by representatives of the Social Democrats, clericals, and Agrarians urged all peace-loving Sudeten Germans to join a Sudeten German National Council, which would negotiate on the basis of the Fourth Benes Plan—which virtually conceded all of the Carlsbad points. The creation of a new German Bohemian Party was in process. This threatened to set at naught the work of Hitler and the "appeasers."

Significantly enough, it was just at the moment that Chamberlain chose to fly to Berchtesgaden to see Hitler. There Hitler informed him in no uncertain terms that "rather than wait he would be prepared to risk a world war." At this crucial moment, when the possibility of a really negotiable policy between the Sudeten Germans and the Czech Government had actually presented itself, Chamberlain chose to capitulate to Hitler's threats of force. Some days later he proposed the Anglo-French plan, that all districts with over 50% German-speaking population should be ceded to Germany. In many of these districts, of course, about half the population would be Czech. The plan assumed—what was definitely not the case—that every German-speaking member of the population wished to be annexed by Germany. The plan involved, in other words, the handing over to Germany of districts with a clear democratic majority.

At this point an interesting disparity in the versions of what took place should be mentioned. Mr. Chamberlain said in his report to the House on the European crisis that, "The British and French Ministers in Prague . . . were instructed to point out to the Czechoslovak Government that there was no hope of a peaceful solution. . . . The Czechoslovak Government was urged to accept the Anglo-French proposals immediately." Harold Nicolson, however, along with other newspaper correspondents on the scene, gave some vital details. "At 2 A.M. on Wednesday, September 21st," Harold Nicolson writes "the French and British Ministers in Prague dragged Dr. Benes from his bed. They informed him that unless the Czechoslovak Government immediately accepted the Franco-British plan he could expect no assistance either from France or from Great Britain in the war which would immediately follow. The Czech Govern-

ment capitulated to this ultimatum addressed to them by their
ally and best friend. In a broadcast to the Czech nation, President Benes informed his countrymen that he had been forced to
yield to 'pressure for which there is no precedent in history.'
Even after the diplomatic visits and while the all-night sitting
was in progress, pressure was applied by telephone calls." The
next day, according to this same correspondent, Hitler had arranged with the representatives of Hungary and Poland to press
their demands simultaneously upon Czechoslovakia. This enabled Britain and France to point to the Czechs that "they were
now faced with a united front of Germany, Hungary, and Poland." These Powers, it was stated, threatened immediate invasion if there were any further delay in acceptance. The President and the Premier were, it is reported, even told that anything short of unconditional acceptance of the London terms
would result in the full partition of Czechoslovakia and its dis-
appearance from the map of Europe. Under these conditions the
Czech Cabinet was forced to accept the Anglo-French plan without consulting Parliament. This Government was overthrown by
nation-wide demonstrations of the people in the early hours of
Thursday, Sepetmber 22nd.

On that same day Chamberlain flew to Godesberg to resume
his talks with Hitler. Two days later he returned with the Godesberg plan, which even the British and French admitted was
hardly suitable for discussion. It proposed the immediate handing over of all districts with over 50% of German-speaking
people, and it proposed the appropriation of other districts as
well. The Godesberg plan was exceedingly vague about the proposed plebiscite in questionable areas, demanded immediate
evacuation and the appropriation of all goods in the areas in
question. The districts marked out by the Germans were to be
handed over intact by October 1st. This included fortifications, all

plants and establishments, materials, railway rolling stock, air-dromes, wireless stations, utility services, foodstuffs, cattle, raw materials, etc.

These demands were rejected by the Czechs. "The proposals," they said, "go far beyond what we agreed to in the so-called Anglo-French plan. They deprive us of every safeguard for our national existence. We are to yield up large portions of our care-fully prepared defenses and admit the German armies deep into our country before we have been able to organize it on the new basis or make any preparations for its defense. Our national and economic independence would automatically disappear with the acceptance of Herr Hitler's plan. The whole process of moving the population is to be reduced to panic flight on the part of those who will not accept the German Nazi regime.

"We rely upon the two great Western democracies whose wishes we had followed much against our own judgment, to stand by us in our hour of trial."

As an answer to this plea the British and French Governments encouraged the Czech Government to mobilize. French mobili-zation came three days later. It looked as if Hitler were stymied. The next day Mr. Chamberlain made a broadcast speech to the nation, which opened in this vein: "How horrible, fantastic, incredible, it is that we should be digging trenches and trying on gas masks here because of a quarrel in a faraway country between people of whom we know nothing." There were numerous hints of what was to come. Mr. Chamberlain said: "I would not hesitate to pay even a third visit to Germany if I thought it would do any good." He further stated: "However much we may sympathize with a small nation confronted by a big and powerful neighbor, we cannot in all circumstances undertake to involve the whole British Empire in war."

Parliament reassembled the next day, to hear Mr. Chamberlain's account. Let us look at that scene through the eyes of an eyewitness, Harold Nicolson: "The House listened in silence to his long tale of pledges broken and of warnings disregarded. The Prime Minister described his flight to Berchtesgaden and how, at his first meeting with Herr Hitler he had derived the impression that the Führer was prepared 'to risk a world war' rather than to abate his demands. In desperation the French and British Governments had forced the Czechs to accept the 'Anglo-French plan' and to surrender their defenses and their territory into German hands. Armed with this plan Mr. Chamberlain had flown to Godesberg. In spite of the fact that under this plan Herr Hitler obtained everything he had ever asked for, he still desired to attack the Czechs. He described the plan as 'too dilatory,' meaning thereby that under this scheme the Czechs would be given time to withdraw some, at least, of their livestock and munitions before the areas were occupied by German troops. 'Imagine,' the Prime Minister said, 'the perplexity in which I found myself.' This remark roused a murmur of sympathy on all benches. Mr. Chamberlain was touched by this demonstration. 'It was,' he added, 'a profound shock to me.' Again a murmur of sympathy passed along the crowded benches. He replaced his pince-nez, leaned forward toward the box on which his papers were spread out and continued his recital. The House waited in tense anxiety for him to reach the events of the last twelve hours. He reached them. 'Yesterday morning,' he began . . . . At that moment a stir was noticed in the Peer's gallery. Lord Halifax, who had been listening intently, was suddenly seen to leave the place. A minute later a sheet of paper was passed down the Treasury bench. It was handed to Sir John Simon, who glanced at it and then tugged at the Prime Minister's coat. Mr. Chamberlain ceased speaking, adjusted his pince-nez, and read the document, which Sir John held up to him. . . . 'I have,' he said, 'something further to announce to the House yet. I have now been informed by Herr Hitler that he invites me to meet him in Munich tomorrow morning. He has also invited Signor Mussolini and M. Daladier. Signor Mussolini has accepted, and I have no doubt M. Daladier will also accept. I need not say what my answer will be.' "

Mr. Chamberlain left for Munich the next day. On Friday, September 30th, the Munich agreement was signed by Hitler, Mussolini, Mr. Chamberlain, and Mr. Daladier. The Czech advisers who were on the spot were not consulted at all. Their material was not considered. Their maps were not examined. "The Czech representatives were not consulted at any stage in the proceedings," wrote the *New Statesman and Nation* on October 8th. "They waited with their maps while their enemies and their false friends divided up Czechoslovakia, on the basis of old maps provided by Hitler. Finally, they were given a two hours' ultimatum for Dr. Benes, and told to take the details of the Munich 'settlement' as fast as possible to Prague."

Under the agreement at Munich, occupation of the "territory of predominantly German character" was to take place in five stages, spread over the period October 1st to October 10th. Four zones were designated to be occupied by October 7th, the fifth zone, to be occupied by October 10th, was to be determined by an International Commission. The final determination of the frontiers was also to be carried out by the International Commission.

The International Commission was further to determine the territories in which a plebiscite would be held and to fix the conditions in which the plebiscites were to be held taking as a basis the conditions of the Saar plebiscite. In this way Hitler's demand that voting rights should only go to persons resident in the territories in 1918 was granted. As there was no census for

1918, but only an entirely unreliable one of 1910, this provision opened up every possible avenue for impersonation and fraud.

Existing installations (fortifications, for example) were to be handed over intact. The Czech Government was to release within a period of four weeks every "Sudeten German" who wished to be released from either the military or political forces and also all Sudeten German political prisoners. No mention was made of the release from German prisons of Czechoslovak subjects, over one thousand of whom had, in recent weeks, been kidnaped and taken to Germany. Great Britain and France were prepared to join in an international agreement of the boundaries of the new Czech state against unprovoked aggression; Germany and Italy agreed to give such a guarantee to Czechoslovakia only when the question of the Polish and Hungarian minorities had been settled.

The whole fiasco was adequately summed up, some days later, by a pro-Chamberlain newspaper: " . . . it is now abundantly clear that Germany's claims to Czechoslovakia have been governed even more by strategic and economic advantages than by solicitude for the German-speaking population. Certain areas inhabited by a majority of Germans have been left to the Czechs. They are poverty-stricken areas. On the other hand, Germany has occupied isolated districts where there is a large Czech majority. In one district where there is a 90% Czech majority, there are three coal mines and the fittings for a fourth one are already installed." The same newspaper added the next day that "in fixing their frontiers the Germans have been careful and clever enough to mobilize the great Czech war industries. Skoda and Explosiva, in which British capital is, or was until recently, interested, are now under the shadow of German guns. What they manufacture in future will be for Germany or with Germany's sanction."

The assets which Mr. Chamberlain turned over to Hitler included 51% of the Czech coal mines, all the important brown coal areas, 39% of the metal industry, 55% of the glass industry, 49% of the textile industry, 35% of the chemical industry, one third of the industrial population of Czechoslovakia and fourteen of the twenty-seven largest towns. Germany received intact the Schoeher line fortifications, built at a cost of fifty million pounds; the Aussig Chemical works, which were the largest on the Continent outside Germany; and virtual control of the Skoda arms works, also the largest on the Continent outside Germany.

Many of Chamberlain's left-wing critics drew the conclusion that Great Britain was arming Germany faster than she was arming herself.

THE PETITION CAMPAIGN

During all this crucial period, when "the lights were going out all over Europe," what was the British Labour party, His Majesty's Opposition, doing to meet the crisis?

Every surrender to Hitler was of course denounced—after it became obvious that there *had* been a surrender. But every manifestation of pseudo-anti-Fascism on the part of the National Government was greeted with unconcealed joy by the Labour party. No hint that the Government's word might not be trusted was uttered till after the betrayal was a fatal reality. Mr. Attlee, for instance, on September 1st, felt that a speech by Sir John Swan at Lanark "must be taken as a warning that there is a limit to the tolerance which has been given hitherto to Fascist aggression." Sir Archibald Sinclair, leader of the Liberals, speaking of that same speech, was critical enough to remark: "I wish it had been much earlier and in plainer language." Sir Walter Citrine's comments are particularly illuminating in view of traditional Labour party tactics. He said: "The visit of the

Prime Minister to Herr Hitler is, I think, a good move. It shows that Mr. Chamberlain is making a determined effort to avoid any possible misunderstanding. *There is no better way of handling such a situation than by personal contact.*" This is reminiscent of Ramsay MacDonald, who "personally contacted" the Labour party into capitulation and catastrophe. The trade-unions had their say through Mr. Ben Tillett, who spoke thus: "This is the noblest act of statesmanlike chivalry known in the last hundred years. Whatever the results of the interview Mr. Chamberlain's conduct will stand out as an example to the world." One wonders if Mr. Tillett still holds the same opinion! It was easy to speak about "preserving peace without sacrificing principles," as Mr. Attlee did in commending Chamberlain's trip to Munich. But these are mere words; in effect the Labour party offered no concrete policy but still clung trustingly to Mr. Chamberlain's coattails.

On the other hand, as far back as July 23, 1938, Sir Stafford Cripps was saying: "A striking and significant gesture should be made by the Labour movement. . . . In my view a conference should be held, with as little delay as possible, a conference of the entire movement, political, industrial, and co-operative, representing many millions of workers and their families, at which this direct challenge should be made. . . .

"There must be no talk of common interests with capitalism or of common dangers, but rather a determination at all cost to use their power to make an end of this Government that has betrayed their interests, alike at home and abroad. In that spirit and with that determination we can in this country give a new lead to the working class throughout the world."

Sympathizers of the Labour party line will undoubtedly point to the Blackpool resolution of the National Council of Labour adopted on September 7th, as evidence that the Labour party did not simply follow along with the National Government. But where in that document is a clear lead given to the British working class? It simply asks the British Government to "leave no doubt in the mind of the German Government that it will unite with the French and Soviet Governments to resist any attack upon Czechoslovakia. The Labour movement urges the British Government to give this lead. . . ." Also, the resolution continued, "The British Labour Movement . . . demands the immediate summoning of Parliament." But what practical political action were the Labour party and the trade-unions prepared to take to bring pressure upon the National Government? Of what avail to summon a Parliament which was overwhelmingly in the power of the National Government, especially when you have no real alternative policy of your own?

Some such action as Cripps proposed, to mobilize working class and anti-Fascist opinion, was the obvious tactic; but the paralyzed hierarchy of the British Labour party were too far gone for such a decisive step. Their action here was analogous to that on Spanish nonintervention when all they could seem to do was to plead with the National Government *really* to enforce the policy. The absence of any clear-cut alternative action on the Munich crisis was to have the same disastrous effect as it had had on Spain.

After Munich a gloomy mood of defeatism swept over the Labour movement of Great Britain. As H. N. Brailsford put it: "A feeling of helpless depression has settled on most of us because we know that failing a miracle, without the capture of some rural seats, Labour unaided cannot win a general election. We see on the Front Bench no magicians capable of miracles." Liberal opinion was equally emphatic in condemning the inadequacy of the Labour party leadership. The *Manchester Guardian* wrote: "Most of us who are not so mesmerized by phrases can only watch and deplore the Labour Party's suicide. Too tired to take the leadership of the British progressive forces, too narrow and machine-ridden to attract and keep new blood, it will meet its fate at the next election." Another Liberal journal commented briefly that "only at Transport House does anyone believe that Labour, unaided, can unseat the Government at the next election." It was this which finally impelled Sir Stafford Cripps to launch his Petition Campaign.

The situation was so grave, he believed, that some affirmative action was needed instantly to galvanize the Labour party. His first step was the preparation of a memorandum to the secretary of the Labour party, Mr. J. S. Middleton, which was submitted on January 9, 1939. Along with the memorandum went a personal letter from Sir Stafford. Since both documents are of the utmost importance, it is necessary to quote them both in full.

LETTER FROM SIR STAFFORD CRIPPS TO MR. MIDDLETON

#3 Elm Court
Temple, E. C. 4   January 9, 1939

To the Secretary of the Labour Party

My dear Middleton:

I wish to lay before the National Executive of the Party the enclosed memorandum as a matter for its most urgent consideration. The urgency arises out of the political news of the past few days and in particular the acute danger of the capture of the Youth movement of the country by the anti-labour elements, together with announced participation of Mr. Herbert Morrison with Sir John Anderson and Mr. Ernest Brown in the launching of the National Register campaign at the Albert Hall.

You will be aware that a very close association has grown up between a number of progressive Youth Organizations over the last year or so and that at the present time many joint activities are planned such as the Youth Pilgrimage, Youth Parliaments, etc. etc.

These activities have brought together, amongst others, members of the Labour Party League of Youth, of the League of Nations Union, of Youth Groups, of the Young Liberty Association, of the University Labour Federation, and of the Young Communist League. These various Youth movements have been active all over the country in co-operation upon such matters as the Spanish and Chinese struggles and various other anti-Fascist activities. This Youth Movement as a whole, apart from the particular sections, is moreover anxiously seeking some sort of political leadership of an anti-Government complexion.

Winston Churchill has made an attempt through Sandys and the 100,000 movement to capture the Youth for reactionary imperialism and was much closer to success than many people may imagine.

That movement is certainly checked and is, I hope, defeated. But the danger remains that some other such political group will make an attempt to take command of this very considerable force of youth opinion to fashion it into the nucleus for a rapidly expanding center party or democratic front.

If this were to happen, and there are already steps on foot from another quarter which may possibly succeed, it would be a first-class political tragedy for the Labour Party and for the country, for it would make even more difficult the defeat of Chamberlain by the forces under Labour leadership. This danger can only be averted if the Labour Party is prepared at once to take up the role of leadership for this combined Youth Movement.

The attempt to segregate and maintain the Labour Party League of Youth isolated from the other Youth movements will, I am certain, result only in the destruction of that body and the divorce of all effective Youth organizations from the Labour Party.

This would have two effects. First it would weaken the Party and its whole appeal to the younger electorate and secondly it would allow a strong and very effective nucleus to be formed at the basis of an assumed opposition movement which might at any moment be diverted into what are substantially Fascist paths.

I regard it as a matter of the utmost urgency—in terms of days and not weeks—that this matter should be dealt with at once by the

Party Executive. I regard it, however, as only one, though momentarily the most important, example of the growing urgency of the situation as regards the whole of a combined opposition to the National Government. This need is in my view emphasized very strongly by the conclusions that will be drawn by the uninstructed public from the appearance of one of the chief Labour Leaders on a platform at the Albert Hall with two of the most reactionary ministers in Parliament. I therefore desire to submit the enclosed memorandum to the National Executive as a basis for the immediate future activity of the Party.

I fully realize that this matter has been dealt with by the Executive upon a number of previous occasions since the joint memorandum was submitted to them in May last by myself, Ellen Wilkinson, Laski and Pritt. The matter has, however, in my view, become so increasingly pressing that I desire to submit this memorandum for their consideration before it is too late to take action prior to the next General Election so that I may feel that I have done my utmost to secure the adoption of what I most sincerely believe to be the only policy which can save the Labour Movement and the people of this country from disaster.

I would ask you to call at once a special meeting of such Executive members as are available in London to consider this memorandum, and to circulate copies of this letter and of the memorandum to them in advance.

In view of the difficulty of summoning the whole Executive for a special meeting, I shall be prepared to accept the decision of those members of the Executive who can attend in London as being the decision of the National Executive itself.

In order that there may be no misunderstanding I desire to put on record that in the event of such a meeting not seeing their way to accept the principles of this memorandum or to take any definite action in the direction indicated, I shall claim the right to circulate it with the exception of those parts which might embarrass the Party, with the object of gaining support within the movement for the views herein expressed.

I asked for an immediate meeting as I understand there may be important developments next week as to the Youth movement if nothing is done or no indication can be given that action is likely to be taken by the Labour Party.

Yours sincerely,
R. Stafford Cripps

MEMORANDUM SUBMITTED TO MR. MIDDLETON WITH THE ABOVE LETTER AND DATED 9TH JANUARY, 1939

During the last 12 months the political situation nationally and internationally has progressively deteriorated.

The menace of the Fascist powers has grown to alarming proportions under the encouraging hand of the British National Government, while at the same time that Government has shown itself completely incompetent to deal with domestic matters. Unemployment remains as bad as ever, working class standards and conditions are tending to decline and agriculture is in a state of chaos.

Democracy has been betrayed and Fascist aggression has been encouraged in Spain, Austria, Czechoslovakia, China and elsewhere to such an extent that even the most vital interests of our own country are now jeopardized.

For these and other reasons a great volume of anti-government feeling has grown up all over the country, even in the least expected quarters, and British Youth is being stirred by these events to a demand for some form of United action against the National Government based upon a real policy of peace.

This state of indeterminate opposition is liable to be swung over to the support of the Government by some international event, by a change in Chamberlain's foreign policy or by an appeal to National Unity if the crisis deepens. It is not at all unlikely that within the next few days or weeks Chamberlain will announce a reversal of his foreign policy upon the basis that he has tried appeasement and it has failed and that he must call on the nation to unite behind him to fight Fascism in what will be a purely imperialistic war. When that moment comes, if public opinion is allowed to remain in its uncrystallized state it will swing behind him, with results as disastrous as those of 1914-18 for the common people of this country and Europe.

There is today in this country the same quality of vague and undirected discontent which has formed the breeding ground for Fascist movements in other countries, and it has in it, for that very reason, real elements of danger so long as it remains without any definite direction or leadership. This is particularly true so far as the younger electors are concerned.

From my experience during the last 12 months in the country, and I believe this must be generally admitted, the strength of the Labour Party has not increased in anything like the same proportion as the intensity of anti-Government feeling.

There has too come into being a very large body of agitation for some form of combined opposition. This agitation, is, I am convinced, the true reflection of the experience of persons of all kinds and classes gained in carrying through combined work upon Spain, China and similar campaigns. Through such work many have become politically conscious for the first time and they realize the possibility of gaining their objective—the defeat of the National Government—by the translation of their co-operative endeavors for humanitarian ends into the field of politics.

The League of Youth, contrary to its own desires, has been rigidly confined by the National Executive in its contacts with other Youth Organizations and has, as a consequence I believe, failed to show any remarkable expansion in spite of all the efforts that have been made by the Party.

The rigidity of Party discipline at a time when many most loyal members are convinced that joint work with other organizations would lead to an increase of power, has led to the weakening of the opposition forces and to discouragement in many areas. The refusal to permit members of the party to co-operate in anti-Government and anti-Fascist work of any kind with other persons or groups active in the same direction, when accompanied by the spectacle of the Leaders of the Movement sharing the Albert Hall Platform with such typical reactionary members of the Government as Sir John Anderson and Mr. Ernest Brown, is not understood by the public generally and leads to the almost inevitable assumption that the Labour Party would rather combine with the National Government than with other opposition forces.

I have examined and re-examined this situation from one point of view and one only. How can we best help to protect the common people of Great Britain from the dangers of Fascism and war that arise out of the present critical circumstances? I regard this question as being identical with—How can we obtain the best chance of defeating the National Government in the next election?

I ask my fellow members of the Executive to consider it objectively from this point of view and to ask themselves, as I ask myself, this further question. Is it not right under such circumstances to put this overriding necessity of defeating the National Government before all other considerations, so as to determine whether there is not something more effective that can be done?

The growth of strength of the Labour Party either in opposition or in organization is not such as to warrant the belief that the Party can defeat the National Government single-handed at a General Election within the next 18 months. During that period of time an election is bound to take place, unless we are already engaged in an imperialist war under the aegis of the National Government before that time has expired.

It is to this last question, as to whether anything effective can be done, that I now address myself.

As I view the situation the following propositions can be accepted as the basis for a calculation of the electoral chances at the next General Election.

1. At the very best the Labour Party and the opposition Liberals fighting independently cannot, under any circumstances likely to exist within the next 18 months, win more than 266 seats, that is all those seats held at present and in addition all those in which there was a Government majority of 3,000 or less at the last General Election. Of these some 38 would be held by opposition elements other than Labour, giving a net figure of 228 for Labour.

2. There are at present 62 seats held by the National Government on a minority (31) or a majority vote of less than 3,000 (31) owing to opposition by two or more parties, of which at least 39 (majorities less than 1000) ought to be winnable if the opposition is combined behind a single candidate.

3. In the remaining 330 seats (omitting Northern Ireland) which

do not fall within category (1) above, apart from some 20 which fall within category (2) above there is little, if any, chance of the defeat of the National Government by a single Opposition Party. A number which may be variously computed, but which I compute in good circumstances as being 25-50 could be, I believe, won by a combined opposition. Such a number if successfully fought would give, with those seats of categories (1) and (2), the following result—Labour, 228 plus (say) half of category (2), 20: 248; other opposition parties, Liberal, I. L. P., Communist, 38 plus half of category (2), 20: 58; category (3), 25 making a total of 331, which would provide a working majority.

4. If the Labour Party and other opposition parties can win only these seats in category (1) and so are in a minority after the next General Election then it means another 5 years of National Government whether in its present or in an equally bad reconstructed form, which event, will in my view, be fatal to democracy and to any prospects for a socialist party for another generation.

If these premises are even approximately correct then they show that the only alternative to the disastrous continuance in power of the National Government—which I assume that nobody desires—is the use temporarily of some tactic which will enable the essential extra electoral strength to be mobilized.

In most of the constituencies of category (3) the organization of the party has never been and is not now strong enough to inspire any hope of a victory at the next election. It is in such constituencies particularly that Labour Party members are turning with a real degree of hope to the prospect of an effective and even winning fight in combination with all other anti-government and democratic forces.

If the above are the only two alternatives then failure to take every step to maximize opposition becomes tantamount to acquiescence in giving the National Government the opportunity of another term of office.

I certainly should not desire to encourage the Party to any combination with other non-socialist elements in normal political times. I have in the past always strenuously opposed such an idea. But the present times are not normal, indeed they are absolutely unprecedented in their seriousness for democratic and working-class institutions of every kind. In such times it is impossible to overlook the fact that a too rigid adherence to Party discipline and to traditional Party tactics may amount to losing the substance of working-class freedom and democracy for the shadow of maintaining a particular type of organization which is, as a mere machine, in itself of no value.

I fully appreciate that the whole case for a chance of tactics is based upon the belief that without that change the Labour Party cannot defeat the National Government at the next Election. I state these views, not because I am defeatist but because I believe that victory will only be based upon a frank appreciation of the true position as it exists. I am confident that the record of the meetings that I have addressed in the past year for the Party will satisfy my colleagues that I have done what little I could to help to strengthen the party in all parts of the country.

In considering what tactics can or should be followed, the following points must be borne in mind:

1. Everything possible must be done to increase the strength of the Party itself in all areas. For whatever tactic is to be employed a strong Labour Party is a vital ingredient.

2. There must be no permanent sacrifice of socialist principles even if a temporary postponement of some items of the Party's program becomes necessary. At the same time it must be realized that with the present urgent threat to democracy and freedom in our country a progressive democratic block dominated by a numerically strong Labour nucleus would be vastly preferable to the continuance of the National Government in any form.

3. The Government that emerges in the event of the opposition succeeding must have a practical program on both foreign and domestic policy including all those measures considered essential by those who are sponsoring it as the minimum necessary for the practical carrying out of a complete progressive policy.

4. The areas of co-operation sought, if any, must be wide enough to contribute effective increase in opposition power but not so wide as to bring it elements so discordant that combined working with them is impossible.

5. The program must be simple, easily understood by the elec-

torate, and must be possible of attainment in a single Parliament.

6. The combined opposition, if any, must be presented to the country in such a form as to provide an effective counterblast to the "National" camouflage which will be used by the Government and also to convince people of all kinds that it is representative of the different interests and classes whom it is desired to attract within the Opposition.

7. One of the greatest assets of such a combination in my view will be its appeal to the unpolitically-minded electorate from the fact that political leaders have shown themselves prepared to drop their particular party aims in view of their urgent determination to meet and deal with the very apparent National dangers.

In this regard it must be borne in mind that the appeal to be successful must not only attract all of the nearly 8 million voters who supported Labour at the last election but at least another 4-5 million voters who have either not voted before or who have given their votes to other parties, the majority of whom, like many of the Labour Party supporters, are not politically instructed.

I believe that the above 7 points include the more important of those considerations which arise from a study of the reactions of public opinion to current political issues. I am, of course, only able to judge of this, as we all are, from the particular contacts that I have in the country and from the study that I have made of the Press, etc. It is always a matter of extreme difficulty to assess the reaction of public opinion, as has been shown by the recent Mass Observation results. I am certain, however, that we are all apt to overestimate the degree of political consciousness and intelligence in the electorate and to underestimate the value of such simple conceptions or slogans as "National," "non-Party," etc., especially in critical times. It is for this reason that I attach very great importance to point (6) above.

As indicated I am convinced that we must consider and decide upon some new tactic of opposition if we are to succeed in defeating the Government. I am, moreover, certain that the course that I am about to suggest would lead to a great strengthening of the Party both numerically and in spirit. If the Labour Party were to come out boldly as the leader of a combined opposition to the National Government, such a step would, I am sure, enormously increase its prestige and popularity in the country, and would bring within the ranks many who are not at present ready to join up because they are not convinced of its power or capacity to defeat the National Government.

It is in the light of these considerations that I suggest the immediate adoption of the following course to be announced by the National Executive and to be considered and approved by a special Conference of the Party called for that purpose alone. In my view Whitsuntide will be much too late for the initiation of such a program. Only the summer months will intervene between that date and a possible general election in the autumn, during which time it is notoriously difficult to carry out a political campaign. Added to this political developments are likely to be such during this and succeeding months as to result in the loss of the present opportunity which exists for consolidating the opposition behind the Labour Party before the Whitsun Conference is held. Once such an opportunity is missed it is unlikely to recur in time to be made use of for the next election. The course that I suggest is as follows:

I. An immediate and special appeal to the Youth movement as a whole upon the basis of combined Youth activities and a special Youth program incorporating the main items which are already to be found in the programs of the various Youth movements and which accord with the Labour Party's own program. The principal of these would be as follows:

1. The T. U. C. Youth Charter.

2. Heads (1) and (2) of the program set out under Head II below.

II. The issue by the Party of a manifesto inviting the co-operation of every genuine anti-Government party, or group of individuals who would be prepared to give support to the following items of policy:

1. The effective protection of the democratic rights, liberties, and freedom of the British people from internal and external attack.

2. A positive policy of peace by collective action with France, Russia, the United States of America and other democratic countries for the strengthening of democracy against aggression and a world economic reconstruction based upon justice to the people of all classes and nations.

3. Co-operation with the Trade-Unions for advances in wages, bet-

tering of working conditions, shortening of hours, raising of work-men's compensation and increase of holidays with pay.

4. Higher standards of nutrition especially for children and mothers.

5. Improvements in the conditions and standards of the unem-ployed, including the removal of the family Means Test.

6. Improved pensions for old-age pensioners and those older work-ers who should be encouraged to retire from industry.

7. Increased educational facilities freely open to all children irre-spective of the parents' income, including an effective raising of the school-leaving age with grants to parents where necessary, and the expansion of nursery schools, secondary and university education.

8. An immediate and serious tackling of the problem of unemploy-ment particularly in such districts as the distressed areas and Lanca-shire by the national planning of industrial development, and of the investment of new capital in industry by rapidly increased public works to improve housing, education and other essential social services.

9. The full utilization of the productive resources of the land by giving planned assistance to agricultural development on the basis of a fair wage to the agricultural worker, a just return to the farmer and an equitable price to the consumer.

10. The national control and co-ordination of all transport services with fair wages for those working in the various industries.

11. National and controlled planning of the mining and allied industries so as to enable fair wages to be paid to the workers and fair terms to be given to the consumers.

12. Control over the financial resources of the Nation through con-trol of the Bank of England and the increase of direct taxation if necessary to enable the above program to be carried through.

The above program could, I believe, be carried through by a pro-gressive Government with a wide popular support led by the Labour Party. It is very doubtful whether a purely Labour Government, even if it had a narrow majority in the House of Commons, could accomplish so much in a single term of office.

III. The statement by the Party that they would be prepared to assist in arranging for and to support combined opposition candidates in such of those constituencies, not at present held by any opposition member, as could offer no reasonable chance of success in a straight fight between any single party opposition candidate and the National Government, provided that such candidate, would agree to support the main items of the above program set out in paragraph (II).

IV. To enter into negotiation with any opposition party or group that accepted the above basis for a combined opposition with a view to making such constituency arrangements as were possible.

V. To concert a nation-wide campaign on this basis to appeal for support and funds for the carrying into operation of this program in conjunction with all other parties, groups or persons who had signified their willingness to participate upon the basis stated.

It would be necessary in such an announcement to state clearly and categorically that:

(a) Neither the Labour Party nor any party group or person joining on the above basis would be expected to relinquish any part of their beliefs or program except for the specific and limited purpose of the present emergency and for the creation of a temporary combination to fight the National Government.

(b) That the Labour Party only took this action because it was convinced that the emergency was such as to warrant and demand the temporary dropping of particular party interests in the cause of national and international salvation.

(c) That the Labour Party remained convinced that the only ultimate solution of the National and International difficulties were along the lines of its fullest socialist program.

I am personally convinced, after giving the matter the most full and prolonged consideration upon all the material available to me, that nothing short of a program along these lines can enable the Party to organize the defeat of the National Government at the next election, and that to continue upon the present line of nonco-operation with any other opposition elements, while co-operating with the Government in such matters as the National Fitness Campaign and the National Register, is to make certain that the National Government will retain power for a further term of years with results that will in my view be disastrous to the freedom and democracy of the British people.

I emphasize that it is only my view of the extreme urgency and the desperately critical nature of the present situation that compels me to submit this memorandum and to ask my colleagues to give it their most sincere consideration, in the earnest hope that the National Executive will in this time of grave crisis for the common people give such a lead as will instil into the people a new hope of peace and salvation and a determination under the leadership of the Labour Party to drive the National Government from office.

R. Stafford Cripps

The meeting of the National Executive for which Cripps asked was duly convened on January 13, 1939. The Cripps memorandum was considered and defeated by a vote of 17 to 3— Sir Stafford, Ellen Wilkinson, and D. N. Pritt voting in favor of accepting the memorandum.

Immediately after the meeting Sir Stafford Cripps sent copies of his document to many prominent members of the Labour party throughout the country, and to every Labour member of Parliament; and included with the document was a reply postcard. Now this action is the crux of the whole controversy on the Petition Campaign. For—rightly or wrongly—the reason given for Cripps's subsequent expulsion from the Party was not his advocacy of a United Front but his breach of Party discipline. The official reason for Sir Stafford's expulsion, which took place on January 25, was this:

"The past campaigns waged over a long period at Sir Stafford's instigation and which were calculated to weaken the unity of the Party and to give aid and comfort to its opponents;

"The wide departure from the Party's Program, Principles and Policy which were the ostensible object of those campaigns; and

"The present organized effort to change Party direction and leadership fundamentally, the National Executive Committee requests Sir Stafford;

CRIPPS IS EXPELLED FROM THE LABOUR. PARTY FOR BEING A SOCIALIST.

OLD LOW'S ALMANACK

PROPHECIES FOR 1937

Copyright Low all countries, from Wide World

A cartoon by David Low which appeared in December, 1936.

"To reaffirm his allegiance to the Labour Party within the meaning of the Constitution, Program, Principles and Policy of the Party; and

"To withdraw his Memorandum by circular to the persons and organizations to whom it was addressed.

"Failing compliance with these requests Sir Stafford Cripps be informed that he no longer fulfills the conditions of membership of the Labour Party, and that in consequence he be excluded."

Leaving aside, for the moment, the question of the Popular Front, let us consider these charges closely. In the first place it is quite obvious that Cripps was advocating a new policy which he was anxious to present to the rank and file of the Labour party for their consideration. Cripps belonged to the Labour party, in which there was, presumably, liberty of discussion, and therefore he was free to present his views to the rank and file. However, he was only entitled to membership if he swore allegiance to the "principles and policy" of the Labour party—which included a principled opposition to any Popular Front proposals. But if, after swearing allegiance, Cripps proceeded to advocate a Popular Front, then obviously he was breaking his oath and was open to expulsion. Further, strenuous objection was made to his circulation of the memorandum; and his continuance in the party was subject to its withdrawal. If he remained in the party he would be free to discuss his program with the rank and file. But how was it possible to discuss if he was forbidden to circulate his views? In other words the position of the Labour party, even on a relatively superficial analysis, was absurdly illogical. In the words of a keen observer of British politics, "This liberty of discussion seems singularly like the liberty of the unemployed to reside at the Ritz Hotel."

Cripps went into this question in some detail in his speech to the Southport (1939) Conference of the Labour party. Over a year earlier, in May, 1938, he said, "Four members of the Executive had submitted a somewhat similar memorandum to the Executive, and, after it had been turned down the only document circulated to the membership of the Party was a one-sided argument stating why the Executive had turned it down. It was obviously hopeless to get any reasoned consideration of the proposal before this conference if only one side—or no side at all—of the question was to be put before the rank and file." One experience, then, with the sham democracy of the Labour party had been enough. The outright contradictions involved in the official party statement are alone enough to indicate that the party bureaucracy were concerned not so much with democracy, or with a Popular Front, as with the fear of putting themselves at the head of a determined working class anxious to seize power. There seems to be no other way of explaining many of their actions; and there is some support for this view. Mr. Cecil Poole, a well-informed M. P., wrote as far back as March, 1939: "I wish . . . that I were perfectly sure, beyond a shadow of a doubt, that all our leaders really did desire to provide an alternative government. Some I know . . . feel that with such an uncertain foreign situation, so desperate an industrial problem at home, and along with both a colossal financial burden to be handled, it is preferable to leave the National Government to extricate itself from the muddle it has created."

What were the objections of the Executive, first, to the points made in the memorandum, and then to the Petition Campaign? Their answer to Sir Stafford was contained in a pamphlet called *Unity—True or Sham,* which was issued on February 2nd. Briefly, their arguments are as follows:

"Some people seem vaguely to suppose that the mere forma-tion of such a Popular Front would at once make Mr. Chamber-lain's position untenable and that he would be compelled to resign, either before a general election or immediately after. Some seem also to imagine that a general election would be precipitated by the establishment of a Popular Front. . . .

"It is proposed by those who are conducting this propaganda that the Labour Party should adopt what amounts to a purely Liberty policy and merge its independence in an ill-defined coalition of parties and groups, having little in common except their opposition to the Government's foreign policy.

"Even if the Labour Party joined with Liberals, Communists, and others in a Popular Front, such a combination would not lead to the defeat of the Government in the House of Commons. This could only happen if a large number of Conservative M. P.'s were to rebel against the Prime Minister and join the Popular Front. There are no signs of any such large-scale rebellion.

"The suggested Popular Front would not be more effective, electorally, against the National Government than the Labour Party itself.

"It is very doubtful whether the Parliamentary Liberal Opposition would join the Popular Front as a body. There is no reason to believe that, even if they did, the Liberal electors could be trusted to follow the advice of their leaders and vote for Labour candidates. It is well known that in many constituencies the absence of a Liberal candidate assists the Conservative rather than the Labour candidate.

"The Communists would, no doubt, be willing to enter such a combination. But their entry would drive away many Liberals and other possible supports and their presence would be electoral liability rather than an asset. . . .

"Their presence would bring some few thousand votes to a Popular Front alliance, but it might well drive millions into Mr. Chamberlain's camp.

"The formation of such an alliance—even if it were practicable —would create more controversy in our own ranks than it would remove. It would take the heart out of many of our most loyal members and would be bitterly resented by many who value the traditional independence of our Party.

"Even if we imagine, for the sake of argument, that a Popular Front combination won the next general election and formed a Coalition Government, such a Government would be inherently weak and unstable, divided in its outlook on both home and foreign affairs, and likely, if it failed to show the necessary unity, courage and decision, finally to discredit democratic institutions in Britain.

"The collapse of the Popular Front Government in France is an object lesson which we should not forget. Both Radicals and Communists soon broke away from their Socialist partners.

"We are asked by Sir Stafford Cripps to accept a Liberal program, but without even the assurance that the Liberal Party would accept it. No Government of the Left, confined within the limits of these most inadequate proposals, could hope to deal either confidently or successfully with the urgent problems of economic and financial reconstruction with which it would soon be confronted. Sir Stafford Cripps invites the Labour Party, in view of the international crisis, to become a Liberal Party. The Labour Party declines his invitation.

"No member of the Labour Party, least of all a member of the National Executive, can be permitted to conduct an organized and privately financed campaign in support of a program of his own manufacture from which all Socialist proposals have been eliminated and in favor of the abandonment by the Labour Party of its political independence."

The first two points made are purely rhetorical, and the second is an obvious misstatement of fact. Sir Stafford's proposals cover a wide range of purely internal, as well as external policies; a glance at his memorandum will prove the point. The third point makes a definite charge that there was no sign that any conservative M. P.'s would join in the revolt against the Chamberlain Government. This was said in spite of Eden's resignation, and the resignation of Duff Cooper, First Lord of the Admiralty, immediately after the Munich Pact. Mr. Duff Cooper's words at that time are worth quoting, since they indicate some of the feeling in imperialist circles over Chamberlain's action. "The Prime Minister," he said, "has confidence in the good will and in the word of Herr Hitler. . . . But I cannot believe what he believes. . . . I have ruined, perhaps, my political career. But that is a little matter; I have retained something which is to me of great value—I can still walk about the world with my head erect." This was unquestionably the attitude of an increasingly large number of people after the Munich fiasco; and an appeal calculated to win these confused and hesitant adherents of the National Government to the side of Labour was well worth making.

As for the response of the Liberals, a few statements from their leaders will show that the move for a Popular Front won wide Liberal backing, and, if accepted, would have received firm co-operation. Sir Archibald Sinclair, the leader of the Opposition Liberals said on January 25: "The Labour Party has now the task of choosing between partisan considerations and the states-manlike lead which Sir Stafford Cripps has given." The next month, in the *Manchester Guardian,* he pointed out a significant coincidence: "When the Fascist troops were battering their way into Barcelona the Labour Party Executive celebrated the occasion by expelling from the Labour Party the most outspoken champion in this country of Spanish democracy, Sir Stafford Cripps." Numerous other communications to the same effect were printed all over the country, both before and after the start of the Petition Campaign.

The Petition Campaign was, essentially, an effort to mobilize this public opinion beyond a petition.

"The Petition of the British People to the Labour, Liberal, and Co-operative Parties" reads as follows:

"We British citizens, looking out on a world threatened as never before by war and Fascism, call upon the parties of progress to act together and at once for the sake of peace and civilization. We ask for a Government that will:

"1. DEFEND DEMOCRACY—protect our democratic rights and liberties against attack at home and from abroad;

"2. PLAN FOR PLENTY—multiply the wealth of the nation by employing the unemployed on useful work; increase old age pensions; ensure a higher standard of life, education, and leisure for old and young;

"3. SECURE OUR BRITAIN—organize a peace alliance with France and Russia that will rally the support of the United States and every other peace-loving nation and end the shameful policy which makes us accomplices in the betrayal of the Spanish and Chinese people to Fascist aggression;

"4. PROTECT THE PEOPLE'S INTEREST—control armaments and the vital industries, agriculture, transport, mining and finance;

"5. DEFEND THE PEOPLE—provide effective protection for the common people against air attack and starvation in the event of war;

"6. BUILD FOR PEACE AND JUSTICE—end the exploitation of subject races and lay the foundations of a lasting peace through equality of opportunity for all nations.

"In the face of the perils that confront us we urge you to combine in every effort to drive the National Government from office and win for us the six points of our petition. To a Government of your united forces we pledge our wholehearted support."

The object of this petition, as Sir Stafford said in the speech which launched the campaign, was "for the political purpose of defeating the present Government." This it would do by convincing the leaders of the Labour party that a sufficient body of anti-Government opinion was united behind the policy of a Popular Front to make it a practical political alternative. "If by next Whitsuntide," Sir Stafford said, ". . . we can mobilize the country against Chamberlain in this way using every progressive force at our disposal for the work, we shall produce evidence that cannot fail to convince the most doubting of the desire of the rank and file of our movement and of the workers.

... It will be clear that there is no intention and no possibility of the formation of any rival party or group or anything else of that noxious kind coming out of this petition."

The Executive's reaction to this appeal was immediate. On March 4th they sent a letter to seven prominent members of the Labour party—George Strauss, M. P., Aneurin Bevan, M. P., C. C. Poole, M. P., Sir Charles Trevelyan, Will Lawther, M. P., Robert Bruce, and Lt. Commander Edgar P. Young—warning them that their participation in the Petition Campaign was contrary to the party rules and constitution. The letter was accompanied by a general declaration of party principles, and a request for adherence to its affirmed policy. The position of Sir Stafford and his colleagues was fairly stated by Aneurin Bevan: ". . . conference of the Party, to be held at Whitsun, will decide between the Executive and the advocates of the Popular Front. In the meantime the Executive has insisted that only its side of the case shall be heard, for if we state our side we shall be expelled from the party, and thus prevented from appearing at the conference. On the other hand, if we bow to the Executive's decision and remain silent, when we do appear at the conference the result may be a foregone conclusion."

Warning was sent to all organizations affiliated with the Labour party, pointing out that "having now dealt with the leader of the 'Popular Front' Campaign, it cannot avoid taking similar action against others who associate with that campaign, and who thereby violate the condition of party membership." In spite of this, by March 10, 1939, 544 Labour organizations had lined up behind Sir Stafford. Seventy-nine divisional Labour parties had accepted the Cripps Memorandum and twenty-seven had expressed their disapproval of his expulsion. One hundred trade-union branches and about sixty Labour youth organizations were included in the body of support for Cripps. It was also admitted that since the start of the Petition Campaign between three and four thousand new members had joined the Labour party.

The Executive could do no more than vilify. They pointed out that Cripps was a rich man and that only a rich man could have launched the Petition Campaign. That a rich man might have used his money to awaken the Labour movement at a critical moment never occurred to them; and, as Cripps pointed out at Southport, the prejudice against rich men "is singularly absent on other occasions." There was actually no discussion of the Popular Front on its own merits. All that the Executive did was to say that the idea was an abandonment of the Socialist Ideal. To this Sir Stafford made cogent answer. "I have had," said he, "a good deal of experience personally in the past in attempting to get a real Socialist policy adopted in the program of the Labour Party, and I have found that many of those who are now loudest in their advocacy of a policy of pure Socialism are the very ones who were most outspoken in their opposition to my proposals on the ground that they would needlessly alarm the electorate. It is true that I have changed my views as regards the political tactics of the moment which should be adopted by the party in the light of the terribly urgent needs of our present time. Others may have done the same, but I believe that to insist today on the pure doctrine of Socialism, all Socialism and nothing but Socialism is a great disaster."

The primary issue was that of democracy within the Labour party. This was the stand which Cripps took at the Southport Conference, which voted upon his expulsion.

"I assert the right of myself as a member of the Party, and of any other member of the Party, to do all in his or her power— including circularizing a Memorandum if need be—to convert the rank and file of the Party to his or her point of view, and so to change the policy or tactics of the Party through a decision of this conference.

"If they are to be expelled and suppressed then the Party will become static and lifeless. A rigid orthodoxy may be right as the condition of membership of a totalitarian organization, which destroys all individual initiative and contributions to policy making, and which denies the right of the rank and file, or of any minority, to have a voice in party control, or even to express its sentiments of disapproval of the decisions of some ruling clique or dictator.

"No democracy, however, can continue to exist, if freedom of discussion, however inconvenient or ill timed, is forcibly suppressed by expulsion and by threats of disciplinary action."

In spite of the magnificent effect of the Petition Campaign in rallying working class and anti-Fascist opposition to the Chamberlain government, Cripps's expulsion was upheld by a conference whose prevailing temper was well described by a delegate, Mr. R. H. S. Crossman, a lecturer at Oxford University. "If the Executive said 2 x 2 = 7," Mr. Crossman writes, "the floor would condemn as an intellectual any one who suggested it equalled four."

IX

WAR IS DECLARED

The moment that the Executive of the British Labour party expelled the man who might have given them a constructive lead in the critical prewar situation, their eventual capitulation to National Government policy could be predicted. Thus, during Chamberlain's blundering leadership in the early months of the war, did they become merely another cog in the British war machine.

After his expulsion, Sir Stafford was still loyal to the Labour party, in spite of the fact that during the Petition Campaign he was often accused of wanting to start a rival party. He, and all the others who had been expelled, applied for readmission, recognizing that "the Labour Party has decisively and overwhelmingly set its face against any proposal for forming a Popular Front against the Chamberlain Government." The reason for this somewhat humiliating decision is worth quoting, for it well expresses the caliber of the man.

"There are some people," he wrote, "who have suggested that we acted with undue haste in applying for readmission so quickly after the conference decision. The issues are too grave and the time too full of peril for Socialism, or Socialists to indulge themselves in false pride." This was not abject capitulation. The leaders of the Labour party had denied that they opposed freedom of expression. If this were so, then in Cripps's view any differences were incidental. What he had objected to was the effort of the Executive to prevent him from circulating his views to the rank and file. That was what the Labour party *had* attempted to do. But since the rank and file had rejected the Popular Front, and since the Executive stated most emphatically that they did not intend to suppress liberty of speech, there was no reason why the expelled members should not have been readmitted to the Labour party. In their letter of May 30, 1939, asking for readmission, the expelled members (Cripps, Bevan, Bruce, Strauss, and Young), made this point clear: "We understand from Dr. Dalton's statement to the conference yesterday that full freedom of opinion and of expression of that opinion is afforded to all members of the Party. If our application is granted we shall exercise that freedom to impress upon the Party the necessity of making effective the opposition to the National Government and to oppose every tendency to co-operate with that Government which we regard as the gravest menace to the working class movement of Great Britain." It was obvious from this that Cripps had abandoned none of his principles; that the only issue at stake was that of appealing to the rank and file of the Labour party; and that once this task has been performed he conceived of his mission as finished. But the animosity of the Labour party Executive to Cripps and his "intellectuals" was too deep-rooted; their professed internal democracy for dissenters was merely a blind.

In June 1939, when the international situation had become so increasingly dangerous and the threat of war so imminent that far-sighted Englishmen were forced to look around for any possible *coup de force,* Cripps was informed that *due to the severity of the international situation the National Executive would not meet for the summer, and thus the application for readmission would have to wait!*

Convinced through first-hand information, that Hitler would strike against Poland within the next two months, and accepting the National Executive's rejoinder as further evidence of the bankruptcy of Labour party policy, he now felt free to pursue the course which he considered to be the only possible remedy. That course in his opinion should consist of some immediate alliance with the National Government itself, since England was now beaten back to the very last line of defense of democracy. The Labour party, by rejecting all forms of united opposition to the Chamberlain Government, had destroyed all possibility of defeating that Government. In the face of this crisis, Labour, Cripps now believed, must force its way into the Cabinet, so that there should be within the Cabinet at least some elements which could influence it immediately toward an alliance with Russia and at the same time possibly inspire some confidence in the German people. For instance, the Labour elements might secure the use of the British Broadcasting Company for spreading true information to the German people. This might check the rising war ferment created by the Hitler "encirclement" propaganda, which was bringing the entire German people behind him. For certainly, from Hitler's point of view, it would be wise to attack in the very near future rather than to delay and risk the falling off of the support of the German people and rising internal discontent.

Sir Stafford had absolutely no idea that he himself should go into such an enlarged Government. At the moment he was out of the Labour party and was technically without influence. There was a very considerable split in the Cabinet and the anti-Chamberlain elements might well have been persuaded, in the face of the immediate peril, to get into the Government certain members of the Opposition.

To be admitted to the Government without becoming a party of mere "yes-men" presented a real difficulty to the Labour party, who were ostensibly in opposition. In fact of policy, however, the Labour party, since the Whitsun Conference at Southport, was virtually pledged to support the Government in all the more vital matters. At that time Sir Stafford was convinced that it would be better for the Labour party to be in the Cabinet immediately, while there was still some hope of averting the catastrophe, than to wait until after war had actually broken out or was manifestly inevitable.

Since Sir Stafford was responsible to no party, he was free to draft and to publish these convictions. Further developed they became Lord Halifax's ringing speech of June 29, 1939, by far the firmest pledge to resist Nazi aggression by any member of the Chamberlain Cabinet up to that time.

The Labour party, consistent with its policy, refused to enter the Cabinet to provide a more united opposition to Hitler.

In the House of Commons, at the end of July and a month closer to war, Sir Stafford discussed with this writer his future political activity. There was a great doubt in England: could there be another Munich? If not, then Labour's influence would be nil unless it entered the Cabinet. On the other hand, if war could still be somehow averted, then there would be a general election in the fall. Cripps declared that regardless of the Labour party's decision on the subject of his readmission he would stand for re-election in Bristol East. (The elections were never held because the war intervened, and Cripps retained his seat.) In the event of a general Labour party defeat—which he felt inevitable —there would be little gained by remaining in England. He would travel to China to pursue further his interest in the Chinese Industrial Co-operatives; to India to see Nehru and Gandhi and to explore personally the turmoil of the Nationalist Congress; to other lands and possibly Russia for new perspectives. He wished to study the world political scene at first hand, and he believed that the heightened sensibility gained by first-hand contact would furnish him with a new clarity for his future work in Parliament.

Since the Labour party refused to offer an alternative to the National Government nothing could be done internationally to prevent the precarious situation from worsening. Great Britain was dickering with Soviet Russia for an Anglo-Russian Pact. Hitler's absorption of Czechoslovakia had proved that the battle cry, the empty slogans of the motives declared in *Mein Kampf* were just a rather gruesome fairy story, and that he was bent on imperial conquest rather than on freeing his "oppressed" German brethren or guarding Europe from the specter of Bolshevism. Impelled by this threat to British imperialism—which might have been foreseen all along, and which was, apparently, by everyone but Chamberlain—the English sent a second-class diplomatic entourage to Moscow to negotiate with the Russians. It seemed obvious that Mr. Chamberlain had qualms about signing a pact with Russia. But such a pact seemed the only possible way in which Great Britain could fulfill her pledge to Poland; and Sir Stafford joined along with others in urging that the pact be signed.

Negotiations with Russia were broken off with the startling news on August 23rd that Russia had signed a nonaggression pact and trade treaty with Germany. Two explanations were offered for this amazing event, one British and the other Russian. The Russians contended that Great Britain had never intended to observe a Russo-British pact if one was signed. Poland and the Baltic States, at Great Britain's instigation, refused to have Russian troops on their soil, although they would welcome Russian airplanes and Russian munitions. This was not only a slap at Russian prestige but indicated, according to the Russians, that Great Britain intended to leave the Poles and the Baltic States to the mercy of Hitler. If the Russians chose to fight single-

handed, well and good; but they had no guarantee that Great
Britain would aid them in any way. And so, according to their
version, they refused to pull Great Britain's chestnuts out of the
fire.

The British told another story to explain the same facts. Lord
Halifax has said that the Russians demanded the right of sovereignty over territory which the army entered to defend. This
would be tantamount to surrendering national independence,
and the states in question refused to accede to the demand.

The fate of Poland, to which country Great Britain sent no
aid, seems to confirm the Russian version; the fate of the Baltic
States seemed to confirm the British one. No doubt both versions
contain elements of truth but neither contains the whole truth.
The Russians did not deny Halifax's charge, and the British
Government has not explained why it did not send an important
delegation to Moscow with full powers to act. Until these crucial
questions are cleared up judgment must be reserved.

With the declaration of war on September 3, British Labour
was in a state of complete subservience to the National Government. There would be no general election now.

Cripps retired from the Bar immediately, and within the week
offered to the Government his *technical services only* since he
was out of sympathy with its politics. It will be remembered that
he was the head of a munitions factory during the First World
War. His offer was not accepted.

On September 27th a document of recantation was presented
to Cripps by the National Executive of the Labour party. He
refused to sign this document because he declared that it demanded that he sign away inalienable privileges of free speech
which the Labour party constitution accorded to each member.
From this point onward he was a free agent.

If the situation was depressing to many far-seeing members of

Parliament, Cripps refused to become downcast, even though Germany had beaten Britain to the punch by getting Russia to sign a pact. Cripps still considered it important to take up Stalin's belated offer to negotiate a trade agreement with Great Britain. In spite of his long-standing difference with the Government, he was still willing to assist Oliver Stanley, head of the Board of Trade, to frame a policy for negotiating with the Kremlin.

The Foreign Office sent William Strang to Moscow. This was the same Strang who had spent a number of months in Poland prior to Germany's attack, attempting to appease the Poles. Cripps contemptuously referred to the move as "a retreat to Moscow." He was eager to heal the breach with Moscow as quickly and as effectively as possible. At the same time, however, the Indian problem was very much on his mind; and he had also been invited by General Chiang Kai-shek to go to China. It is irrelevant to speculate about which possibility he would have acted on. The Russians solved the problem for him by declaring war on Finland. Negotiations with Russia by the Chamberlain Government were now out of the question. In the last days of November 1939, therefore, Cripps left London on the first leg of what was to be almost a half-year trip around the world, visiting in turn India, Burma, China, Russia, Japan, and the United States.

Before leaving England, he had been actively interested in all the Government's problems, either writing personally in the *Tribune* or joining with his colleagues in statements on important questions. The most crucial of all these questions, immediately before the war, was that of the Russian-German Pact and the consequent Soviet appropriation of half of Poland. This move stunned the Left, whose first reaction was to ask, as did Sir Stafford, "Why blame Russia?" He wrote then: "It is recalled that Britain gave the guarantee to Poland without the least consultation with Russia. Secondly, it is remembered that Chamberlain dismissed as premature the Russian proposal that an immediate conference be called to consider the widest possible front to resist further German aggression following upon the German occupation of Prague. Then there occurred the prolonged negotiations in Moscow conducted on the British side by a subordinate Foreign Office Official, negotiations entered into with ominous reluctance by the Chamberlain Government. On the top of all this came the rejection by Poland of the Russian military proposal to send two armies through Poland against Germany."

This was how the situation presented itself to the British Left. In view of Chamberlain's collusion with Fascism in the past it seemed clear that the Russians were merely protecting themselves.

The Russian invasion of Finland, however, was not so easily swallowed by the British Left. The protests of the Communists against unprovoked aggression in Manchuria and against the Fascist attack on Loyalist Spain were still too fresh in the minds of Western radicals. The editorial board of the *Tribune,* of which Sir Stafford was a member, felt impelled to make a collective statement on Finland because, as they said, "The obligation rests upon us to guide Socialist thought to the best of our ability for the welfare of the workers." Cripps was at this time in India but he did not issue any statement announcing his disagreement with the point of view expressed in the collective statement; so it can be assumed that he accepted at least its main outlines. These are best expressed by the following paragraph: "It is useless to conceal from ourselves that this action of the Soviet Union has profoundly shocked Socialist opinion throughout the world. The diplomatic preparation for the invasion smelt more of *Mein*

Kampf than of the Communist Manifesto." One by one the
arguments in favor of the Finnish invasion are disposed of. "We
have spent years in teaching the workers to detest aggression,"
the editors write. "All that detestation is directed against Socialism when aggression and Socialism are identified." But the
editorial concluded with a warning to the British Labour movement not to allow the war against Nazism to be turned into a
war against Socialism.

Sir Stafford Cripps and Aneurin Bevin published in the
Tribune an article on the outbreak of the war which, at that
time, seemed to define the task of the British working class
movement. "Our immediate objective," they wrote, "must be
clear. Whatever else may be entailed in the present war there
is the possibility and purpose of arresting the progress of Fascist
aggression. So long as that purpose is behind our efforts, every
good Socialist will do his utmost to assist the anti-Fascist forces."
But the issue was unfortunately not as clear and simple as that.
"A very heavy responsibility rests upon the British Government
and upon those who have allowed that Government to remain
in office during the last vital months." Later, the *Tribune's*
editorial board felt it incumbent upon themselves to discuss the
question of war aims more completely, and proceeded to do so
in an article which laid down the essential principle: "Socialists
can have no aim in war except to get rid of what is evil for the
working class in the world wherever it may be found."

But what were the war aims of the Allies? The late Robert
Dell, Geneva correspondent of the *Manchester Guardian* and
The Nation, told of the French war aims, which seemed to be
to split Germany up into her original feudal states, and to unite
the Hapsburgs, the Wittelsbachs, and the Hohenzollerns to rule
again over a decentralized Germany. Chamberlain seemed to
have no war aim other than the defense of Britain's own imperial

interests through the destruction of Hitlerism—an aim disguised as a defense of democracy, of international morality, and of the spirit of fair dealing in international relationships. Duff Cooper, however, revealed in America that the British, too, would like to see the Hapsburgs restored, and that this could only be done along the lines suggested by the French. "But can Socialists legitimately support a Government pledged to such reactionary— not to say fantastic—war aims? What would be the fate of Socialists under the new Holy Alliance? The answer is unmistakable. Therefore," said the editors of the *Tribune*, "in a sense it is academic to talk under the existing circumstances of any peace aims that a Socialist could accept, since it is impossible to get the present Government to adopt such aims or to carry them out. In order to make any reality of such a demand it is necessary as a first step to change the government of this country." Assuming that this has been done, the next question to ask is: What sort of Europe would Socialists want? The essential answer to this is given in the following statement: "We, the working class, are in fact fighting a war on two fronts, the one against Fascism abroad and the other against oppression and exploitation in our country. To win, we must defeat both enemies and therefore in our peace aims we must consider the domestic as well as the international situation."

The editors of the *Tribune* were thus proposing a policy little different from the Federal Europe plan outlined by G. D. H. Cole in his important pamphlet, *War Aims*. This plan—vaguely referred to favorably in one of Mr. Chamberlain's speeches— proposed a European state composed of all nations: a League of Nations based not on consent but upon the delegation of sovereign powers to a decisive authority. The plan first achieved prominence with the publication of Clarence Streit's book *Union Now* in 1939, and it seemed to have captured the imagination of the British Labour movement. Certainly it seemed to be the only answer to Europe's economic problems, but the difficulties in the way of its achievement were apparently insuperable. For, as was pointed out in the *Tribune,* "If we want a federation of all the countries of Europe, as most of us do, then we must see to it that our country has an economic system that makes such a federation possible with other countries."

For Cripps, however, this problem was indeed insurmountable. What would and could be done, beginning now, to "make such a federation possible?" That was the pressing question. Leaving England, for the moment, seemed one way of getting to the core of the problem—perhaps to the answer.

X

FACT-FINDING AROUND THE WORLD

No SOONER had Cripps left London in late November 1939 than insinuations began to appear in the Left press (sections of which opposed the war at that time because it was "phony" and "imperialist") to the effect that Cripps was off to India on a mission of colonial appeasement for the British Government.

It was asserted that Cripps was out to secure from Jawaharlal Nehru an agreement to a compromise "solution" of the whole Indian conflict along a line originally proposed by the British Labour party and subsequently adopted by the British Government. It was declared that the Labour party first proposed the establishment of an all-party consulting committee in India and that this was subsequently suggested by the Viceroy in his reply to the Indian Congress demand for a statement on British war aims, and actions consistent with the aims. (Mr. Claude Cockburn, editor of *The Week,* quoted Mr. Dalton as having spoken to this effect at a semiprivate gathering at Cambridge.) The Labour leaders believed that there was a fair chance of overcoming, by these means, the Indian opposition to co-operation in the war.

In addition, it was rumored that before leaving for India, Cripps—though officially outside the pale of the Labour party— had had lengthy discussions with his former colleagues and that consequently there seemed to be no doubt that the proposals which he was to make to Nehru would have the approval alike of the Labour party and the British Government. This contention was based on the allegation that during Nehru's visit to London in 1939 there had been a close collaboration between Nehru and Cripps. A kind of "Temple-man's Agreement" was supposed to have been reached regarding Indian policy. The assumption was that Sir Stafford would at some imminent date occupy a position, if not of power then at least of great influence in a government based upon a victory of the Popular Front. Mr. Cockburn averred in *The Week* that "The current hopes of the success for the Cripps mission seem, so far as our investigations disclose, to be founded on certain assumptions about the position of Nehru himself, who is declared in certain—possibly wishful-thinking—London circles to be moving to the Right." This idea was apparently based on the fact that during the conflict in the Indian Nationalist Congress over the re-election of Bose to the presidency, Nehru, who had been expected to support Bose against the Right, retired from the melee to a mountain retreat and from there issued a statement condemning both factions. Other rumors were that Nehru had lost much personal influence and that he was committed in any case to a policy of nonviolence "more Gandhi than Gandhi."

Whatever personal contact there may have been between Sir Stafford Cripps and Nehru, the real situation in India had developed beyond the point where negotiations or compromise proposals could have the dimmest chance of influencing the Congress majority. But even this fact tended to confirm the allegation that Cripps had gone to India to impede the situation in the interests of Chamberlain's Government. This was, of course, sheer nonsense.

Cripps had a certain amount of knowledge of the Indian situation, acquired as a result of ten strenuous years in active parliamentary politics, and a close proximity to colonial problems. He went to India to discuss the total situation with the leaders of the various political parties. He wanted (1) to find out the immediate demands of the opposing groups in India and (2) to see whether there could be devised a formula which would meet not only the basic demands, immediately, but would also be in consonance with a long-range solution.

Cripps had no desire to act against his own fundamental convictions. He felt that the basic demands of the Nationalist Congress could be co-ordinated with the demands of the other groups. After discussions with Indian leaders of all shades of opinion he wrote (December, 1939) a draft constitution for Indian Dominion status. This was his contribution to the situation. The document was submitted to the Colonial Office in the hope that it could be of some use. A short time later, in January 1940, he departed for Burma.

When he returned to England six months later, he expressed his feelings about India in some detail. "The man whose opinion counts most today in India and who has the greatest power is Gandhi," Cripps wrote. "The Congress Party will follow his lead, and Jawaharlal Nehru, whom I regard as the best statesman in India, gives Gandhi his complete support. Because Gandhi appears to be 'moderate' in his methods and anxious to avoid civil strife, it is a complete mistake to imagine that he is weak or that he is prepared to give up the things for which he and Congress are fighting.

"Within Congress there are many shades of opinion on diverse subjects, but upon one point they are unanimous, that India must be given the right to determine freely and without restraint her own future constitution.

"There is no doubt whatever that the communal difference between Hindus and Moslems is a difficult factor in the situation. The position is complicated by the fact that the religious differences are often stirred up and exaggerated to serve what are in reality class ends. The controllers of the Moslem League are drawn almost entirely from the professional, landlord, or industrialist class of well-to-do Moslems, whose interests are quite different from those of the Moslem masses. By aggravating religious passions these leaders can bring in behind them a large bulk of the 80 millions of Moslems who inhabit India. They would like to see the return of the Moslem domination of India, to which they look back with pride and longing, but as this is impossible they have regarded the continuation of British rule as on the whole the lesser of two evil alternatives. The other is the government of India by the peasants and workers through adult suffrage and a democratic Indian constitution. They fear this latter alternative even more than they dislike British rule. It is for this reason, that they have refused to support the demands of Congress.

"The crux of the whole situation is whether the British Government will acknowledge the right of India to determine its own form of Government and constitution. So far it has refused. Apart altogether from questions of expediency, which would seem to point very strongly to the avoidance of conflict in India at the present time, we must ask ourselves whether the 250 million Hindus are to be denied self-government in a United India because 80 million Moslems either are afraid of it or put forward an impractical suggestion for the division of India in order to prevent the Indian peasants and workers from obtaining the control of their own country.

"In truth, if the 80 million Moslems were left to make their own political decision without any injection of communal animosity, the great majority of them would support the Congress Party's program. In fact many of them do today. Actually the

President of the Congress is himself a Moslem and there are
many Moslem organizations which oppose the Moslem League
and support Congress in its demands.

"The attitude that is being adopted today by the British Government is that they can and will do nothing further until the
Hindus and the Moslems settle their differences. This gives the
reactionary leaders of the Moslem League the power to prevent
the people of India getting self-government almost indefinitely.

"It is this attitude that the British Government is in fact encouraging whether consciously or unconsciously. There are real
religious animosities and difficulties but these would be capable
of accommodation were it not for the added economic factors
dealt with above."

Although his trip was laden with political implications it was
Cripps's first long absence from national politics. It afforded him
an opportunity to relax a bit. Adventures along the way invited
his graceful humor to relatively free play, and when, later on,
they were told to a few friends, we Americans present admired
the homey character of the tales and the Lincoln-like qualities
of the narrator. In India, his hosts had arranged for Cripps to
ride in their modern trains. In the most luxurious of these were
showers which afforded Cripps and Wilson, his friend and secretary, relief from the intense heat. But after the first experience
they became hesitant; on this "Pullman-luxurious" train with
such modern accommodations as showers there were no towels!
On the occasion of his visit to Gandhi with Nehru and Wilson,
Cripps had started to bend down to assume the squat cross-
legged position on the floor of the little thatched hut when
Gandhi motioned him to a stool. He looked at Gandhi quizzi-
cally and the latter replied with a pointed touch of humor: "You
sit on the stool, Cripps, as a concession to your English middle

age." Cripps could not but laugh over such solicitude from a man who is more than a score of years older than he.

When, accompanied by Geoffrey Wilson, he visited an Indian maharajah who is well known for despotic ways, he attempted to teach him by contrast some of his own democratic ideas. The Maharajah sent his bodyguard and a fleet of automobiles to Cripps's hotel to bring him to the palace. As they left the hotel, Cripps entered the automobile at the head of the line. His secretary, Wilson, was shoved off to another car in the rear. Cripps was taken by surprise. Wilson—Cripps's protégé—had traveled everywhere with him in almost the role of a son. Cripps said nothing, but after the meeting with the maharajah had come to an end and they left the palace, Cripps grabbed Wilson's arm and almost dragged him into the first automobile. All the way back to the hotel an empty automobile followed in case Cripps should decide to throw his secretary out of the car in which he was riding!

In Burma, W. H. Donald, adviser to Chiang Kai-shek, came to meet Cripps and Wilson to escort them to Chungking. The three had a splendid dinner before retiring early, preparatory to a start at dawn up the Burma Road. In the morning, Donald was nowhere to be found. Insistent questioning finally brought out the information that Donald had left some time during the night. When Cripps arrived in Chungking, about a fortnight later, he was met by Donald. With curiosity rather than annoyance, he asked Donald why he had disappeared. Donald replied: "Our intelligence discovered a Japanese assassination plot." Cripps looked shocked. "Why didn't you tell me?" "Oh," Donald replied, "your life's worth a very great deal but the Japanese were less interested in taking yours than mine."

Chungking was perhaps the turning point of a new development in Cripps's life. He had come to China to study the Chinese

Industrial Co-operatives, about which he was enthusiastic, and to find out the true nature of the relations between China and Russia. The British Ambassador to China, Sir Archibald Kerr, was a rarity in the British Foreign Service, and for the first time on his trip Cripps felt very much at home with a diplomatic compatriot of his own country. It was at dinner with Kerr, the Russian Ambassador to China, Donald, and the Chiang Kai-sheks that Cripps remarked that even though Russian and British relations had reached an impasse as a result of the Russian war with Finland, he would like to do what he could, and that if he were invited to Moscow he would be very glad to go. We know that the Russian Ambassador transmitted this information to Moscow. Shortly afterward Cripps made his adventurous journey to Moscow. In the thirty-six hours he was there he did not hesitate to point out to Molotov that the Finnish war was a blunder in the eyes of Britain and the rest of the world, and that the only way in which the whole situation could be remedied would be for the war to come to a speedy end. It has been suggested that these arguments convinced Stalin that, instead of taking all of Finland as he probably could have, he should content himself with simply rectifying the borders and then make a comparatively reasonable peace with the Finns.

Cripps was the first white foreigner to pass through Sinkiang since 1934. He had the opportunity to visit the important though unknown towns strung along the highway which had been built through that great province of China and which runs for almost a thousand miles across plain, mountain, and hitherto trackless desert. This highway is part of a long through-route linking up Alma Ata, capital of the Kazakistan Soviet Socialist Republic, with Chungking, the capital of "Free China." Cripps relates that it is perhaps the most romantic road in the world not merely because of the country through which it passes, with its incredibly beautiful mountains and deserts, but because for long distances it runs over the route of one of the oldest caravan tracks in the world, the "silk road" of Marco Polo which had been immemorially in use when Columbus first discovered America.

Conditions in Sinkiang, when Cripps made his trip in early 1940, had greatly improved since the civil war which had placed a benevolent military governor in power. The province was now enjoying the advantages of peaceful development. A great highway across the north of the province had also been built and others as well, and a through air service had been established from Chungking to Moscow which stopped at Hawi, Tiwha (better known to the outside world as Urumchi), and Ila. It was by this air route that Cripps flew to Moscow and returned again to Chungking.

It was supposed that Cripps's hurried visit to Moscow was to gain the fullest elucidation of the policies of Russia toward Finland. But he was equally concerned with impressing upon the Kremlin the practical danger of England turning to an accord with Japan to offset the Russo-German agreements. He also tried to impress upon the Kremlin the need for a total reorientation of international policy so that expanding Fascism could be met by a solid opposition.

In spite of the rivalries within the Kuomintang and the feudal temper of many Chinese officials, Cripps felt that "China can no longer be regarded as a colonial country, whose markets and whose developments are to be regulated and arranged by outside powers." He wrote: "China has now achieved a full stature of independent nationhood both through the rapid progress that she has made toward a true national unity and by reason of the heroism with which she has successfully defended herself against aggression by Japan.

"The Nationalist sentiment among the Chinese people as a

whole was not very marked before the Japanese attack. The fierceness and brutality of the Japanese aggression has, however, acted as a powerful cement in binding the Chinese together under the leadership of their Generalissimo Chiang Kai-shek. The effect upon the people has been to knit them together in a firmer bond of unity and to increase their determination to resist the common enemy. So far from damaging the morale of the Chinese civilians, their devastation has been a major factor in the growing resistance of China. The appalling behavior of the Japanese soldiers toward the Chinese women and girls in the occupied areas as well as the purposeful popularization of the opium and drug habits have become notorious in all parts of China and provide a further powerful influence toward uniting the Chinese in north, south, east, and west in mutual sympathy and determination to drive the Japanese out of their country.

"If the new constitution is passed in a form broadly corresponding to the present draft, as is probable, then there will be ample opportunity, for all who wish, to make their political opposition effective within the democratic structure. Herein lies the great safeguard for the future of China.

"This new constitution is not only a great hope for China, wisely proposed even in the stress of war, but it also offers the possibility of a stabilizing force in favor of democracy in every other country of the world where democracy still survives. It is for this reason that I regard it as the special interest of the United States of America and of Great Britain to nurture and strengthen this bold experiment in the Far East.

"The preparing of China for its democratic government—so much importance attaches to the practical experience of and instruction in democratic methods that is being given through the Chinese Industrial Co-operatives. The setting up throughout

China of some thousands of small, self-governing co-operative units of production is not only providing work—instead of charitable relief—for refugees from the Japanese-occupied areas and increasing the production of most urgently needed supplies for the military and civil population, but it is also laying a foundation for the permanent structure of political democracy. The development of this peaceful and constructive co-operative organization in China has already received considerable help from other democratic countries, and its extension is one of the most effective ways in which any individual democrat can help toward the emergence of a successful democratic government in China.

"Nationalism is by no means necessarily democratic, indeed the experience of the world since the last World War has been in precisely the contrary direction. It has become almost an accepted thesis in many quarters that violent nationalism shows itself in totalitarian forms of government, while the alleged weakness of the democracies is associated with their international outlook. It is certainly a possibility that Chinese Nationalism, which is today very strong, may turn toward—or perhaps the more accurate expression would be, may remain linked to— a totalitarian form of government. Such a government exists today in China though those in charge of it are most of them genuinely anxious and determined that it should become democratic in form within the present year. That it should remain totalitarian in form would not perhaps be of vital importance to the Chinese so long as the war lasts, but it would probably lead to a civil war after hostilities with Japan had ceased. At least there would be a danger of China ending up as an important unit in some totalitarian grouping in the Far East.

"The ultimate safety and peacefulness of the Far East depends upon the Chinese people being able to turn their pacific ideology into practical political action, and not upon the wishes or ambitions of any small controlling group in China. At the present time it is certain that the Generalissimo, who is the real power in China, wants to see a Chinese democracy, but he is also determined and primarily determined upon victory for the Chinese people over Japanese aggression. It may be that external influences will be such that in order to obtain the latter objective the former intention will have to be sacrificed.

"It is therefore necessary for the democratic powers of the world who are interested in the Far Eastern situation to reconsider their policies in the light of the considerations that are outlined above. To achieve this, China must be given support; and, if in addition the development of democracy is looked for, then the support must come at least in large part from those powers that believe in and practice democracy themselves."

"Russia today desires nothing more than the independence of China as a bulwark between herself and Japan and as an ally in resisting Japanese aggression. This attitude is obviously consistent with the best interests of Russia herself, so long as the integrity of the Chinese government is maintained. It might, however, come about that in new and different circumstances such a policy would no longer be considered the safest for Russia.

"There is, however, one matter in which the democratic powers have an advantage in spite of the manner of their past interference in Far Eastern affairs. The Chinese today do not want to become a totalitarian nation, and this applies to the Generalissimo as well as to his people. They are truly anxious to develop a form of democracy suitable to their own needs and their own traditions, and they turn naturally to the other democracies rather than to the totalitarian states to give them help.

"If the democracies will help China in a form that she can

accept without losing her independence, then they can do a great deal to influence China's development in a democratic sense. But to do this they must realize that the old days of the exploitation of China in the interest of western industrialists and financiers are over. The New China will not tolerate the practices that were once made possible through the corruption of Chinese officialdom. Co-operation in the development of Chinese industry and raw material supplies they will welcome but only upon the basis that China maintains the control and direction of her own resources. If it is sought to impose other terms or if assistance is withheld, then China will be forced to seek help from her totalitarian neighbors, for she would rather take that risk than allow herself to be treated once again as the subject matter of foreign exploitation.

"No permanent and peaceful settlement will be possible in the Far East, unless there exists, when that peace is made, a strong Nationalist Government of China with a democratic foundation.

"The present prospect of any such settlement is remote, and will continue to be so until the military elements in Japan come once again under civilian control. The attempted division of China by the setting up of the puppet central government under Wang Ching-wei at Nanking will not expedite the solution of the difficulties. It will prove a failure, though by providing an alibi for the Japanese military it may prolong their stay in China.

"The cardinal need today is to maintain and reinforce the National Government of Chungking so that when the moment arrives to conclude the settlement that Government will be able to insist upon a just and reasonable peace in which the integrity and independence of China will be assured by the inherent unity and power of the Chinese democracy."

Cripps left China for Japan in the second week of March 1940. He stayed in Japan only a short time, but long enough to observe the tragedy of the country in its many contrasts:

"The simple and charming ways of old Japan and the harsh, cruel drive of modern mass production. The enlightened and cultured civilians and the cruel and corrupt military machine which dominates the country with its Nazi philosophy. The liberal-minded civilians are powerless in the grip of the militarists; and, however much they may desire, as many sincerely do, to behave with decency and restraint, they are forced to follow the policies of the dominant military caste.

"Economic conditions, too, are not happy in Japan. The first thing that I noticed on reaching Japan was the general shortage of all kinds of commodities and services.

"There will be no sudden collapse of Japan unless external powers intervene, but the slow process of exhaustion has already set in and so long as the Chinese National Government retains its strength and unity it is inevitable that Japan will have to withdraw from China sooner or later. It may take years but nevertheless it is certain unless we and other powers create conditions favorable to Japan.

"The Japanese are now demanding as the condition of the cessation of war that China should enter into an anti-Russian pact with Japan, that the present status of Manchukuo should be recognized, that Japan should have a permanent position of preference in the Chinese markets, and that Japanese troops should remain stationed in the northern parts of China and Inner Mongolia.

"Such conditions are fantastic and would mean the permanent subjugation of China by Japan. The Chinese will have none of them because they are confident of their capacity to wear down their enemy.

"No final peace will come in the Far East until the military power is overthrown in Japan and the Japanese people can treat with the Chinese people; then at least there will be a basis for agreement, for both peoples are happy, simple, honest folk who demand nothing better than peace and the right to control their own lives."

Cripps arrived in the United States on April 1, and spent an evening with Charlie Chaplin at the actor's estate, where various parts of *The Dictator*, which was then in production, were acted out for him. On the following day, Cripps flew to Washington.

He remained in the United States for ten days, during which time he talked with Government officials, saw old friends, and spoke at a number of meetings. The most important of these were an off-the-record talk to the National Press Club, and another sponsored by the Chinese Industrial Co-operative Movement, which he addressed jointly with Pearl Buck.

He sailed for England on April 10 on what was to be the last trans-Atlantic voyage of the Italian liner *Rex* prior to Italy's entrance into the war.

XI

ENVOY

CRIPPS ARRIVED in London at the end of April 1940 to find England reeling under Germany's successes in Norway and in time to participate in the final *coup de grace* to the Chamberlain Government. On May 7th began the full-dress debate on the Chamberlain Government's blundering policies, a debate which Cripps regarded as the "most momentous that has ever taken place in the history of Parliament." On May 8th he made his final major speech in Parliament before he went to Moscow.

"What is constantly said," Cripps charged, is that "you must not attack the Government because it will endanger the country. There are times when the only safety of the country is attack upon the Government, and it will be a grave dereliction of duty on the part of the Members of this House if, being honestly convinced that it is necessary to challenge the issue, they take no steps to do it."

Since this debate casts much light on the purposes and effects of Cripps's trip, it is worth quoting the official proceedings in some detail.

"SIR S. CRIPPS: Before I come to deal with events in Norway I want to give the House a very short impression of some views I gathered while I was away, upon one particular point, which, I think, is material so far as the matter under discussion is concerned. It is a perfectly trite and true saying that the on-lookers often see most of the game, and there have been, especially in America, but in all neutral countries, many very keen observers of the war in Europe. They are perhaps not so oppressed or encouraged by immediate events as are those who are here intimately taking part in day-to-day affairs. However isolationist the Americans may be upon the subject of participation or assistance in this war, they are at present strongly pro-British in their sympathies as a whole. But that has made them all the more keen observers of the conduct of this war and has developed in them a very sensitive judgment as to how the war has been conducted.

"Upon certain points I found, in contact with Americans of every sort and kind, almost unanimous agreement. Uniformly, they take the view that the efforts of this country have been ill-organized and have been permeated with a spirit of indecision and a lack of boldness that would seem to rise out of the failure to appreciate the extreme seriousness of the war situation. I do not think that I met anybody, excepting, of course, British officials and members of the American administration, whose lips were sealed upon such matters, who had a good word to say for the British Government as at present constituted. Of the Prime Minister and the Chancellor of the Exchequer they were scathing in their criticism, and the question that was put to me more than any other while I was in America was, Why was it that the British people, if they desired to win this war, did not bring about a change of Government? Certainly they regard such a change as essential, and measure the necessity in weeks and in months.

"SIR WILLIAM DAVISON (Kensington, South): What reasons did they give?

"SIR S. CRIPPS: If you will apply to Mr. Stimson he will give you the reason as regards the Chancellor of the Exchequer, and if you apply to many others they will give you the history from the time of Munich onward about the Prime Minister, and these are full and sufficient reasons.

"SIR W. DAVISON: Let the House of Commons know what they are.

"SIR S. CRIPPS: I am trying to inform the hon. Gentleman and others what American opinion really is. They are certainly of the view, and this was made clear by the American Press, that the prestige of this Government has suffered another serious blow in the events which have taken place in Norway. These criticisms were so markedly universal in America that it was absolutely impossible for anybody to overlook them. When one returns to this country after an absence of some months, trying in the meantime to observe from a distance the development of events, one is at once struck by the depressing atmosphere which prevails in this country. In the Far East, for instance, in such a place as China, however difficult material matters may be for these people, one senses an intense feeling of hope and of life. In this country there seems to be no conviction of success for a just cause. (Hon. Members: 'Oh.') A desire, but no conviction. There is doubt and despondency widely expressed on all sides.

"No one will convince me that the spirit has gone out of the British people, but it is obvious that undecided and half-hearted leadership has created a sense of frustration in the people where bold leadership would give confidence and courage. In almost every Department of the Government the same fatal indecision and lack of realization of the urgency of the situation seem to rule. Indeed, it is hardly possible to detect in some cases where the Government have yet made up their mind that this country must be organized for victory regardless of all costs. There are constant calls made by Ministers for great and united efforts by the people, but they have wholly failed to organize those great and united efforts. Whether it is foreign policy, supply, strategy, or any other matter, there exists today an opportunist indecision, now apparently favoring one line of policy and now favoring another line of policy, and it is this hesitation and vacillation which is paralyzing the efforts of our country, and which is fatal to our chances of victory. . . . Now, Mr. Speaker, the Government seems to be in a state of almost perpetual fear of something. They are sometimes afraid because of the wicked efficiency of our enemy and are sometimes frightened by some possible action in this country itself. They are dodging along a circuitous route, attempting somehow or other to avoid the objects of their fear. There is only one fear which ought to influence the Government in these circumstances, and that is the fear of British democracy, which ought to drive them into bold and resolute action. The recent campaign in Norway is, I believe, absolutely typical of their indecision. I believe their prime blunder in this campaign goes further back than the time of the German occupation of the coastal ports of Norway.

". . . . It is not some isolated blunder or mistake from which we are suffering. There will always be isolated mistakes, however good the direction of affairs may be. We are suffering today from the inability of our leaders to concert and carry through definite policies, from a lack of leadership of the people. The Government in their oft-repeated pleas for unity mistake their own safety for that of the country. No one can fail to observe the rising tide of criticism, even in the ranks of the Conservative party. The people of this country are not afraid of the truth, nor will they hold back from any sacrifice that is necessary. But they will not stand wasteful and inefficient administration or doubtful and hesitant leadership in times as critical as these.

"Every hon. Member today has a duty which I believe far transcends any party loyalty; it is a duty to the people of the country as a whole. To allow personal interests or party loyalty to stand in the way of necessary changes of government is at the present time to act as a traitor to one's country. We as a

House bear the ultimate responsibility to the people so long as we pose as a democracy. If we shirk that responsibility we join the Fifth Column as Hitler's helps. The Prime Minister intervened today in order to make an appeal to the House to give the Government and himself their support in this critical time. I never thought that I should be present in this House of Commons when in a moment so grave a Prime Minister would appeal upon personal grounds and personal friendship to the loyalty of the House of Commons. I trust that those revealing sentences which he spoke will show that he is unfit to carry on the government of this country."

Winston Churchill succeeded Neville Chamberlain as British Prime Minister on May 11, 1940, the day after Hitler invaded Holland, Belgium, and Luxembourg. Eleven days later, with Holland subjugated, Belgium on its last legs, and Hitler's motorized forces driving toward the Channel ports, Parliament made Churchill war dictator of Great Britain for a minimum of two years.

The extent of Russian help to Germany was still one of the things the British wanted to know. Unofficial sources announced in London on May 25th that Cripps had been selected to head a mission on trade matters to Moscow to "see what he can find." On May 28th, Cripps left London, flying by way of Rome and Athens. He left without credentials. London knew that Italy was about to enter the war, and there was no time to get credentials ready for Cripps. As G. E. R. Gedye said in a dispatch from Moscow later, "The first essential was to get him through Italy before the war broke out." A day after his departure it was announced that he would lead a British mission to Moscow on economic questions. Then the Russian wireless announced that the Soviet Government could not accept Sir Stafford or any other special envoy and suggested that if His

Majesty's Government wished to reopen trade talks this could be done through the British Ambassador in Moscow and the ordinary diplomatic channels. Cripps was in Athens when this new development came. It was clear that the Soviet objection was not directed against Sir Stafford personally, since he was a left-wing Labourite, but against the anomaly of a status under which he would have ambassadorial power but not ambassadorial rank.

The official Russian press said: "In reply to a proposal of the British Government regarding the sending of Cripps to Moscow as a special extraordinary delegate of the British Government, People's Commissar of Foreign Affairs Molotov instructed Maisky (Soviet Ambassador to London) that the Government of the USSR could not receive either Cripps or anyone else in the capacity of special or extraordinary delegate. If the British Government really desires to conduct trade negotiations and not merely confine itself to talk about some nonexistent turn in relations between Britain and the USSR, it could do so through its Ambassador in Moscow (Sir William Seeds) or through another person holding the post of Ambassador in Moscow if Seeds is going to be replaced by another person."

While Britain and Russia discussed the issue, Cripps, sight-seeing in Athens, awaited the ruling on his status as envoy. He decided that regardless of the outcome he would retain his seat in the House of Commons.

On June 4th it was announced that the USSR had accepted the appointment of Cripps as Ambassador to Moscow in place of Sir William Seeds, who had returned to England on indefinite leave in January. Sir Stafford's appointment was officially announced on June 6th.

Between that date and June 13th, when he reached Moscow, he was received by the Prime Minister and the Foreign Minister of Bulgaria; he visited with Rumanian leaders in Bucharest; he had a harrowing experience on the Balkan flight when lightning bolts went through the plane and his flight was delayed at Odessa. With Cripps went Geoffrey Wilson, his private secretary who had been appointed Third Secretary of the Embassy, and Mr. Lascelles, a career diplomat who had been in the Moscow embassy before, an unusually good Russian scholar, and an expert in Soviet affairs.

Cripps wasted little time. Within a few days he had talked at length with Molotov, in spite of the fact that his credentials had not yet arrived. It was on this occasion that Sir Stafford remarked to another diplomat: "Of all the various occupations I thought I might follow, that of Ambassador was never among them. When any one addresses me as 'Your Excellency,' I involuntarily glance over my shoulder to see whether some Excellency is standing behind me!"

On July 1st, Cripps met Stalin and discussed a number of vital matters. Cripps was noncommittal, but London later said that "one result hoped for here is the consummation of an old agreement whereby Russian timber was to be exchanged for British tin and rubber." In addition, perhaps as a damper to any undue optimism which might result from the meeting, it was reported that Stalin had advised Great Britain through Cripps that the Soviet Union was determined to remain neutral in the European War and that Moscow saw no reason to fear German domination in Europe. On August 1st, at the formal approval of the annexation of Bessarabia and the Baltic States before the Supreme Soviet, Molotov said: "It is difficult to expect that Soviet-British relations would develop favorably in view of Britain's previous hostile acts against the U.S.S.R. even though Cripps's appointment reflects a desire on the part of Britain to improve relations."

Sir Stafford leaving the Foreign Office upon his return from Moscow in June, 1941, to "report."

The signing of the British-Soviet pact in Moscow, July 12, 1941. Behind Sir Stafford, who is seated, is Josef Stalin. On the left (leaning over) and on the right are other members of the British delegation.

Notwithstanding the discouraging attitude taken by the Kremlin, G. E. R. Gedye wrote from Moscow on September 18th that "If Sir Stafford, who appears to have the necessary willingness to wait patiently for his opportunity, and, as his reception by Stalin proves, to understand perfectly the realities of the situation, enjoys the complete support of his government, it seems as if nothing could long delay the natural clash of Soviet and German interests in the Balkans."

Cripps was apparently willing to wait patiently—he had learned to do so during many years at the Bar. From September onward to June of the following year he did a hard routine job, which consisted mainly of watchful waiting.

In October he made a trade offer whereby Russia would get rubber, machinery, and tools if she paid for them in war materials that would be passed on to China. In the same month, in conversations with the Soviet Vice-Commissar of Foreign Affairs, he tried to work out a basis for the settlement of Anglo-Russian differences over Soviet absorption of the Baltic States. At the same time the Soviet Union rejected British protests regarding Soviet participation in the Axis move for control over the Danube. Despite Soviet snubs, Britain was still bidding for Russia's good will. In return for a more benevolent attitude on the part of Russia, Britain would (1) not associate with anyone in an attack on the USSR, (2) guarantee Russia a voice in the peace settlement after the war, and (3) grant *de facto* recognition of the incorporation of the Baltic States into the Soviet Union. Russia, however, did not reply to this offer.

But one may say—not on the authority of Cripps himself, of course, but on that of persons who talked with him and saw him at work in Moscow during those dreary months—that he never lost confidence that Britain and Russia would be brought together on the same side against Nazi Germany. One reporter says that Cripps predicted in the winter of 1940-41 that Russia and Germany would be at war *before the end of June*. It may have been more than coincidence, then, that Cripps arrived in London "to report" just ten days before Hitler invaded Russia on June 21, 1941.

Hitler, in his speech seeking to justify the attack, sought to lay upon Cripps, by name, part of the blame for his break with Russia.

The next development was that Cripps was raised to the rank of Privy Councillor and on June 27th he was back in Moscow, accompanied by a British Military Mission.

An Anglo-Russian pact of mutual assistance was concluded on July 12th and signed by Cripps and Molotov. The agreement, the signing of which was witnessed by Stalin and Vishinsky and by members of the British Military Mission in Moscow, declared that:

1. The two Governments mutually undertake to render each other assistance and support of all kinds in the present war against Hitlerite Germany.

2. They further undertake that during this war they will neither negotiate nor conclude an armistice or treaty of peace except by mutual agreement.

In the House of Commons on July 15th, Prime Minister Churchill said: "The Foreign Secretary and Sir Stafford Cripps were indefatigable in carrying matters to a swift conclusion. The agreement which has been signed cannot fail to exercise a highly beneficial and potent influence on the future of the war. It is, of course, an alliance, and the Russian people are now our Allies."

XII

"DEMOCRACY UP TO DATE"

I<small>T HAS BEEN</small> suggested by some of his critics that no man has thrown away greater political opportunities than has Sir Stafford Cripps. These critics acknowledge his courage and independence, and his parliamentary ability which brought him a large following among the more forward-looking elements in the Labour party in the dark days after 1931. They recognize also the hard work which he put in for the Labour movement as a whole, thereby winning the personal respect of wide sections of the Labour party which did not agree with him politically. They aver that had Cripps really come to know the Labour movement, had he studied how to win its support, he might have become its political leader, and the party itself might have been in a much healthier state than it was before the outbreak of war.

The very fact, however, that he consistently maintains his principles alienates certain of his colleagues and presents as good a reason as any for his not having assumed leadership of the party.

The support which Cripps has received in the Labour party has been due mainly to two factors: The first of these is the political awakening of sections of the British middle class who in recent years have grown more and more alarmed as a result of the Fascist threat to the British Empire. The second source of Cripps's support has been the widespread feeling of frustration in the Labour movement. Whole sections of the move-

ment were suspicious of the party control because of its failure
to give a lead in periods of political turmoil such as the Spanish
Civil War. The leadership of the Labour party was only too
willing to line up behind the Government in a foreign crisis;
eager to compromise, eager to institutionalize their political behavior along traditionally conservative lines.

Two factors were intimately related to the basic conflict between Cripps and the National Executive of the Labour party.
First, there was the fear on the part of the National Executive
that Cripps would weaken and split the party, and second, the
fear on the part of the trade-union leadership that the party
might become truly political and, to that extent, get out of their
control. The newly found love of the trade-union leaders for
Socialism pure and unadulterated, when they expelled Cripps in
1939, did not mean a turn to revolutionary ideas. It did not involve for a moment the slightest change in the party's program.
It meant simply that the one way in which the trade-union
leaders could hold complete control of the party was to take
over Cripps's essential arguments and to eliminate him from the
movement by claiming that only they could put the arguments
into effect. An important point is that Cripps as an individual
could not have been as effective as he was if the Labour movement had not been so full of frustration. There was no provision
for intelligent political discussion and interchange of opinion
among members of the party; consequently there was no effectively organized pressure for intelligent political action brought
to bear by the rank and file against their leadership, which was
acquiescent to the Government and deaf to the demands of the
Labour masses. The political awareness of the membership of
the Labour party, as a result, was on such a level that the
trade-union block could always retain its power.

To Cripps, on the other hand, the political education of the party was extremely important. He wrote at great length, for example, about the problems of the transition to Socialism in Britain. He believed in 1939, as in 1929, that there was a chance of achieving Socialism in Britain by peaceful and constitutional means; but his reasons for thinking so were rather different, due both to his growing appreciation of the change in the nature of world capitalism in recent years and to his observation of the methods of capitalistic groups in other countries.

In 1932, he wrote the pamphlet, *Can Socialism Come by Constitutional Methods?* in which he outlined his view of the difficulties and possibilities of Socialism's achievement. At that time, he already appreciated to the full the events of 1931. He saw that the capitalist class in Britain would stop at nothing to defeat parliamentary action if this action involved the transference of their financial and political power. The financial crisis of 1931, used as it was for dangerous political purposes by the dominating class, showed also how powerful and how subtle were the weapons which this class had at its command. With these facts in mind he reviewed the situation with far greater clarity than could most of the Labour leaders. They were able to believe in the methods of gradual change because they had not, most of them, realized in the least the forces they were up against. Cripps did realize these forces, and as a result he was able to produce an analysis of the tactics that were likely to be required. I shall quote from his pamphlet at some length, for it sheds very important light on Cripps's whole relation to the Labour party.

After laying bare the tactics of the Tory and Liberal parties in forming the National Government in 1931, he drew certain lessons to be learned from these events.

"The ruling class will go to almost any length to defeat parliamentary action if the issue is the direct issue of their financial and political control. If the change to Socialism is to be brought about peacefully, a Socialist Party must be fully prepared to deal with every kind of opposition, direct and indirect, and with financial and political sabotage of the most thorough and ingenious kind.

"The first requisite in bringing about a peaceful revolution is to obtain a parlimentary majority of adequate size to carry all necessary measures through the House of Commons. This majority must be definitely and irrevocably pledged to Socialism and must not depend in any way upon the assistance of merely radical or humanitarian elements. Given such a majority, success or failure will be proved in the first full parliamentary term. Unless during the first five years so great a degree of change has been accomplished as to deprive capitalism of its power, it is unlikely that a Socialist Party will be able to maintain its position of control without adopting some exceptional means, such as the prolongation of the life of Parliament for a further term without an election. Whether such action will be possible would depend entirely upon the temper of the country, and this in turn would depend upon the actual results which the Government could show.

"The most critical period, however, for a Socialist Government will be the first few months of power. But there will be even before this a time of great crisis for the country and of vital importance to the Socialists. As soon as it becomes apparent to the capitalists that the Socialists will have a majority, plans will be laid for countersocialist activities. For a period the capitalist Government must normally remain in power, but obviously they will take no active steps to assist their successors, and their successors may be powerless themselves to act. This period would usually last for a few days, but if the outgoing Government decides to meet Parliament and not to resign until after a Parliamentary defeat, the period may be prolonged into weeks.

"From the moment when the Government takes control, rapid and effective action must be possible in every sphere of the national life. It will not be easy to detect the machinations of the capitalists, and when discovered there must be means ready to hand by which they can be dealt with promptly. The greatest danger point will be the financial and credit structure of the country and the Foreign Exchange position. We may liken the position that will arise somewhat to that which arose in August, 1914, but with this difference, that at the beginning of the war the capitalists, though very nervous and excited, were behind the Government to a man, whereas when the Socialist Government takes office they will not only be nervous and excited, but against the Government to a man. The Government's first step will be to call Parliament together at the earliest moment and place before it an Emergency Powers Bill, to be passed through all its stages on the first day. This Bill will be wide enough in its terms to allow all that will be immediately necessary to be done by ministerial orders. The orders must be incapable of challenge in the Courts or in any way except in the House of Commons. This Bill must be ready in draft beforehand, together with the main orders that will be made immediately upon its becoming law."

Clearly, Cripps had come to grips with the situation, in a concrete way, quite unlike the vague wishful thinking of other Labour leaders on the subject of constitutional reform. He went on to describe in detail the immediate measures that would be necessary to counteract the various forms of sabotage in which the capitalists might be expected to indulge. He saw that the House of Lords was one of the chief bulwarks of the existing basis of society; its prime function was to put a brake on "rash experiments" and new legislation of all kinds, and it fulfilled this function admirably. Obviously it would be the first instrument to be called into play to block Socialist legislation. It is true that since the passing of the Parliament Act in 1911 the House of Commons has been able to override the Lords in certain cases; but the Lords still have the power to block any legislation for two years. Obviously no government trying to bring in Socialism would be able to survive the two years during which it was waiting for its first socialist measures to become law under the Parliament Act. The whole force of finance would inevitably be directed toward the destruction of the Government. The abolition of the House of Lords was therefore in Cripps's view one of the first essentials.

The question remained, could this be done constitutionally? Cripps believed that there was a chance that it could, but his arguments on this point are not wholly convincing. In his article in the *Political Quarterly* of 1933 ("Democracy and Dictatorship") he wrote as follows:

"The method of abolishing the House of Lords is not entirely simple. Fortunately, we, in this country, are endowed with a flexible, and not a rigid, constitution, which provides us with a safety valve against revolution in the form of the power of the Crown, on the advice of its Ministers to create a sufficient number of Peers to ensure the passage of any bill through the Lords. Since constitutionally the Crown is obliged to accept the advice of its Ministers so long as they have the confidence of the people, the Cabinet is able to demand the creation of Peers in any case where the House of Lords defies the clearly expressed will of the electorate. To refuse to create Peers in such an event would be an unconstitutional action by the Crown and if unconstitutional action were taken a revolutionary situation would at once arise. The Crown must in case of doubt exercise its own judgment as to whether or not the Government has received a clear mandate at the polls for the passage of the particular Bill in question. It is in order that there may be no possible doubt as to what such judgment will be that it is so important to impress upon the electors as clearly and unequivocally as possible that the immediate abolition of the House of Lords is demanded.

"If a clear demand is expressed by the electors we must assume that the Crown will act upon it, and by the creation of a sufficient number of Peers the Bill abolishing the House of Lords can be passed into law. If, however, for any reason, the creation of Peers were to be refused it would be necessary for a Socialist Government to make an immediate appeal to the country on that single issue. We need hardly contemplate the case of an unconstitutional refusal, and, in any event, it is of course impossible to foresee what action any government would take in a revolutionary situation."

Events of recent years have not added plausibility to the sentence, "We need hardly contemplate the case of an unconstitutional refusal"; but at the time when these words were written, over three years before the abdication of Edward VIII, and before all the other barely constitutional actions of the Government had taken place, the hope was excusable. But even then Cripps was being unduly optimistic. His suggestions in the pamphlet were even less convincing, read in the light of later events. Here he suggests:

"Should the Crown refuse (to create the necessary Peers) there would then be two alternative lines of action open to the Government, first, immediate resignation throwing the responsibility back upon the capitalists, or second, an unconstitutional continuance of power with a total disregard of the Lords."

He himself recommends the former alternative, and prophesies as follows:

"The capitalist Government, in a minority, would have to accept office, or an immediate second general election would ensue, on the sole issue of the right of the Lords to obstruct emergency legislation. On such an issue the Socialist Party would, I think, be in a strong position, and, provided they could beg, borrow, or steal the funds to fight the election, would have a second and perhaps even greater success. In this event the capitalists would have to yield. . . ."

This was not a hopeful outlook, when one considers the tactics of the governments in Europe during the last ten years. Cripps chose this first alternative, because he thought that to remain unconstitutionally in power in spite of the Lords would raise a conflict that "would throw the country into confusion and would almost certainly result in an uprising of the capitalists which would have to be quelled by force, and would lead to the very difficulties that it is most desired to avoid."

Considering the time when they were written, his ideas shed a good deal of light on a very confused matter. While most of the other parties to the dispute tended to conduct the argument on the lines of " 'Tis—'Tisn't!" Cripps really did make an attempt at an objective and dispassionate review of the question whether a constitutional change to Socialism was possible. Though it may seem now that Cripps was erring on the side of optimism, he was doing so far less than were any of his colleagues except Harold Laski.

This discussion and analysis was continued in Sir Stafford Cripps's last book *Democracy Up-To-Date,* published in late 1939.* The problem here is handled in its broader aspects. Sir Stafford puts forth the idea that changes should be instituted not only after a Labour majority is elected but before, in order to facilitate the election of a Labour majority. The problem

* London: G. Allen and Unwin.

which the book deals with is stated succinctly in the opening pages. "French democracy," Sir Stafford writes, "has been forced into the acceptance of a dictatorship and has had to acquiesce in its own suspension. British democracy is rapidly approaching the same condition as is apparent from the apathy of the electorate, the lack of interest in the House of Commons and its proceedings, and the invalidity of public opinion to control the Prime Minister . . . ."

The question, therefore, is no longer whether Socialism can come by constitutional methods; the question is rather whether democracy as a political system has enough virility to prevent itself from relapsing through sheer inertia into some form of tyranny. Peter Drucker, in his suggestive book, *The End of Economic Man,* published in 1939,† predicts the eventual decline of democracy simply because it provides no emotional security but only a freedom which is steadily being proven an illusion. As Sir Stafford sees it, the problem is to make democracy function again; and being a lawyer he proceeds to examine the process of democracy as it functions in England. "We must realize," he says, "that democracy has to function practically through a number of imperfect human beings brought together in committees, councils or Parliaments. These men and women become incapable of carrying out their democratic functions unless there is devised some form of procedure which enables them to exercise their power at the right time and in the right way."

The solution, as Sir Stafford conceives it, consists in streamlining the democratic process so that it will truly serve as an instrument of democratic change. The most important element, of course, because it is the primary one, is the electoral system. Here Sir Stafford proposes some drastic revisions. The representative character of the electoral system will, he says, "be deter-

† New York: The John Day Company.

mined by the degree with which the electoral system throws up true representatives of the majority view of the electors in each constituency." Accordingly the disproportionate influence which wealth plays in elections should be eliminated. This should be done by having the state finance the elections. Voting, too, should be compulsory, "for every citizen should be made to take at least that amount of interest in the political life of the country.

"There are many other amendments and alterations to the electoral law such as the abolition of plural voting, and the redistribution of seats, now long overdue, that are highly desirable, but the most important factor is so to regulate the election of representatives to Parliament that neither wealth nor class influence can give a candidate any advantage over another."

There are indications that these proposals may soon come to pass. Since May 1940, the Labour party has been in active collaboration with the Churchill War Government. This collaboration is perhaps of secondary importance to the fact that the leadership of the British Labour party no longer fears absorption by the Tories. The presence in the War Cabinet of Ernest Bevin as Minister of Labour and of Clement Attlee as Lord Privy Seal, is indicative of Labour's great power. In addition there are other Cabinet ministers who are members of the Labour and the Liberal parties.

The major question that poses itself today when the overt manifestations of Tory domination are giving way under the stress of war, is whether or not the present position which the Labourites and the Liberals enjoy will at some future date be turned into state power. In *Where Do We Go from Here?* published in 1940,‡ Harold Laski says that the traditional rulers of Britain must accomodate themselves to the needs of democ-

‡ New York: The Viking Press.

racy and thus resolve the central contradiction of modern society. Both the Labour and the Liberal parties realize that the National Government, between 1931 and September 1939, was concerned in its foreign policy primarily with appeasing Hitler and Mussolini, and with hopes that Hitler would turn toward the wide reaches of the Soviet Union's Ukraine to meet the needs of *Lebensraum*. The Labour and Liberal parties must realize, too, that, while Churchill was opposed to such a policy, he was also a staunch defender of the Empire. One of the most troubling questions facing these two parties is whether or not Prime Minister Churchill can—and will—free himself from the traditional practices of the Conservative party, and whether the accommodation which Laski speaks of can be effected. For one thing is clear, and that is that neither the Labour party nor the Liberal party desires to be a partner with the ruling class for reasons of ruling class expediency.

In the past, as has been shown in earlier chapters, the Labour party's undemocratic structure evoked a number of reformist campaigns within the party. Each time the party bowed to the will of the trade-union leadership in suppressing the campaigns. It is an axiom that a political party must possess an able and responsible leadership. Such leadership is essential to interpret, co-ordinate, and make effective the dynamic inter-relationships of the party with a realistic political program. An examination of the speeches, writings, and activities of the Labour party's leaders before the outbreak of war showed that this necessary leadership was in the minority and came almost exclusively from the Constituency membership.

While this state of affairs has profound implications for the future, it would be academic and absurd to become defeatist, since the impact of the total war effort, a purgative for party factionalism, has already elevated Ernest Bevin—trade-union leader—to a position second only to that of Churchill, and has at the same time utilized the talents of Sir Stafford Cripps— leader of the Constituency groups—as British Ambassador to Moscow. More than that, Bevin, who has eschewed political action in the past for trade-union organization, is being forced to think—and act—politically. This sophistication process is acting not only on Bevin and the trade-union mind he represents, but on the whole British people, who are being forced, equally, to think in more egalitarian, less caste-conscious terms. It is a result of no minor importance, for in the past both the British Labour movement and the British masses as a whole have acted like a beaten class in relation to the Conservative, imperialist ruling class at home and at the same time as an upper class in relation to their colonial brethren.

It is to the credit of both Labour and an awakened opposition that they realize that the problems facing the democratic countries of the world today are, perhaps, more pressing than at any other time since the beginning of the first World War. The rise of Fascism has pushed the democratic way of life to the point where any defeat at the present moment might easily mean the complete triumph of reaction. All the institutions of our political, social, and economic life are immediately menaced. While on the one hand, the Fascist drive for world hegemony provides a direct challenge to the methods of political democracy which have grown up within the framework of our economic system, the pressure of that economic system, on the other, has forced certain elements within the democratic countries into more and more open attacks upon minority groups and the political organizations of the working masses. Thus, both internally and externally, the democratic countries of the world find themselves facing foes whose strength cannot be denied; whose strength, indeed, becomes more obvious as the issues sharpen, and as the inadequacies of old-line thinking become more nakedly revealed.

Sir Stafford Cripps has displayed in his political career and in his most recent ambassadorial activity, an aversion to the dogma which would make ideological considerations more important than reality. As one of the results of the World War the same aversion may soon be felt by British trade-union and Labour party leaders. This hope, best expressed by Sir Stafford in the final paragraphs of *Democracy Up-To-Date,* which was written immediately before the outbreak of war, may well conclude this book:

"We can best demonstrate our sincere attachment to liberty and to liberal forms, not by looking backward and clinging to the old methods which may have sufficed in the past, but by looking forward to the needs of the future. We must first examine what is needed immediately to cope with the vastly complex circumstances of the present time, and then determine to carry into practice that which we decide to be necessary as a foundation for future democratic government, as to the needs of which we must keep our minds flexible and alert.

"I believe that there is in Great Britain today a great fund of genuine desire to maintain and to increase the measure of democratic freedom which the common people enjoy. At the same time there is, I am certain, a lack of realization of the urgency of the self-contained dangers that are threatening our democracy. A disintegration has set in, which will, unless steps are taken to arrest it, bring destruction to our liberties.

"However good the principles we advocate, they can achieve nothing unless we devise the practical forms that will make them effective in our government.

"The only alternative to a revision of our machinery of government is the suppression of democracy by some form of total-itarianism, not because the people will wish to destroy democracy, but because they will be persuaded to believe that that democracy has been proved unworkable and incapable of providing them with the protection of the standards that they want.

"One safeguard in such circumstances is for those who believe truly in democracy and liberty to combine together to revise the form of their democratic machinery so as to enable it to provide the people efficiently with their needs while at the same time perserving their liberty in those things that are essential.

"If, then, there can be put into this machine the energy of the people's democratic will to liberty, a workable and efficient form of government will result. To stress the unessential liberties, or to demand the continuance of privilege and license for a limited class in society in the circumstances of today is to invite the rapid destruction of our democracy.

"A great satisfaction can often be derived from speaking in somewhat vague terms of great new principles and from picturing some Utopia in glowing words. Principles and policies must, of course, be altered with changing times, and the working out of these is a matter of prime importance for the future, but the most humdrum task of keeping the mechanism of our democracy in a fit state to function is of the first importance if ever we are to be able to achieve, through democracy, new policies, or reach, by that road, the Utopia of our visions."

APPENDIX

"IF I WERE FOREIGN SECRETARY"

BY SIR STAFFORD CRIPPS

(In the *World Review of Reviews,* June, 1936)

The title to this article is the Editor's responsibility, but in a world of topsy-turveydom I am prepared to join in the phantasy!

Hitherto the main determinant in the Foreign Policy of this country has been the necessity for supporting British Imperialism, as an essential to the continuance of capitalism in Great Britain. The similar desire in other industrialized countries brings into being a sharp economic clash throughout all phases of international life.

The whole structure of world politics is built upon a foundation of economic competition. What is advantageous for the capitalists of one nation is of necessity bad for their rivals in other countries. Bilateral treaties are as much economic weapons as tariffs, quotas, or colonial monopolies. In this atmosphere of day-to-day antagonism it is of little use to ask nations to sign pacts for the renunciation of war, or to agree to put aside the armaments which they manufacture to reinforce their economic arguments. The state of affairs which we describe as "peace" is in reality only the absence of war. True peace implies something much more than mere restraint from physical aggression. So long as economic aggression continues it is impossible to have a true state of political peace. Physical disarmament requires as a corollary economic disarmament.

The prime necessity today is to turn the minds of the peoples and the nations away from the inevitability of force as the solvent of economic problems. The fact that every nation is today rearming, while all alike disclaim the desire for war, proves that this rearmament is regarded as an essential factor in the economic struggle that continues unceasingly.

Great Britain has more influence in world politics than any other power, and that influence is not derived from her large armaments alone. It is the result of her commanding economic position in the world as the pioneer imperialist power since the industrial revolution.

I should like to see the power and position of our country used to launch the world out into a new conception of international relations, where the Governments would determine their foreign policies with a view to world economic co-operation.

Such a proposition coming from a great imperialist power like our own would, I believe, go some way toward removing the war-mindedness of the peoples of the world.

It is not possible for any British Government to compel acceptance of such an objective by other Governments, but it is a policy of despair to discount too heavily the effect of such a lead honestly given.

The proposal must be sincerely meant and the implications of it must be fully realized.

If competition is to be eliminated as the basis of international economic relations, it is impossible for this or any other country to retain its imperialist conquest and privileges.

Monopoly territories and markets are as inconsistent with a co-operative organization of world trade as are private property and the private ownership of the productive means inconsistent with a just and equitable distribution of wealth within a single country.

Imperialism must be liquidated if co-operation is to take its place. The process of liquidation, so far as the British Empire is concerned, has already gone some distance. The Dominions are already free and self-governing countries, and it is unlikely that we shall be able to retain much longer the control of India.

Our Eastern possessions are threatened by Japan and we have allowed Italy to become a strong and hostile neighbor in North Africa. The outlook for the imperialist is an unhappy one; what remains of our Empire will be held only by a succession of desperate wars. The workers will be as freely sacrificed in the losing struggle to maintain British imperialism as they were in the struggles by which it has been won and maintained.

We still, however, control and influence large portions of the earth's surface, and we could make a very remarkable contribution to the solution of the world's economic difficulties by the offer to pool those resources in favor of a group of powers who were prepared to abandon imperialist exploitation.

It is idle to attempt a solution of our difficulties on the basis of maintaining any form of exploitation of the so-called backward races. Whatever is done must be upon the basis of trusteeship in its fullest sense, that is co-operative assistance by the more "advanced" nations to educate the more backward nations in self-government and in the development of their economic life.

It was some such conception as this that was popularly supposed to lie behind the setting up of the mandatory system under the League of Nations. Unfortunately mandates granted to imperialist powers are nothing but an extension of their imperialism.

The U. S. S. R., in her treatment of some of the autonomous or semi-autonomous republics coming within the vast continental area under her control, has shown what can be done in assisting backward peoples to develop their cultural and economic life. Exploitation is not a necessary incident of such a development, and such exploitation does not increase the prosperity of either the exploiting or exploited nation, though it does temporarily increase the wealth of the capitalist class in an empire.

The colonial or imperial problem is only a part and in some cases a small part of the economic difficulties of the larger nations. The co-operation which forms the basis of peace must extend throughout the whole economic life of the nations who are prepared to co-operate. Exploitation of their own peoples is as inimical to peace as is the exploitation of foreign peoples. The nations who are willing to come together to lay this foundation for a peaceful world, must be prepared not only to liquidate their imperialism but to do away also with their capitalism.

My first proposal then as the objective at which we must aim is a world confederation of Nations based upon economic co-operation in the utilization of their own natural and manufactured resources, and in the development of the world's backward areas for the benefit of the backward peoples.

As a beginning Great Britain would offer to group itself and its colonial empire with any countries that were equally prepared to change over from the imperialist conception of world organization to the co-operative socialist conception.

The group would become governing trustees of all the colonial dependencies of the constituent countries, retaining them within the economic group but giving them the fullest measure of cultural and economic freedom within that grouping.

Thus would be constituted the nucleus of a true League of Nations based upon economic unity, and not attempting, as does the present League, to superimpose political peace upon economic war.

Such a group would be open to all nations that accepted its principles, and around this nucleus could be gathered a circle of nations not yet ready to accept the full implications of those principles in a somewhat looser alliance.

It would not be possible to draw up the full covenant of co-operation at once. Like all sound building it would take time, but in the transition period the closest treaty alliance could be maintained.

Great Britain, Socialist France, Communist Russia, Spain, and perhaps the Scandinavian countries might all of them be prepared to enter the group. Other democratic countries could obtain great economic advantages by adhering more loosely to the group in the first instance, with the ultimate certainty that they would be drawn within it by their own economic interests.

All forms of federation necessitate the giving up of some part of their national sovereignty by the federating nations. A supreme council of the group nations would have to be set up, to whom by stages, slowly at first, such incidents of sovereignty as the levying of customs duties between the units could be handed over. In the early stages treaties and agreements would suffice to consolidate the feeling of unity within the nucleus.

Although the primary basis of unity would be economic, there would too be worked out a common program of defense. So long as aggressive Fascist and imperialist powers remained it would be essential to provide protection for the new peace system against their possible attack. A block of countries such as I have mentioned, knit together by common economic interests in a permanent alliance, merging into a confederation, would be much more formidable defenders, than the same group linked only by temporary political interests.

Today an alliance between the U. S. S. R., France, and England would be powerful, but it would lack cohesion because it could have no motive behind it but temporary political expediency. Its liability to disintegrate at any moment and so provide opportunities for aggression to an opposing power group, rob it of any possibility of giving stability to the world.

A co-ordinating general staff would be the first step to the effective combination of defense forces, which might reduce the necessities for national armaments in each individual country. This would be followed by an amalgamation of the national defense forces into a single defense force for the group, just as today the states of America have pooled their defense forces.

Again I emphasize that these things could not be accomplished in a day, nor would the speed of that accomplishment be so vital once the course had been determined and the world knew of its development.

In the west I have no doubt that America and Canada would look sympathetically toward such a group and might indeed be prepared to align themselves with it to some extent in Far Eastern matters.

The smaller nations, seeing a firm foundation for peace, would undoubtedly cling around this strong permanent nucleus rather than ally themselves to some aggressive nation whom they feared.

The danger of war would not disappear. Neither Japan, Germany, nor Italy would suffer a miraculous conversion to common sense. The door would remain open to all these nations, and it might well be that the economic prosperity of the group of nations would exercise a powerful influence in persuading the peoples of those countries not yet members of the advisability of dropping aggression and its dangers so as to benefit by co-operation and its safety.

To put the future at its worst, if the nations in the toils of dictatorship are to be compelled by their economic circumstances to become aggressive, such a scheme as I have sketched would provide the maximum of protection for those who were attacked.

Japan in the East would hesitate to open war with Russia if it were known that France and England at least would be firmly on the side of Russia. Hitler would think twice before engaging the hostility of a similar group. Today he is angling for the friendship of England or France in order to isolate Russia; once he could be assured that no such division was possible the alternative avenue of economic co-operation would have great attractions.

Such co-operation could be by treaty only, as no Fascist state could be allowed within the close-knit economic group, but co-operation by treaty might well end in the downfall of Fascism by the penetration of the ideology of socialist co-operation into the minds of the German people.

The most important immediate result of the scheme I have outlined would be the sense of permanence and direction given to the foreign policy of a group of major powers. The present doubts and fears of tragedy encouraged so largely by the traditional conservative foreign policy of our National Government, would turn to expectancy and hope for the slow but sure building up of a state of real peace.

Today the National Government first treat with France, then make a naval agreement with Germany, turn again to France, and show no signs as to their attitude towards Russia and Japan. They hope that, when war breaks out, they may jump on to the side of victory. The uncertainty of their position in the power groupings of today is a constant source of irritation. No country can rely upon them as an ally or an enemy!

This opportunism is a necessity for an imperialist Great Britain with her "far-flung" interests the world over. We are forever trying to balance interests here there and everywhere so that we may save ourselves and our possessions whenever trouble may arise.

The world will get tired of *"perfide Albion"* and we shall be set upon one day and left an isolated carcass to be picked by the new imperialist vultures. Robbed of our Empire and with no socialist confederation to take its place, we shall indeed be the victims of a most unhappy end.

We have still the chance to begin the building of an alternative structure of economic life for the world. Within that structure we can plan the abundant use of the world's abundance, or at least of a considerable part of it. We can provide a far greater measure of safety from aggression, a true collective security because the objects we desire to secure are common to all the people of the world, and not just to our own group of capitalist exploiters.

Of those who would say "Utopian" and "impossible" I ask what alternative exists? The League of Nations, which, because it has no economic control and can never get rid of economic war, cannot impose political peace upon the world? That has been proved already in the case of Japan, Germany, and Italy. What is the good of waiting sentimentally for the next inevitable failure? Power groupings on the prewar model accompanied by a scale of rearmament far exceeding that of the decade before 1914, will inevitably land us in a worse tragedy than any the world has yet experienced. As M. Litvinov so wisely remarked at Geneva, now the realists have so patently failed in what they called realism let us try what they decry as Utopian.

"TWO YEARS OF WAR AGAINST HITLER"

BY SIR STAFFORD CRIPPS

(In *Izvestia*, September 3, 1941)

Today, Wednesday, September 3, is the anniversary of Great Britain's entry into a war which represents the most tragic and terrible assault upon freedom that the world has ever witnessed. Under it country after country has been beaten to its knees and millions of Europeans have been reduced to a condition of slavery and suffering. All this has been done in the name of the so-called New Order, when in reality it is nothing more than an attempt by a gang of Nazi hooligans to drive the world back to the ignorance and cruelty of the Dark Ages.

For two years the people of Great Britain and of the British Dominions and their allies have fought stubbornly to guard the world from this evil thing. They have known times of great suffering at the merciless hands of the Nazis, who have rained down death and destruction on women and children in their attempt to break the morale of free peoples. They have experienced reverses and defeats, but never have the followers of Hitler been able to break their spirit of resistance.

Because Hitler knew that the Soviet people stood for something different and better than his policy of brutality and enslavement of the common people, he decided that in spite of his pledged word he must attack them too without warning. His Nazi arrogance made him confident of swift victory, after which he had planned to turn for the final assault upon Great Britain before completing his world domination by the conquest of America.

Little did he know or understand the intense love of their homes and country which fills the hearts of Soviet citizens! He was blinded by his own lust for power so that he could not recognize the gallant strength of the Red Army, Navy, and Air Force.

But now, as the third year of war opens, he must look with different eyes upon the folly of his attack upon the Soviet Union. With the flower of his army stricken on the fields of the Soviet land, and with thousands of his tanks and airplanes reduced to scrap, he must now look with ever-growing fear at the mounting forces of the enemy he once despised.

In the west, too, night after night and day after day, an ever-increasing force of British planes rains down destruction upon the industries of Germany. In the occupied territories Hitler encounters more and more difficulties as the stubborn peoples of those lands put up a courageous resistance to his domination.

Arrayed against him now stand side by side two of the greatest nations of the world, Great Britain and the Soviet Union, backed by the gallant forces of their allies, by the hopes of tens of millions of Europeans and by the almost inexhaustible resources of the American continent. Though great trials and suffering still lie before our peoples, this third year of war opens in conditions full of hope and with absolute certainty of eventual victory for the cause that we defend against the villainous aggression of Hitler and his minions. We have decided to fight together to the last in this great battle for right, and in that decision rests the certainty of Hitler's defeat.

I send my greetings to the great Soviet people and assure them that the British people will do their utmost to help in every way that they can. Our admiration for the magnificent achievements of the Soviet forces by land, sea, and air is unstinted; we acclaim the determination of every man, woman, and child to protect the homeland from the brutal invader, and we are confident that this spirit of courage and determination will bring our two countries to a final and successful issue in our struggle, when the world will once and for all be freed from the terror and suffering of Hitlerism.

ACKNOWLEDGMENTS

I have had the benefit of the criticism and the advice of a number of persons during the gathering of the material, and the writing of this book. I am indebted to Messrs. Gerald Heald, Granville Slack, Angus Macmillan, and Geoffrey Wilson—Sir Stafford's confidential secretary—for material concerning Cripps's legal career; to the late George Lansbury, Herbert Rogers, Lt. Commander Edgar P. Young, R. N., Harry Pollitt, Lt. Col. J. V. Delahaye, William Mellor, the late Marquess of Lothian, Herbert Morrison, St. John Reade, Victor Gollancz, and Mrs. Sidney Webb (Lady Passfield) for material concerning Sir Stafford's political career; to the late Lord Parmoor—the father of Sir Stafford—Lady Marian Parmoor, Lady Isobel Cripps, John Cripps, and Sedon Cripps (the second Lord Parmoor) for reminiscences concerning the family background of Sir Stafford; to President Eduard Benes and Ambassador Jan Masaryk of Czechoslovakia for conversations after the outbreak of war concerning the Munich crisis; and especial thanks to Miss Gwendoline Hill—Sir Stafford's confidential secretary before September 1939—and Professor Harold J. Laski of the London School of Economics for the many conversations and arrangements made in my behalf.

The opinions expressed in this book are of course my own and do not necessarily correspond with the above. I wish to acknowledge my thanks to the research staffs of the Labour party and the Conservative party of Great Britain for permitting me to use their private libraries. To Joseph Frank, Samuel Barron, Bertha Shurtok, Marian Robb, Audrey and Selden Menefee, for the numerous editorial and galley problems, I add my grateful thanks; and to Richard J. Walsh, for his kind personal interest, wisdom, and help, a profound acknowledgment.

INDEX